From Fetus to Child

'There is much more continuity between intra-uterine life and earliest infancy than the impressive caesura of the act of birth would have us believe.'

Sigmund Freud, *Inhibitions, Symptoms and Anxiety*

The use of ultrasonic scans in pregnancy makes it possible to observe the fetus undisturbed in the womb. Dr Alessandra Piontelli has done what no one has done before: she observed eleven fetuses (three singletons and four sets of twins) in the womb using ultrasound scans, and then observed their development at home from birth up to the age of four years. She includes a description of the psychoanalytic psychotherapy of one of the research children, and the psychoanalysis of five other very young children whose behaviour in analysis suggested that they were deeply preoccupied with their experience in the womb.

Dr Piontelli has discovered what many parents have always thought – that each fetus, like each newborn baby, is a highly individual creature. By drawing on her experience as a child psychotherapist and psychoanalyst as well as on her observational research, she is able to investigate issues relating to individuality, psychological birth and the influence of maternal emotions during pregnancy. Her findings demonstrate clearly how psychoanalytical evidence enhances, deepens and supports observational data on the remarkable behavioural and psychological continuities between pre-natal and post-natal life.

From Fetus to Child is a pioneering work which will raise many questions in the reader's mind. It will be of great relevance and interest not only to psychoanalysts, psychologists and ethologists, but to all those working professionally with young children. Its descriptions of behaviour in embryo, with which all human beings can identify, make it a fascinating book for a much wider audience.

Dr Alessandra Piontelli is an Associate Member of the Italian Psychoanalytical Society. She trained in medicine and neuropsychiatry in Italy and as a child psychotherapist in England where she became part of the teaching staff of the Tavistock Clinic in London. She is now Visiting Professor at the Department of Child Psychiatry, University of Turin and has a private practice in Milan.

The New Library of Psychoanalysis was launched in 1987 in association with the Institute of Psycho-Analysis, London. Its purpose is to facilitate a greater and more widespread appreciation of what psychoanalysis is really about and to provide a forum for increasing mutual understanding between psychoanalysts and those working in other disciplines such as history, linguistics, literature, medicine, philosophy, psychology, and the social sciences. It is intended that the titles selected for publication in the series should deepen and develop psychoanalytic thinking and technique, contribute to psychoanalysis from outside, or contribute to other disciplines from a psychoanalytical perspective.

The Institute, together with the British Psycho-Analytical Society, runs a low-fee psychoanalytic clinic, organizes lectures and scientific events concerned with psychoanalysis, publishes the *International Journal of Psycho-Analysis* and the *International Review of Psycho-Analysis*, and runs the only training course in the UK in psychoanalysis leading to membership of the International Psychoanalytical Association – the body which preserves internationally agreed standards of training, of professional entry, and of professional ethics and practice for psychoanalysis as initiated and developed by Sigmund Freud. Distinguished members of the Institute have included Michael Balint, Wilfred Bion, Ronald Fairbairn, Anna Freud, Ernest Jones, Melanie Klein, John Rickman, and Donald Winnicott.

Volumes 1–11 in the series have been prepared under the general editorship of David Tuckett, with Ronald Britton and Eglé Laufer as associate editors. Subsequent volumes are under the general editorship of Elizabeth Bott Spillius, with Christopher Bollas, David Taylor, and Rosine Jozef Perelberg as associate editors.

IN THE SAME SERIES

NEW LIBRARY OF PSYCHOANALYSIS
15

General editor: Elizabeth Bott Spillius

From Fetus to Child

An Observational and Psychoanalytic Study

ALESSANDRA PIONTELLI

TAVISTOCK/ROUTLEDGE
LONDON AND NEW YORK

First published in 1992
by Routledge
11 New Fetter Lane, London EC4P 4EE

Simultaneously published in the USA and Canada
by Routledge
a division of Routledge, Chapman and Hall Inc.
29 West 35th Street, New York, NY 10001

Typeset in Bembo by LaserScript, Mitcham, Surrey
Printed and bound in Great Britain by
Mackays of Chatham PLC, Chatham, Kent

British Library Cataloguing in Publication Data
A catalogue record for this book is available from the British Library.

Library of Congress Cataloging in Publication Data
Piontelli, Alessandra, 1945–
From fetus to child : an observational and psychoanalytic study / Alessandra Piontelli.
p. cm. — (New library of psychoanalysis : 15)
Includes bibliographical references and index.
1. Child analysis—Case studies. 2. Behavioral embryology—Case studies. 3. Child
psychology—Longitudinal studies. I. Title. II. Series.
[DNLM: 1. Child Behavior. 2. Child Psychology. 3. Fetus. 4. Prenatal Exposure
Delayed Effects. 5. Psychoanalytic Interpretation. 6. Psychoanalytic Therapy—in
infancy & childhood. 7. Twins—psychology. W1 NE455F v. 15 / WS 105 P662f]
RJ504.2P56 1992
155.4—dc20
DNLM/DLC
for Library of Congress
91–5236
CIP

ISBN 0–415–07436–3
0–415–07437–1 (pbk)

To Filippo and Roberto

There is much more continuity between intra-uterine life and earliest infancy than the impressive caesura of the act of birth would have us believe.

Sigmund Freud, *Inhibitions, Symptoms and Anxiety*, SE 20: 138

Contents

Editor's preface

Dr Alessandra Piontelli, a medical practitioner, child psychotherapist, and psychoanalyst, has written an original and controversial book. In it she does something no one has done before. She observes eleven fetuses (three singletons and four sets of twins) in the womb using ultrasound scans, and she then observes their development at home from birth up to the age of four years. She includes a description of the psychoanalytic psychotherapy of one of the research children, and the psychoanalysis of five other very young children whose behaviour in analysis suggested to Dr Piontelli that they were deeply preoccupied with their experiences in the womb.

The study is, as she says, ethological, preliminary, and descriptive. It cannot prove or disprove hypotheses. Her central finding is that there is a remarkable continuity of behaviour before and after birth. This finding is at once striking and obvious – obvious, that is, once one has had such clear descriptions of it. Like Freud, who said that it was his fate to discover what every nursemaid knew (infantile sexuality), Dr Piontelli has discovered what many parents have always thought – that each fetus, like each newborn baby, is a highly individual creature. The newborn baby is not 'nature' waiting for 'nurture' to interact with him. In Dr Piontelli's view, nature and nurture have been interacting for so long in the womb that it is impossible to disentangle them; even the idea of nature and nurture as separate entities comes to seem much too crude to be useful.

Dr Piontelli describes the fetal observations, the ensuing post-natal observations, and the analysis of the small children in meticulous detail. It makes fascinating reading. The twins Marisa and Beatrice hit each other in the womb and continued to do so after birth as soon as their motor development allowed it. The twins Alice and Luca stroked each other in the womb through the dividing membrane, and at the age of one year a favourite game of theirs was to stroke each other from either side of a curtain. Marco, who buried his face in the placenta as if it were

ix

a pillow, four years later insisted that his mother get him a pencil case shaped like a pillow. Pina, the most adventurous fetus until a near miscarriage, showed a similar pattern after birth – great adventurousness soon followed by claustrophobia and near panic. Dr Piontelli is not claiming, however, that all the behaviour of the research children can be attributed to their pre-natal experiences; she makes clear that much also depends on their interaction with their parents.

Dr Piontelli's study may well raise many questions and doubts in the reader's mind. Are ultrasounds really safe, psychologically as well as medically? Did she find what she wanted to find, and would it not have been more 'scientific' to have had a different observer doing the post-natal observations? Does not the fact that the parents saw and discussed the scans seriously affect their behaviour towards their children, and therefore contaminate the findings about continuity of behaviour? One is very struck, as Dr Piontelli notes, by the way the observing obstetricians ascribed adult meanings to fetal behaviours – 'he is using the placenta as a pillow', 'look how badly he treats the cord', 'definitely this one doesn't like to be disturbed'. But how can one be sure that such attributions are meaningful when they occur in an environment that is not yet truly social? Is it likely, as Dr Piontelli (and one of the fathers) suggests, that fetuses may have some awareness of 'me/not me' sensations? And what, overall, are the implications of these findings for psychoanalysis, both its theory and its therapy?

Nearly all these questions Dr Piontelli anticipates and answers in her own way, but, as with any radically new work that upsets established ways of thinking, doubt and disturbance will remain. As she says, she hopes the findings of this work will form the subject of further research both descriptive and experimental.

Elizabeth Bott Spillius

Acknowledgements

Amongst the many people who have helped me throughout my studies and the final version of this book my deepest thanks are due to the following: to all the families who so generously let me share such an important part of their lives and to all the parents who have entrusted their children to my care; to my editor, Elizabeth Bott Spillius, whose reading of the manuscript and whose advice, comments, patience, intelligence, and respect have made the publication of this book altogether possible; to Mario Cornali, Silvano Ponzi, Professor Giuseppe Accinelli, Alessandra Kustermann, Alessandro Zorzoli, Professor Costantino Mangioni, Patrizia Vergani, Silvana Mariani, Nadia Roncaglia, who have all been of invaluable help in various ways; to Hanna Segal, Betty Joseph, Ruth Riesenberg-Malcolm, for supporting and encouraging me through various stages of my work; to Peter Fonagy and Nicholas Temple for their helpful comments and important advice; to Alicia Etchegoyen for helping me find some bibliography which was not available in my country; to Chris Benton for so patiently and skilfully revising my English; to Laura Matteini for assisting me with the difficulties of computer work; and finally to my husband for his unfailing support. I also want to thank the *International Journal of Psycho-Analysis* and *The International Review of Psycho-Analysis* for their kind permission to reproduce copyright material. Ultimately all the responsibility for what I say in this book remains mine only.

Introduction

My aim in this book is to describe a preliminary study of pre-natal life and its impact on the future development of the individual. Through ultrasound scans I observed eleven fetuses (three singleton pregnancies and four sets of twins) monthly five or six times, usually from about the sixteenth week of pregnancy until just before their birth. I then observed the infants after they were born, using the method of infant/mother observation developed by Esther Bick (1964). These observations took place weekly until the infant was a year old, then monthly until the age of two, and then two or three times a year until the age of four. In one case I was asked by the parents to undertake psychotherapy of the child when she was three years old. I will also briefly report the analyses of several very young children (aged two to three years) in whom experiences of their fetal past seemed to play an important part in their current pathology, although these children had not been included in my pre-natal observations.

My findings suggest a remarkable continuity in aspects of pre-natal and post-natal life. Each fetus had characteristic ways of behaving which were to some extent and in some form or other continued in post-natal life. Such continuity occurred in spite of the vast changes of birth and the nature of the containing environment. I do not want to assert, however, that 'nature' is more important than 'nurture'. What I think my findings *do* suggest is that the interplay between 'nature' and 'nurture' begins much earlier than is usually thought, and that certain pre-natal experiences may have a profound emotional effect on the child, especially if these pre-natal events are reinforced by post-natal experiences.

Essentially this study is exploratory and descriptive, a preliminary examination out of which I hope that hypotheses will emerge that can be tested by further observations and perhaps more rigorous methods.

The study combines certain aspects of fetal behavioural development, ethology, and psychoanalysis. As this combination of interests is somewhat unusual, I think it may help the reader to know the circuitous path by which I came to it.

My interest in fetal life and in the origins of mental and biological life is longstanding, dating back to a time even before I began to work in the psychoanalytic field some twenty years ago. It was mainly this interest in fetal life that prompted me to study medicine in the first place. Although obstetrics and embryology continued to be a central interest throughout my medical career, neurology, psychiatry, and finally psychoanalysis seemed to offer other and even more fascinating standpoints from which I could attempt to explore what lay in the depth of our minds.

In 1971 in Italy I met Mrs Martha Harris from the Tavistock Clinic of London. She was lecturing on, among other things, the method of Infant Observation as described by Esther Bick (1964). She encouraged me to continue my observational and psychoanalytical studies and, with her invaluable support, I then moved to London during the early 1970s in order to widen and deepen my psycho-analytical education.

During my English years I had the opportunity of coming into contact with and being supervised by many leading psychoanalysts, all of whom have left a deep mark on my thinking. Amongst them was Esther Bick herself, who supervised my psychoanalytic work with a young child for several years and who then also encouraged me to observe another infant under her direct supervision. While living in London I also worked in and taught child psychotherapy at the Tavistock Clinic. Infant Observation is central to the Tavistock Child Psychotherapy Training and, together with child analysis, increasingly became my main interest.

Other parallel interests during these and the following years were directed, albeit in a rather amateurish fashion, towards ethology and anthropology. Only somewhat later was I in fact to realize that the sort of 'naturalistic' observations of infants I was taught to conduct 'in the field' first by Martha Harris and then by Esther Bick had much in common with the methodology of observation used in ethology and anthropology.

I will mention here only some of the main features of Bick's method of Infant Observation as many other psychoanalysts have written thoroughly about it after Bick's original paper in 1964. (See among others: M.Harris 1969, 1975, 1979, 1982; W.E.Freud 1975; Miller *et al.* 1989; Pèrez-Sànchez 1990). As in much ethological, ecological, and anthropological research, infants are observed weekly from birth in the natural surroundings of their homes by a 'participant observer' trying to fit in as much as possible with the routine and the 'sub-culture' of the household. The main subjects of the observation (usually the mother–infant pair) are left free as much as possible to interact in their ordinary way, with the observer refraining from giving 'expert' advice, directions, and unsolicited comments. At the same time the observer tries to be sympathetic and receptive to all the members of the family and is always aware that they have allowed the observer into the privacy of their home. Central to this kind of observation of infants is the assumption that their behaviour has a meaning within the context of the nascent relationships with the people populating their worlds. As in ethological research, which usually deals with non-verbal behaviour, the observer assumes that a vast repertoire of behavioural patterns common to the entire human species underlies and is expressed in the pre-verbal behaviour of the infant.

As in ethological research, inferences about observed behaviour can later be more systematically checked against cumulative data collected from a series of subsequent observations.

Bick is not of course the only person to have observed infants, although the combination of 'naturalism' of the setting and the psychoanalytic slant in interpreting the observations is peculiar to her approach. Anna Freud (1953, 1965), Isaacs (1933), Mahler *et al.* (1975), Middlemore (1941), Spitz (1955, 1957, 1965), and Winnicott (1958), amongst others, though with different methods and varied settings have all made fundamental contributions to our understanding of early infancy through observation. Meanwhile the field of infant and child observation has been further enriched by the rapid development of more structured observations and experiments on infant and infant–maternal behaviour by developmental psychologists, although the hypotheses that have been examined in these studies have not been based on the sort of 'naturalistic' observations of Bick, Harris, and other psychoanalysts. Piaget is the pioneer in this field (1936) but Brazelton's (1962, 1974) and Emde's (1980, 1989) work is of special relevance for psychoanalysis, as is the work of Daniel Stern (1977, 1985), who gives an especially important discussion of the relation of these developmental studies to psychoanalysis.

The first 'ethological' observations were initiated by Darwin with his famous *The Expression of the Emotions in Man and Animals* published in 1872, and with the study of his son Doddy, published in 1877, reporting the first careful observation of an infant. Another study similarly conducted on his son was published a few years later in 1882 by Preyer, who is generally regarded as the initiator of fetal studies. These observations are regarded as having started a long tradition of observational studies of infants.

Bick's method, though closely related to the kind of naturalistic observation and fieldwork used in anthropological and ethological disciplines, is generally little known outside British psychoanalytical circles. Much more famous are the ethological researches conducted on the human infant by John Bowlby and Mary Ainsworth at the Tavistock Clinic in London. John Bowlby himself had appointed Bick as head of the Child Psychotherapy Training which began at the Tavistock Clinic in 1948. From the very beginning Infant Observation, although not yet in the manner in which it would be finally formalized, began to be practised in this course. It is probably no coincidence that Bick had also studied and obtained her Ph.D. in Vienna under Charlotte Buhler at the same time that Konrad Lorenz was studying there and coming in touch, through Karl Buhler, with American behaviourist psychology. This was prior to Freud's flight from Vienna. Though Bick had no opportunity of meeting Freud while she was studying in Vienna after herself fleeing from Poland, she was greatly influenced by his thought and subsequently, after moving to England, trained in psychoanalysis with Melanie Klein. Klein also exerted an influence on Bowlby as he himself, while refuting Klein's (or Freud's) views on instincts and drives, often acknowledged in his early works.

The name of Konrad Lorenz is well known in the field of ethology and he has had a profound effect on its development (1939, 1949, 1978). Perhaps less known in psychoanalytic circles is the work of H.F.R. Prechtl, one of the leading authorities on fetal behaviour (as well as on neonatal neurology). He began his first studies with Lorenz starting with the study of an obscure lizard before moving on to the observation and the examination of the human infant (see Chapter 1 for references and description of his work). Thus a thread of continuity links the figures whom I regard as major inspirations for my work: from Freud to Klein to Bick and Bowlby; from Darwin and Preyer to Lorenz; from Lorenz to Bowlby; from Lorenz to Prechtl.

Unfortunately the various sciences related to man have now become highly compartmentalized as well as specialized, rendering it very difficult to maintain a truly interdisciplinary approach. Such compartmentalization, although probably enhancing our knowledge by deepening each single and specific field, has also brought with it an unfortunate closure towards different areas of investigation. An ethologist, a behavioural neurologist, or an ecologically oriented psychologist, for example, could easily frown at the 'non-scientific' conclusions reached by an observer trained in the psychoanalytical field, while a psychoanalyst might dismiss much of the evidence coming from ethological studies as being too unemotional and superficial for someone used to speculating about the depths of the human mind. Yet careful observation is fundamental in each of these disciplines.

It was in fact, as I have said, with Infant Observation that I first began my training in the field of psychoanalysis, and the first babies I observed are now twenty years old. As I have kept in touch with most of them I am always struck by the degree of continuity, even predictability, in some of their behaviours since birth. The longitudinal study of two such infants was written in book form in the late 1970s and was finally published a few years later (Piontelli 1986). Its title, *Backwards in Time*, clearly indicates my growing interest in what lay back in our pre-natal past.

For a very long time, however, my interest in fetal life was mainly retrospective, focusing as I was on the apparent regressions to it that I observed in some of my patients. While working intensively with younger children, in particular, I met daily with very vivid phantasies and representations of life inside the womb and of birth. The same applied to dreams and phantasies reported by some of my adult patients. Some of my most 'regressed' patients seemed to live as if they were still in an unborn state, closed inside a 'mental womb' which rendered them almost totally impervious to life in the outside world. This sort of regression was particularly striking in one of my adult patients whom I used to think of as 'the big fetus', as, among many other manifestations, tall and strongly built though he was, he used to curl up like an enormous fetus on my couch while declaring emphatically his wish and intention to enter inside me with all his body. His intentions at times seemed so serious that I had to arrange for someone equally strong to be present in a room next door should I have needed help. It was actually while trying to treat this patient that I began to think of engaging actively in some kind of direct study of pre-natal life. This same patient, however, also made me realize how distant he or any other adult patient actually was from the concrete reality of our pre-natal past.

Through inferences from the re-living in the transference of what might have been the emotions, defences, and mechanisms operative in a patient's past, even the pre-natal past, one can certainly gather many ideas for the formation of hypotheses about pre-natal life. Such reconstructions, however, are always very much coloured by the accretions and distortions of later life and cannot be considered faithful accounts of the events and the emotions felt in a more or less distant past. In treating severely regressed patients, though dealing with more primitive functioning, one is also only apparently closer to early life, as each severe regression carries with it something fundamentally different from the original non-pathological stages one is referring to.

As Hanna Segal, whose direct supervision and teaching has also been fundamental for my work, says in her *Introduction to the Work of Melanie Klein*:

> The psychopathology of the earliest phase of development is, not surprisingly, the most obscure and difficult problem in psycho-analytical research. It is the phase of development the most remote in time from the actual age at which we see our patients, when their earliest experiences are certain to be modified, distorted and con-fused with later ones. Furthermore, when observing the behaviour of infants, the younger they are the more difficult it is to interpret. Difficulties encountered in the study of the earliest phases in normal development are very much increased in the presence of patho-logical phenomena; the more disturbed the infant is, the more remote is his experience from the observing adult's introspective experiences.
>
> Nevertheless the study of this phase is of paramount importance. We know that the fixation points of psychoses lie in the earliest months of infancy. Furthermore, we know that in psychological illness regression occurs, not to a phase of development that was in itself normal, but to one in which pathological disturbances were present, creating blocks to development and constituting fixation points. We are entitled, therefore, to assume, and our clinical experiences have amply confirmed this assumption, that, in so far as the psychotic regresses to the earliest months of infancy, he regresses to a phase in development which already possessed pathological features in his infancy.
>
> (Segal 1964:54)

Working with adult patients made me feel that one could not aim to achieve a faithful picture of the happenings and the possible emotions of pre-natal life just through clinical work and the tools of transference and counter-transference. Though deep down we can probably all still feel 'in our bones' some of the sensations of or the emotions pertaining to fetal life, it is certainly not possible to derive much exact information from such sensations alone.

Reconstruction in analysis of babyhood (as well as its direct observation and testing) was and is certainly rendered much easier by the fact that we have all been babies once, and also by the fact that babies, with their reactions, development, and behaviour, are easily and constantly available for observation in everybody's everyday life. Whilst the fact of having all been babies once helps us to understand better the emotional impact that real babies or infantile aspects in our patients elicit in us, the direct observation of babies in daily life helps us to confirm and reinforce, as well as to correct or reject, our intuitions. But just as psychoanalysis without observation can lead to sterile speculation, observation without the fundamental tools offered by introspective analysis can easily lead to false beliefs and superficial theories. Though babies have been available for our observation since the origins of mankind, it was mainly with the advent of psychoanalysis that we began to look at early infancy in a different light, and only lately in the history of mankind have babies been given the dignity of human beings with already complex feelings and emotions. Some of the psychoanalytic theories about babyhood may in the end prove to be wrong, but nobody would deny they have at least had the fundamental role of awakening ordinary people as well as researchers to the largely ignored world of early childhood.

As Anna Freud remarks:

In recent years direct observation has added much to the analyst's knowledge concerning the mother–child relationship, and the impact of environmental influences during the first year of life. Moreover, the various forms of early separation anxiety became visible for the first time in residential institutions, creches, hospitals etc., not in analysis. Such insights are on the credit side of direct observation. [On the other hand she added that] None of the discoveries were made before the observers were psychoanalytically trained, and that the most vital facts . . . remained unnoticed by direct observation until they were reconstrued from analytic work.

(A. Freud 1965:24)

Freud himself drew attention to the limits of observation and the need to combine it with psychoanalysis. He states in the *Three Essays on Sexuality*:

The direct observation of children has the disadvantage of working upon data which are easily misunderstandable; psychoanalysis is made difficult by the fact that it can only reach its data, as well as its conclusions, after long detours. But by cooperation the two methods can attain a satisfactory degree of certainty in their findings.

(Freud 1905:201)

Until quite recently we knew very little about intrauterine life and the direct observation of it seemed to belong to the realm of voyeuristic phantasy. Fetal life, because of its sheltered nature, was often regarded either as a totally separate world, as if life only really began with the act of birth, if not even much later (the fetus in this case was seen as a complete Lockian *tabula rasa*) or else, at the other extreme, fetal mental life was subjected to the wildest adultomorphic speculations such as attributing to it very complex phantasies and foresights into its future life. In any case the fetus was always compared to the adult and any reconstruction of its life and functioning took a retrogressive pathway using adulthood as the reference point and reaching the fetus backwards from it.

Medical sciences and technological advances have recently helped us greatly in shedding light on fetal life and, thanks to ultrasounds, we now know much more about fetal behaviour and development. When I decided to study fetal life more closely, I knew of course that what I would observe would basically be motor and somatic manifestations. I decided that it was only through observing how a fetus then develops as an infant and child that I could have a basis for developing hypotheses about the role of fetal life. Through the already established links of infant observation and child observation with psychoanalytic theory, I hoped to understand something of what the child's fetal experience might have meant to it. And, unlike the usual situation in ordinary infant observation, child analysis, and adult analysis, I would know a good deal about the material reality of the individual pre-natal experience. In other words, I hoped to link a new field of observation (the fetus) with a familiar field of observation (the infant and child) and with psychoanalytic thinking.

I had no specific hypotheses. As this was such a preliminary study I had little idea of what I was looking for. I only had in mind that I wanted to extend the method of Infant Observation to life before birth and to follow some fetuses and their mothers before and after birth. I wanted to see if it was possible to detect some kind of continuity or discontinuity between the two stages and what sort of continuity or discontinuity it would be. But I had no idea of what one could actually observe and expect to find. A preliminary descriptive and observational phase is central to and characteristic of ethological and anthropological disciplines, and the formation of hypotheses usually only takes place during the course of this preliminary phase. Hypothesis formation rather than testing was therefore and still largely is my aim.

Preliminary stages

When I decided to engage in some kind of study of fetal life I began reading the currently available literature on fetal life brought about by the recent advent of ultrasounds; with such a non-invasive, non-damaging technique, albeit with some limitations, it had now become possible actually to see and observe the undisturbed fetus in its natural environment. Chapter 1 of this book consists of a brief review of this literature.

Though this reading gave me a fundamental basis for my knowledge of the milestones of fetal development and an essential view of its physiology and pathology, the fetus seemed to emerge from the literature as an absolutely anonymous, though highly skilled and sophisticated, creature: I learned what a fetus was capable of doing at a certain age and stage of development, but still could only picture it as a rather amorphous being.

Soon I decided to try to observe fetal life personally with ultra-sounds. Other research on fetal movement was being carried out at the hospital I had contacted at the time. Very much following the lines of Prechtl's work and that of his co-workers, a team of obstetricians was trying to repeat and thus check his observations. I spent about a year watching ultrasound scans and learning how to interpret them.

At first it took me quite a while to get used to the images on the screen and to acquire confidence in my capacity to decode what was being shown on it. At the same time, following mostly ethological concepts, I was trying to form in my mind a kind of 'ethogram' of the fetus within its natural environment. Therefore for a while I sat through many observations as a simple onlooker in order both to get accustomed to the visual images and to form a better idea of what one could aim to look for. What struck me during this time (about one year of almost weekly observations of several pregnancies) was the richness and the complexity of movements one could observe right from the early stages. Long before mothers could perceive any of these movements, their babies could suck, stretch, scratch, yawn, rub their hands and their feet. I was also struck, particularly in the earlier stages, by the freedom of movement each fetus could enjoy in the amniotic fluid. With the full impact of gravity at birth this freedom is lost at least for a while, and in this respect a baby may seem a much more impotent creature than its predecessor.

I realized almost immediately that my previous stereotyped vision of fetuses was changing into one of increasing differentiation and personalization. As my experience developed I was more and more struck by the individuality of movement of each fetus and by their preferred postures and reactions. I could no longer regard the fetuses I was watching as non-persons, as each of them seemed already to be an individual with its own personality, preferences, and reactions. Each fetus also seemed to relate differently to its own environment and the various components that went to make it up. This was evident not only from what I would observe on the screen, but also from the frequent comments made by the obstetricians and the mothers and their companions. Everybody ascribed motives to the behaviour of each fetus, very much as is done with animals or with babies in ordinary life. All the observations were also interspersed with remarks like 'he is a nervous type', 'this one will become a dancer', 'he is very calm', 'she is a sort of reflective type', 'she has a good character', or 'he is using the placenta as a pillow' or 'look how badly he treats the cord'. All the observers seemed to take it for granted that some kind of motive could be ascribed to each single action of each single fetus and that one could also read from the different types of attitude and activity some indication of the child's future temperament. More or less the same comments were repeated for each fetus each time.

This tendency to 'anthropomorphize' or to 'adultomorphize' the fetus is so strong and so universal among the observers of fetuses (and of babies as well) that it may be dismissed as unscientific and unreliable. In the case of a single observation such judgments and attributions of meaning carry little conviction. When the behaviour is repeated in observation after observation, however, one becomes increasingly convinced that the behaviour has a consistency and meaning which needs to be understood, even if the meaning may not be that which is so readily attributed to the behaviour by the initial observers. Longitudinality cannot tell what the fetus or the infant feels – hypotheses only become more plausible if they can be checked against repeated future observations.

At this stage I decided to focus on a few mothers and their fetuses and to follow them throughout pregnancy and during the first years of the baby's life to see if what had been an impression of some early markers of temperament could then find confirmation or disproof in the subsequent development of the child after birth. Having made this decision, I found that many unforeseen problems still lay ahead and had to be considered and overcome step by step.

The first and fundamental question was of course that of the safety of ultrasonographic observations in general both for the mothers and their unborn children. Again a thorough review of the most up-to-date literature on this topic was required. From all such publications it emerged that no ill effects have so far been attributed to ultra-sonographic examinations of the fetus with the intensities commonly used for such observations, and, indeed, generally the absolute safety of this procedure has been underlined. Quite recently the American Institute of Ultrasound in Medicine (AIUM 1988) stated officially that 'There are no confirmed biologic effects on patients or instrument operators caused by exposure of intensities typical of present ultrasound instruments'.

All the principal studies on fetal motility and behaviour (see Chapter 1) have been conducted with lengthy (up to twenty-four hours) and frequent (weekly or even daily) ultrasonographic recordings. When it came to deciding how frequently and for how long to observe the fetuses to be selected, however, I opted for a particularly conservative and safe approach. Weekly observations as with Infant Observation in the post-natal stages, though they would have certainly added precious information as well as 'scientific respectability' to my study, seemed to me to be untenable. First and foremost I did not want to expose anybody to even faintly remote or hypothetical risks, and secondly I did not want to overburden mothers with too frequent visits to the clinic and with some discomfort particularly during the later stages of pregnancy. Therefore I decided to limit the sessions to five to six observations during the mothers' monthly visits to the clinic when ultrasounds were routinely performed anyway to check the growth and development of the fetus. As with Infant Observation, a duration of about sixty minutes for each session seemed to me to meet the requirements of absolute safety while not causing too much discomfort for the mother and for whoever was going to hold the probe. (It is frequently not realized that current probes looking vaguely like portable phones which are gently applied to the abdominal wall of the mother are in fact very heavy for those holding them. Several devices have now been designed to hold the probe in place, particularly during studies of fetal behaviour, but none of these were available in the two hospitals where I conducted my study.)

Another potential unfavourable effect now frequently attributed to ultrasounds, particularly within psychoanalytical and psychological circles, is that of interfering with or interrupting the mother's phantasies about her child-to-be by introducing reality too harshly and too prematurely into the delicate balance of her mental processes. This harsh and non-biological confrontation between reality and phantasy could in turn affect her moods and therefore indirectly her fetus and subsequently her relationship to the child once it was born. Other authors, however, point out how the visualization of the unborn fetus seems in general to be greatly reassuring for most mothers and to facilitate bonding. This could be particularly important for those mothers having to undergo a Caesarean section who often complain of a feeling of 'unreality' when confronted with their child, as the fact of not having gone through the natural stages of the birth process often makes them feel that the child has come 'out of nowhere' and therefore does not properly belong to them.

Though we do not have any instruments to measure such subtle changes and correlations and we can only rely for the moment on macroscopic information, I was well aware of this problem which will certainly need much further investigation in the future. On balance, having observed the visible effects that ultrasounds seemed to have on mothers during my preliminary year of acquaintanceship with them, it seemed to me that none of the mothers I had observed appeared to be obviously negatively affected or influenced by the sight of their child on the screen. The reactions varied from interest and excitement to reassurance, and in a few cases to indifference and blankness according to the basic personality of the mother. These observations, albeit superficial, preliminary, and certainly not conclusive, encouraged me to continue with my project.

Most of the mothers I subsequently chose to follow in the pre-natal and the post-natal stages, simply 'forgot' about the ultrasound observations, seldom mentioned them again in the following years, and seemed to continue to relate to their children in their own natural and particular way. The scientific role of the observer as well as her project of research also seemed to be soon accepted and almost 'forgotten' by most mothers, busy as they were looking after their newborn children. Of course this apparent 'forgetting' does not mean that the mothers were not profoundly influenced by the experience of the research and that it may well have affected the way they responded to their children. I doubt very much, however, whether this factor alone can account for the consistency of pre- and post-natal behaviour though it may well have been a factor.

As I describe below, I and the obstetricians asked the mothers to participate in the research, explaining what it involved, and all those we asked agreed to take part. Since my aim, as in Infant Observation, was to observe the behaviour of an undisturbed fetus in its natural environment, no stimulation other than the ultrasound procedure itself was applied during the observations. In the case of some fetuses who, for example, were unusually motionless, the obstetricians agitated the mother's abdomen after the observation was over in order to check that the fetus was able to respond and move normally. Needless to say, if any emergency had been revealed, the scan would have been stopped immediately in order for the obstetricians to take appropriate action.

The scans were recorded on videotapes, thus permitting a future more detailed analysis of the behaviour being observed.

With the parents' and obstetricians' permission, I also tape-recorded their spontaneous comments during the observations, except for two occasions when a mother withheld permission temporarily. This audio-recording gave an extra element of precious information in judging retrospectively if what had been noted and commented upon at the time would find any confirmation in the subsequent development of the children. Whilst videotaping and audio-recording were not thought to be appropriate in the post-natal stages, during the already highly technical ultrasonographic observations video- and audio-records seemed to be much less obtrusive than they would have been in a home setting and were soon forgotten in the heat of the observation.

Each fetal observation had a strong emotional undertone. Such intangible emotional undertones are generally lost in the review of the faithfully accurate videotapes. In anthropological research in particular the observer becomes an important tool of research by adding to the records of the observations those subtle emotional parameters that no videotape can record. Whilst registering the behaviour, the observer can also describe his reactions, his impressions, emotions, and so on, as well as the type of behaviour that may be elicited by his presence in the field. Therefore, in addition to video- and audio-recordings, I decided to take some notes after each fetal observation, registering the impressions and emotions elicited in me by the events and the interchanges taking place during the observations, thinking that these too could be potentially useful in the case of a retrospective review of this study.

Another important issue I had in mind was whether to have different observers studying the pre-natal and post-natal stages, to reduce a potential bias due to pre-conceived expectations. Though this aspect is usually considered irrelevant in ethological research, it needed some consideration here as my studies were to be applied to the much more emotional situation of human beings. Already during my preliminary exploratory observations, however, as well as in my long experience with Infant Observation, I had noted how important it was for mothers not to feel that they were just subjects of scientific inquiries or examination; they needed to be allowed to establish a 'human' relationship with whoever was observing them too, and continuity was very important to them. In the transcription of most of the tapes (see Chapters 2 and 3) it will be noted that I was mostly silent during the ultrasonographic observations, but much non-verbal contact was established with mothers during the scans whilst verbal contact in the form of general interest was usually sought by me and by some of the mothers before and after the scans. As taught by Bick, I avoided direct questioning as such and no questionnaire was used. I left it to the mothers to volunteer whatever information they wanted to tell me. By the time their children were born, most of these women were already strongly attached to me and looking forward to my visits in the privacy of their homes. If one accepts the view that a well-trained observer may himself become an important tool of research, continuity of observer seems to be essential for the spontaneity and the continuity of the observations, particularly in this exploratory research. Therefore I decided to do both the pre-natal and post-natal observations myself.

However, I do not want to minimize the criticism that such continuity of observer may have influenced my results, and the possibility of having separate observers for the ultrasound scans and post-natal observations will be one of the factors I shall consider in future research.

Throughout this study, as I have already remarked, my 'counter-transference' feelings were carefully monitored and accurately recorded in separate notes, trying to keep the actual recording of the events taking place during the observations as free of them as possible. This will be reflected in the actual layout of this book, where those observations that I report in detail are in fact kept as separate as is possible from my interpretations and summaries of them. This inevitably leads to repetition, but has the merit of allowing the reader to compare raw data with my inferences about it. The detailed reports of observations are taken directly from my notes and/or transcribed tapes and are enclosed in quotation marks.

As I have described above, my method of observing the babies and mothers post-natally followed the method of Infant Observation described and taught by Esther Bick (1964), which is close to the method of 'participant observation' used by anthropologists and ethologists. I realized of course that I was interested in and therefore looking for any consistencies or contradictions that I would find with the pre-natal observations, but I tried to put these expectations to one side of my mind while making and later recording the home observations so that I could allow the behaviours of the baby, the mother, and the other members of the family to emerge as freely as possible. The frame of mind of the psychoanalytic observer of infants is close to the 'free-floating attention' recommended by Freud (1912).

As with psychoanalytical sessions, I made notes only after the home observations in order to avoid interfering both with the spontaneity of the interchanges taking place and with the possibility of registering and responding freely to the emotions arising during the observation itself. After each observation I tried to recollect and record as many random facts as possible, keeping them as far as I could separate from my inferences about them. As is common practice in naturalistic observations, the language of each recording was kept wherever possible descriptive, non-selective, and non-specialist.

As with ethological research, the review of this study was mostly retrospective, and when re-reading my notes and transcribing tapes I found it almost unbelievable how much I had recorded without my remembering it. As I have already indicated, I had tried to concentrate on observing and recording the ongoing situation and feel I was largely successful in doing so. It was only later when reviewing and comparing my notes to prepare this book that my appreciation of the continuities of pre- and post-natal behaviours began to crystallize for me out of the mass of observational detail. The concordances were often so dramatic that I was amazed that I had not been more aware of them at the time.

I am aware that the reader is likely to think me disingenuous when I say that I was not very much aware of such continuity when I was making the observations. It would not be unreasonable to think that I wanted to believe that there were continuities and therefore found them. Further, in some cases the reader may find it possible that the mother, having seen the scans, told her young child about them, which may have influenced the child's behaviour. I cannot disprove either allegation though neither fits my experience. I hope that the presentation of the material, even though it has to be selective, will at least make clear some of the bases for my assertion of continuity, which is indeed the central finding that I report in this book.

Field techniques

Once these preliminary considerations were clear in my mind, my plan was submitted to the ethical committee of the hospital for approval.

Mothers were then contacted through the hospital when they came for a routine check-up. No criteria of selection were used in choosing them. The first mothers who happened to be there on that day were approached by my colleagues, I was introduced to them and asked if they would like to participate in the research. All the mothers who were approached accepted enthusiastically the idea of the scans and follow-up visits at home. Several other mothers who were there on that day were equally enthusiastic, and many more mothers than we could actually observe wanted to participate in the study. Most of them said that it would have been interesting as well as reassuring to be monitored so closely during pregnancy. The observations seemed in fact to be perceived as extra care and extra attention to be given to just a few privileged mothers.

Where the husband was not present at this initial contact with the mother I said that I would like to talk to him if possible and tried to arrange to meet. After carefully explaining that I wanted to observe their yet unborn children in the pre- and post-natal stages to see whether or not one could detect some kind of continuity in their behaviour, I told all the mothers that they were under no obligation to continue this study unless they wished to do so and were therefore free to withdraw from it at any stage. Informal consent was also obtained from the parents regarding any possible future publication of the material collected during the observations. I then explained that, once the baby was born, I would visit them at home once a week, each visit lasting about one hour, until the baby was one year old and that, subsequently, the visits were to become monthly during the second year and then two or three times during the following years. During my visits mothers were encouraged to continue as much as possible their daily activities undisturbed by my presence. It is perhaps not often realized how easy it is to fit in with the routine of family life particularly when an infant seems to dominate it for a while and when the focus of the observation is that infant. Mothers are usually very busy and most of their activities centre on the child, while the observer and their scientific aims are easily left rather in the background.

Most mothers very much welcomed the presence of a sympathetic observer ready to listen to them, giving them an opportunity to talk about themselves, their child, and their problems. It is also seldom realized how very lonely many mothers feel nowadays in the isolation of the all-absorbing task of looking after a young child. Nuclear families and modern high-rise apartment blocks do not offer them much possibilty of contact or of sharing their experiences or of receiving help from their neighbours and friends. Though most of the mothers volunteered a lot of information about themselves, their families, and their work during the course of our prolonged acquaintanceships, on principle I never asked them any direct questions and left it very much up to them whether they wanted to tell me anything or not. Sharing or not sharing important information was considered to be in itself a significant feature of the observation.

My first ultrasonographic observations were started in 1983. Mothers were invited to come to the clinic in the early afternoon, after meals, and the observations took place in a dark, quiet room. They were allowed to bring whoever was with them into the room and most of the time they did in fact come accompanied by someone. Besides myself, one or two obstetricians were also usually present. As my ability to interpret ultrasounds increased, I gradually took over the actual process of performing the observations, thus alleviating the usually very busy obstetricians. By the time I came to observe twins the probe was mostly in my hands.

My original plan had also been to be present at each delivery – the delivery being often regarded as a highly important and often traumatic event for the child as well as a turning-point, setting mental and emotional life in motion – but unfortunately this was only possible once (see Giulia – Chapter 2), because the obstetricians, certainly too busy dealing with more vital matters, almost always forgot to phone me. In all cases, however, I was able to obtain detailed reports about the delivery and about the attitude of the mother and of the baby during the following hours. The observations then, as I said, continued at the hospital and at home.

Singleton pregnancies

Since the type of observation I used is enormously time-consuming, particularly if note-taking has to be accurately performed after each observation, and since I already had in mind for reasons I will explain later to observe several twin pregnancies, the number of singleton pregnancies I followed in the pre- and post-natal stages was in the end restricted to three. However, my experience of fetal behaviour was already based on the many pregnancies which I had been able to follow in the course of the preliminary year of acquainting myself with scanning techniques. Chapter 2 of this book presents a detailed description of the three singleton pregnancies and children I observed in the pre-natal and post-natal stages. Some preliminary results of this study have already been published (Piontelli 1987).

Twin pregnancies

Why twins?

My reasons for studying twins were slightly different from the usual controversy of nature versus nurture that has attracted so many scientists to study twins since the publication in 1876 of Galton's paper 'The history of twins as a criterion of the relative powers of nature and nurture'.

Some kind of study of twins had been in my mind long before starting my preliminary ultrasonographic observations of single pregnancies. A generic interest had been further stimulated several years before this research during a brief psychotherapeutic consultation lasting just a few sessions over the span of three weeks. A very young (eighteen months) and very intelligent child was brought to me by his sensitive parents whom he seemed to be driving mad with his incessant restlessness and lack of sleep. When I first saw Jacob, while his parents were explaining all his troubles to me, I noted that he seemed to move about restlessly almost if obsessed by a search for something in every possible corner of the limited space of my consulting room, looking for something which he never seemed able to find. His parents commented on this, saying that he acted like that all the time, day and night. Occasionally Jacob also tried to shake several of the objects inside my room, as if trying to bring them back to life. His parents then told me that any milestone in his development (such as sitting up, crawling, walking, or uttering his first words) all seemed to be accompanied by intense anxiety and pain as if he were afraid, as they put it, 'to leave something behind him'. When I said very simply to him that he seemed to be looking for something that he had lost and could not find anywhere, Jacob stopped and looked at me very intently. I then commented on his trying to shake all the objects to life as if he were afraid that their stillness meant death. His parents almost burst into tears and told me that Jacob was, in fact, a twin, but that his co-twin, Tino, as they had already decided to call him, had died two weeks before birth. Jacob, therefore, had spent almost two weeks *in utero* with his dead and consequently unresponsive co-twin. The simple realization of this, as well as the verbalization of his fears that each step forward in development, starting from the first warning signs of his imminent birth, might have been accompanied by the death of a loved one for whom he felt himself to be responsible, brought about an almost incredible change in his behaviour. All this in turn facilitated an intense process of mourning in his parents who had until then been unable to express the intense pain, anxiety, and guilt that the event had caused them. This episode had always remained in my mind, together with a desire to know more about the mysterious link which often unites twins. Such a link, as well as the awareness of a terrible loss, in Jacob's case seemed to date back to his experience before birth.

One of the most intense debates within the psychoanalytical movement centres on the psychological birth of the human infant; its capacity to live mentally and emotionally in the outside world once out of the narrow boundaries of the womb. On the one hand are the analysts who consider that the infant is not psychologically born for at least the first few months of its post-natal life and regard it as an ego-less creature still living inside a kind of post-natal womb. On the other hand are those analysts who consider mental life to be operative from birth, and for most of them the actual event of birth is regarded as the turning-point that sets mental functioning in motion. Only with meeting other human beings after birth do they consider that the infant begins to feel and think. Very little mention can be found in psycho-analytical literature of the possibility of mental life, ego functioning, and awareness in the fetus and of the possible bearings of this previous stage, fetal life, not only on the future development of the individual, but also on the mental functioning of the baby.

Recently, however, much interest has been centred on the effect of maternal influences on the fetus during pregnancy. Many psycho-analysts believe that maternal emotions and even phantasies can have a strong impact on the fetus and therefore may determine the outcome of its future personality as well as its future sanity or pathology, but here again the fetus is considered almost as a non-entity and in its extreme form this view tends to consider the fetus as a totally malleable 'tabula rasa' on which the mother leaves her imprint, and pregnancy is regarded as important only in so far as her state of mind is concerned.

All debates on the origins of mental life are rendered even more heated by the objective difficulties encountered in studying it. When I first decided to observe fetal life with ultrasounds it seemed to me that the observation of twins, starting from the pre-natal stages, could be of great importance in developing at least tentative answers to the questions raised by these differing views of infant development. In particular I wanted to observe what happened when two fetuses were contained in one womb. Several questions and hypotheses were in my mind. If one postulated that mental life proper and relationships only began after birth with the meeting of other human beings, what consequences could be derived from the presence of another similar creature inside the womb? Is the fetus anyhow too immature and therefore the presence of the other twin totally irrelevant for the development of its future mental and emotional life? Or, if not, could this perhaps entail a more precocious awareness of another living entity similar to, yet different from, oneself? Could this, in other words, bring about a precocious psychological birth? And, further, could a relationship between two twins be observed already *in utero*? Could this precocity of relationship influence and in some extreme cases even obliterate any future relationship? Are there similarities and/or differences in the pre-natal behaviour of twins? Is individuality already evident at such precocious stages as for single fetuses, or does the fact of living in the same environment somehow blur any individual spur? And, in the case of monozygotic twins, does the fact of having the same genoma mean automatically the same reactions and the same behaviour? And if one hypothesis is that maternal phantasies, emotions, and states of mind have a deep impact on the fetus, what about twins: are they both affected in the same way by them? If one follows the extreme view of the all-importance of the maternal state of mind during pregnancy, both twins should receive the same kind of imprint.

I therefore decided to observe twins before and after birth, and, as in the case of singleton pregnancies, I first read the current literature on twins, especially the obstetrical literature, and then observed several twin pregnancies by ultrasounds before selecting four pairs of twins to follow in both the pre- and the post-natal stages.

During my study of twins I decided to delay the beginning of the observations by about two weeks (eighteenth to twentieth week) compared with singleton pregnancies. As with singleton pregnancies the observations then continued at monthly intervals till the end of pregnancy. Each mother was therefore subjected to an average of five ultrasonographic observations lasting about one hour each. No stimulation was applied during the observations.

Chapter 3 of this book deals with a detailed description of the four twin pregnancies and, therefore, eight twins I observed in the pre- and post-natal stages. Some preliminary results of this study have already been published (Piontelli 1989).

Child analysis

The second and complementary (if one may so call it) line of research I decided to pursue was to extend my studies by using the psycho-analytical method with patients who were still close, in a chronological sense, to the event of their birth.

Though I already had a lot of experience of treating children parallel to my observational studies, I decided to concentrate for a while almost exclusively on the treatment of several very young children. So far I have treated twelve young children all under four years of age.

While longitudinal observational studies can help us to understand how certain behaviours, emotions, and defences may have originated in the subjects under observation, child analysis can help to understand what the remote emotional experiences of our young patients, including perhaps emotions starting from their pre-natal past, might have been and might have felt like.

It is not my aim here or later in this book to explain the principles of child analysis, nor its techniques, as these are generally well known. In the treatment of my young patients I adhered mostly to the technique of child analysis as described by Melanie Klein (Klein 1926, 1929, 1930, 1932, 1961).

Many important papers and treatises have been written on this technique as well as on other approaches and on child analysis in general. Full discussion of this topic would certainly take me too far from my central theme. My accent here is on the importance that child analysis can have for the study of fetal life. Very few psychoanalytical theories, however, and very few authors who have written on fetal life will be mentioned here. This is not because I regard the work of my predecessors or contemporaries as having no influence on my work, but, rather, because the work of so many of them starting from Freud has been so essential to it that I feel I cannot do them justice in a few simple quotations. A review of psychoanalytical literature on fetal life is also beyond the scope and length of this book. This too does not mean that I consider psychoanalysis as a less important tool of research than observational study. Psychoanalysis has become so much a part of our daily life that I feel it would be inappropriate to enter into detail about its principles and theoretical approaches. I only wish, therefore, to stress a few points here.

Since its origins psychoanalysis has never been just a 'cure', but more properly its therapeutic aspects have always been linked with its use as a tool for research, albeit of a particular kind. Freud himself considered his interest in the depth of our mind to be closer to that of a scientist than that of a healer, and child analysis in general has contributed greatly to a better understanding of mental functioning in adults.

Though child analysis largely suffers from the same limitations as adult analysis when trying to reconstruct the past of our patients through their present manifestations in the transference, certainly in child analysis one deals with subjects who are still very close in time to the actual event of their birth and for whom their pre-natal past is not yet a very remote past. Presumably in young children one can find either actual memories of their peri-natal state or at least traces of it still relatively undistorted or coloured by the accretions of later life. If their pre-natal life and/or birth has been disturbed or traumatic, it may still be possible to observe its reverberations on the actual state of mind of the child.

In working with very young children (I am referring here to patients between the ages of two and three as were most of my young patients) one often has the added advantage of knowing a good deal about their actual pre-natal and peri-natal history which, unless actively dis-couraged, parents are usually keen to describe. In addition, in child analysis we also have the chance to make first-hand acquaintance with the child's parents and therefore we can form a fairly direct impression of them and of what the child's early object relations might have been like.

When analysing very young children, as in Infant Observation, one deals mostly with non-verbal communication. With children who are not too severely regressed or disturbed, one often has the opportunity of testing intuitions through the actual responses and reactions (verbal or otherwise) of the child to our interpretations.

21

In one case (see Giulia – Chapters 2 and 4) I had in fact the unusual opportunity of following the same child with serial pre- and post-natal observations and then of treating her later (though only twice a week for just over one year) with psychoanalytic psychotherapy. In this child's case one could see how the psychoanalytic method can clearly enrich, as well as confirm, many of the intuitions reached through simple observation. Giulia's case also shows us how, though temporally and spatially living in the post-natal world, many of the elements observed during her pre-natal past are still re-lived in her present. Had I not known how far back many of these elements dated, I might certainly have attributed at least some of them to much more recent conflicts arising from and within her post-natal environment. When seeing a child like Giulia for a consultation like that described in Chapter 2 without knowing so much about her previous past, one could easily wonder if her present dramatic state of closure towards the outside world and her obsessive search for food could be linked perhaps to some traumatic event and deprivation she had suffered in her infancy or more recent past.

Whilst certainly Giulia's pre-natal and early post-natal observations cannot give a complete picture of the infinite variables and complexities shaping each unique human being, the direct observation of some features of her distant pre-natal past as well as of her very early post-natal life has undoubtedly added for me a different dimension to the study of the phenomena to be observed in the consulting room.

The five other children whose case-histories are briefly reported in Chapter 4 illustrate how aspects of their current psychopathology were seen and interpreted by me as being connected with their pre-natal experience. All these children, albeit in their own peculiar, mostly non-verbal way, seem to have been able to communicate to me what some of their pre-natal experiences might have felt like.

I am well aware of course that one could argue that I was seeing in my child patients only what I wished to see and that the same phenomena could have been given other meanings. Yet the responses and the evolution in analysis of some of these children (particularly of the three less severely disturbed ones – see Cases Nos 4, 5, and 6 in Chapter 4) has added conviction to my intuitions and consequently to my formulations.

Had I not observed several infants pre- and post-natally, I would have certainly looked at the phenomena I was at the same time seeing in the consulting room in a different light, and, similarly, if I had not, right from the start, worked clinically with young children while carrying out the pre- and post-natal observations, these would have had much less depth and conviction.

Though the chapter on child analysis may seem less central to the themes treated in this book, the analysis of many of my young patients was certainly central to me during this study.

Concluding remarks

Some hypotheses and considerations of a more speculative nature deriving from my observations and psychoanalytic work will be described in Chapter 5. These should be taken as simple working hypotheses to be tested by further observation and psychoanalytical examination.

My central finding, as described above, is that there is a remarkable consistency in behaviour before and after birth and that many small children show signs after birth of being influenced by experiences they had before birth.

This book will certainly be disappointing for anyone looking for certainties and definitive answers. I hope nevertheless that it will make interesting reading and will open new perspectives into this age-old, yet still almost totally new and complex field, as well as making the fetus seem a less foreign and alien creature than we usually consider it to be. The continuum uniting all of us with our pre-natal past will I hope become evident to any reader.

Unfortunately, with the limited means at my disposal it was impossible to gather a large number of observations comparable to those of the customary medical, biological, or even psychological research. This fact, however, is usually a general and almost intrinsic condition of psychoanalytical and observational research, which is more conducive to depth and longitudinal study. One normally tends to favour in it depth of understanding, each single individual under study and the length of longitudinal observation, rather than statistically meaningful numbers. Such depth and length are enormously time- and energy-consuming, yet in psychoanalysis and in Infant Observation alike one can learn more, within their particular frame of reference and angle, from the detailed description and analysis even of one single case history than from a collection of more anonymous data. A cooperation of all such branches of scientific study of human behaviour and development will enhance the possibility of further scientific progress and understanding in these fields.

Much more simple and direct observation of fetal behaviour in general will still be needed before one can have a picture of it sufficient even to try to formulate more sophisticated ways of interpreting and quantifying it. When Jane Goodall first ventured into the forests of

Gombe near the shores of Lake Tanganyika to study the largely unexplored behaviour of our close phylogenetic relatives, the chimpanzees, she first carried out a very thorough and detailed, as well as 'humane', observation and recording of chimpanzee behaviour, before adding, almost twenty years later, tables and charts and laboratory testing to her original work (Goodall 1986, 1990). Explorations into fetal life are still largely like explorations into a distant and faraway world, and, as I said, when approaching the pre-verbal world of the human fetus one has certainly a lot to learn from the methodology and conclusions (albeit adapted carefully to man) of such disciplines as ethology which deal with non-verbal behaviour. As Hinde (1982) says, ethologists 'regard a descriptive base as essential for tackling all the problems with which they are concerned' and N. Tinbergen in the introduction of the 1969 reprint of his famous *The Study of Instinct* warns us that no natural science can afford to rush through the preparative descriptive phase and through exploratory watching of natural events before developing an experimental attack and plunging into quantification and experimentation (Tinbergen 1969).

Perhaps quantification and experimentation may never be fully applicable to this type of study which centres on the individual and his inner as well as his environmental world.

Studies on human beings are also rendered much more difficult and debates about them more heated by the fact that we are studying subjects from our own species, and this inevitably entails emotional and often irrational responses in us all. When it comes to studying the realm of the 'innocence' of childhood and even more so the 'sacred' realm of maternity, one can inevitably expect much emotional disruption and dispute. My case histories also lack the asepticity that could render them 'scientifically' more acceptable and less emotionally stirring, following as they do the tradition of case-history illustrations once so frequently used in medicine and so brilliantly carried on by Freud. This tradition unfortunately runs the strong risk of being lost.

Summary of aims of research

1 To discover, by ultrasonographic and post-natal observations, whether or not there are continuities of behaviour before and after birth.
2 To investigate with pre-natal and post-natal observations of twins issues relating to individuality, psychological birth, and the influence of maternal emotions during pregnancy.

3 To complement the observational part of the research by the psychoanalysis of very small children in order to study the way such children live out and express certain pre-natal experiences in the treatment situation.

1

Fetal behaviour and fetal environment

My aim in this chapter is to provide some basic information for those psychoanalysts and lay readers who are interested in these areas of research but have little time for deepening them.

When approaching the field of fetal mental life, one has to rely principally on data made available by medicine and biology in order not to fall into the realms of pure imagination and wild speculation. Though there is more to the mind than simple movement, it is mainly through the somatic manifestations of the fetus that one could hope reasonably to infer something about its possible mental functioning.

Within the vast realm of medical and biological research, I will refer in particular to investigations in the field of fetal behaviour as it can be observed with ultrasounds. In pursuing my interest in the beginnings of mental life, I decided to concentrate mainly on the study and observation of fetal motor-behaviour, both because this was more easily accessible to my direct experience and did not require extremely specialized skills and because it was also closer to my previous practice of observing infants and young children. In Infant Observation too one has to rely mostly on overt behaviour to infer the mental and emotional experiences of the baby, as movement is seen to represent a means of communication with its physical and human surroundings.

Moreover, through motility fetal perceptions can also be investigated indirectly, as perceptual mechanisms are often associated with particular motor mechanisms and their output can only be observed after it has activated some kind of motor response. Central mechanisms too can be 'seen' in action in the coordination and activation of various motor mechanisms. Therefore, through motion one can deduct important information about sensory and higher functions of the brain. Selected findings on these will be also reviewed in this chapter.

These areas of research have now become extremely specialized and incredibly extensive. I will therefore only be able to give a rather superficial outline of them. One could too easily get lost in the meanders of histology, neurophysiology, or neurochemical transmission and all too far removed from the macroscopic interest of the psychoanalyst in the anfractuosities of the mind.

Contrary to many popular beliefs, no fetus develops in pure isolation and its behaviour is also a reflection of the interaction with its pre-natal environment. Hence at least a rough knowledge of some of the characteristics of the fetus's habitat is also essential for the comprehension of fetal actions and reactions. Therefore, after discussing in some detail fetal movement and the sensations and stimuli reaching the fetus, I will try to describe briefly certain aspects of intra-uterine environment.

These areas of research are rapidly and continuously expanding and therefore by the time this book is published it may well be that other findings will have become available and some of those mentioned here may have already become obsolete. I hope, however, that my indications will be useful to readers and will stimulate their desire to deepen their knowledge in this fascinating field.

Fetal motility

Early investigations

Fetal motility began to be investigated scientifically only towards the end of the last century, and, before ultrasounds were introduced, several techniques were used to study it.

On the one hand one had the possibility of relying on the direct palpation of movements through the maternal abdominal wall often accompanied by auscultation with a stethoscope. Particularly important and incredibly 'modern' were the observations and intuitions of Preyer. As early as 1885, he wrote in his classic book *Spezielle Physiologie des Embryos* that fetal movements started probably long before the twelfth week of pregnancy and he considered fetal motility to be spontaneously generated and not a mere response to outside stimuli. He believed that the movements to be seen in the newborn were similar to those of the fetus and he recognized the abnormality and excess of movements of deformed fetuses. He also described fetal drinking of the amniotic fluid. All this was to be confirmed by the advent of ultrasounds, as, for instance, the onset of spontaneous

27

motility was seen to start at 7.5 weeks post-menstrual age (Ianniruberto and Tajani 1981; de Vries *et al.* 1982), and sucking and swallowing movements have now been clearly visualized.

Generally speaking, though, apart from several brilliant but unverifiable intuitions, such studies permitted only a rough estimate of the quantity of clearly perceptible movements during the later stages of pregnancy.

More detailed observations were obtained through the study of non-viable aborted fetuses, particularly through the observation of their responses to various kinds of stimulation. Several observations were derived from such studies. In 1928 Minkowski described the spontaneous and induced motility of pre-agonic aborted fetuses from the second month of pregnancy. More recently Hooker (1952) and Humphrey (1978) continued along the same line of research and examined elicited movements in detail. The critical condition of the observed fetuses, though, rendered these observations less reliable when it came to formulating principles about the physiological condition of the fetus.

The same applied to many pioneering studies on lower animals (Carmichael 1933; Coghill 1929; Kuo 1932; Windle 1940), with the obvious added difficulty of drawing information from different species. Moreover, an interest in the origins of reflexes and neuromuscular development prompted these researches. Though these studies were certainly very thorough, these authors held the view that reflexes represented the fetus's earliest neural functions and that fetal movements were only induced by external stimulation. Many spontaneous movements were in fact only visualized later with the advent of ultrasounds and their contemporaneity with movement patterns elicited by stimulation was then observed. We can now state almost with total certainty that fetal motility is endogenously generated and not a mere response to external stimulation (Prechtl 1984, 1989).

Fetal motility was also investigated in premature infants particularly by Gesell (1945) and by Saint-Anne Dargassies (1966). Gesell noted that the 'fetal-infant' remained 'true to its fetality' even though born before its time and Saint-Anne Dargassies noted that neurologic maturity was primarily related to gestational age and not weight.

Another means of obtaining information on fetal movements was to rely upon accounts from mothers of their sensations. Several researchers, such as Walters (1964), Edwards and Edwards (1970), and Sadowsky *et al.* (1979), recorded and classified movements perceived by mothers. The first fetal movements (quickening) are usually perceived around the sixteenth week. Their presence was found generally to be a sign of well-being of the fetus, while their

28

disappearance or diminishing below a certain frequency, a phenomenon described as 'movement alarm sign', was found to be connected
with fetal distress (Sadowsky and Yaffe 1973).

All these methods, though clinically useful, had the disadvantage of
being highly subjective and could not, for obvious reasons, be applied
to the early stages of pregnancy.

Ultrasonographic investigations

A real breakthrough in the study of fetal motility and of fetal life in
general was represented by the advent of ultrasounds, as they permitted
the observation of the undisturbed fetus within its natural
environment.

Ultrasonographic observations were described for the first time in
1971 by Reinold, who observed fetal movements between eight and
sixteen weeks post-menstrual age. (It should be remembered that while
embryologists when speaking of embryonic or fetal age refer to
conceptional age, it is now common practice in obstetrics to refer to
gestational or post-menstrual age, as for the patient it is usually much
easier to remember the first day of her last period rather than the
supposed date of conception.) Reinold classified fetal movements into
two groups: (1) strong movements involving the whole body, and (2)
slow movements limited to fetal parts. A similar classification was made
by Juppila in 1976. In the meantime technological advances brought
ever clearer and more detailed images. In 1980 Van Dongen and
Goudie described a more detailed study on the progression of
movements between seven and twelve weeks. A classification of
individual movement patterns was first developed by Birnholz *et al.*
(1978) and subsequently by Ianniruberto and Tajani (1981) and by de
Vries *et al.* (1982).

Other authors (Manning *et al.* 1979; Roberts *et al.* 1979; Patrick *et
al.* 1980, 1982; Rayburn 1980; Visser *et al.* 1982) concentrated on the
study of movement during the later stages of pregnancy.

Spontaneous fetal motility emerges and becomes differentiated at a very
early age. The first type of pattern, still unclear and hazy, seems to be
represented by the transient class of the so-called 'just discernible' (de
Vries *et al.* 1982) or 'vermicular' movements (Ianniruberto and Tajani
1981); small shiftings of the fetal contour lasting from half a second to
two seconds which appear between seven and 8.5 weeks of gestation
and disappear from the fetus's repertoire two weeks later. According to
Prechtl (1989) the first visible movements appear at about 7.5 weeks
and consist of slow flexion and extension of the vertebral column with

passive displacement of arms and legs. The repertoire expands rapidly from ten weeks onwards (at ten weeks, for example, hand and face contacts, stretches, yawns, jaw opening and movements of the tongue can be observed; by twelve weeks hand and mouth contact, sucking and swallowing as well as fine finger movements can also be observed) until by fifteen weeks it can be considered almost completed.

No neonatal pattern can be considered to originate at birth, as the fetus has already the full repertoire of movements which will be found in the neonate. The only difference lies in the quality of movement, most probably because of the increased influence of gravity after birth. Besides movement, no other function is seen to originate at birth either. According to Prechtl, the 'impressive continuum of neural functions from prenatal to postnatal life' is made possible by 'the large set of pre-adapted functions which emerge through prenatal life, mainly during the first half of gestation' (Prechtl 1984).

Different fetuses of the same gestational age, under normal conditions, show identical patterns of behaviour, though the quantity of movement can vary, within certain limits, from one to another. From the eighth week, within the range of its capacities, the fetus shows clear individual initiative and choice of movement (de Vries *et al.* 1988). The differences between individuals are considerable and seem consistent throughout pregnancy (Rayburn *et al.* 1983; Prechtl 1989). Each fetus has its own pattern of daily activity and such patterns appear to be unrelated to the time of the day in which the mother is awake (Rayburn 1982).

Purposeful actions were observed early during gestation by Ianniruberto and Tajani (1981). Very frequently and very early on one can, for instance, observe fetuses introducing their thumbs into their mouths.

Some types of movement are observed only during limited periods of time in the course of pregnancy: apart from vermicular or just discernible movements, jerky movements can be observed only between the ninth and the twentieth weeks and scissoring and extension of the legs between the thirteenth and the twenty-fifth week.

Some quantitative changes also occur during gestation. General movements, for instance, increase in incidence from eight to ten weeks, and then reach a plateau and remain at this level for the first six months. Isolated arm movements, rotation of the head and sucking movements all increase gradually in incidence over the first half of pregnancy (Prechtl 1989). Breathing movements gradually increase until about thirty weeks and hiccups reach a maximum at thirteen weeks, then gradually decrease (Trudinger *et al.* 1980). The rate of changes in fetal position reaches a climax at thirteen to fifteen weeks, then, probably due to a question of space in the uterus, decline (de Vries *et al.* 1982).

When the integrity of the nervous system is impaired qualitative changes in motor patterns precede quantitative changes (Prechtl 1989). Changes in the quality of movement, such as their becoming slow and sluggish, are considered to be a poor prognostic sign. In some cases acute fetal distress causes an exaltation of motricity, and movements then become abrupt, forceful, and frantic. Since motor functions are usually spared for a long time even following substantial and irreversible damage to the nervous system, a normal motricity does not by itself rule out fetal distress or guarantee the integrity of the central nervous system. The presence, however, of an alteration in movement can generally always be linked to severe organic damage (Ianniruberto and Tajani 1982). Milani-Comparetti (1981) postulated that fetal distress, particularly if of a hypoxic nature, resulted not only in a decrease in movement, but also in a regression towards more primitive patterns.

Normal fetuses usually show some kind of activity within ten minutes of observation (Roberts *et al.* 1979). Natale *et al.* (1986) with twenty-four-hour ultrasonographic observations have calculated that the fetus is active during about 14 per cent of the time between twenty-four and twenty-eight weeks of gestation.

Ultrasounds have also made it possible to compare the subjective assessment by the mother with ultrasonographic recording of fetal movement (Gettinger *et al.* 1978; Sorokin *et al.* 1981). All studies showed that mothers felt less movement than detected by ultrasounds and that the variations between individuals were very pronounced. Though fetal movements were felt by the majority of women, there were some mothers who seemed to be quite insensitive to them (Hertogs *et al.* 1979).

Each fetal movement, whether large or small, after thirty-two weeks is associated with fetal heart rate (FHR) acceleration, and nearly every large acceleration is associated with fetal movements as seen with ultrasounds (Hon and Quilligan 1968; Sorokin *et al.* 1982; Rabinowitz *et al.* 1983).

Ultrasounds have rendered it possible to visualize other fetal activities such as *hiccups* (a frequent and unclear, though apparently not worrisome occurrence) and *swallowing* and *micturition* with subsequent changes respectively in the volume of the stomach (Vanderberghe and de Wolf 1980) and of the bladder (Campbell *et al.* 1973; Visser *et al.* 1981).

Healthy human fetuses, from the tenth week onwards, periodically perform *breathing movements* (Boddy and Dawes 1975). Fetal breathing movements are paradoxical in nature, the anterior fetal chest moving inwards and the abdominal wall outwards. Their incidence increases with increasing gestational age (Trudinger *et al.* 1980). Such movements are not perceived by mothers and are irregular, shallow, and episodic and show a considerable diurnal variation in frequency. Fetal movement was generally found to be present during the intervals of apparent fetal 'apnoea' (Marsal and Genser 1980).

Fetal eye movements have also been visualized (Bots *et al.* 1981; Birnholz 1981, 1985). Fetal eye movements begin at between sixteen and eighteen weeks (Birnholz 1981; Awoust and Levi 1984; Prechtl and Nijhuis 1983), and by twenty-three to twenty-four weeks rapid eye movements (REM) are seen to appear (Birnholz 1985, 1989).

Pre-natal movement plays a necessary role in the fetus's normal physical and behavioural development (Hofer 1981; Moessinger 1983): normal muscular, skeletal, neural, and behavioural development are all facilitated by fetal activity, whilst altered morphological and behavioural development are likely to be the consequence of grossly modified fetal behaviour (Smotherman and Robinson 1988). For instance, the periodic swallowing and expulsion of amniotic fluid was found to be relevant for the normal development of the lungs (Vyas *et al.* 1982) and regulating the quantity of the fluid itself (Prechtl 1984). Pre-natal breathing is considered to represent an important practice that facilitates the performance of the complex neuromuscular action needed immediately and constantly from birth. Frequent changes of position may prevent adhesion and local stasis of circulation in the fetal skin (Prechtl 1984). Prolonged physical inactivity, as can be observed in congenital myopathy and in various neural dysfunctions, was seen to result in such physical anomalies as various joint contractures, facial and skin deformations, growth deficiency and pulmonary hypoplasia (Moessinger *et al.* 1982; Moessinger *et al.* 1983). Fetal breathing and fetal eye movements are examples of preparatory movements anticipating post-natal functions.

Fetal activity is highly influenced by the state in which the fetus appears to be, and fetal states should be taken into account when examinations of fetal motor activity are performed, particularly, as will be explained later, during the advanced stages of pregnancy (Campbell 1980; Marsal and Genser 1980).

Fetal behavioural states

According to Prechtl's definition:

Behavioural states are temporary stable conditions of neural and

32

autonomic functions known as sleep and wakefulness. They are characterized by a distinct behaviour of certain variables in concert. Observation or recording of such variables (e.g. eye movements, heart rate pattern, breathing pattern, EEG pattern, motility) provide a method for monitoring behavioural states over long periods.

(Prechtl 1985:91)

The direct study of fetal *sleep–wakefulness* is certainly fraught with difficulties. In contrast with the newborn, respiration is not continuously present, opening or closing of the eyes cannot yet be observed, nor can an electroencephalogram (EEG) be recorded except after the rupture of the membranes.

Researchers trying to record the intrapartum fetal EEG have developed a variety of electrodes, but contamination of the fetal EEG by fetal electrocardiogram (ECG) still remains a major problem.

Traditionally, therefore, fetal EEG and its maturational evolution has been studied in both full-term and pre-term infants (Parmelee *et al.* 1968; Graziani *et al.* 1974; Parmelee 1975; Werner *et al.* 1977; Lombroso 1978; Dreyfus-Brisac 1976; Dehkharghan 1984; Anderson *et al.* 1985; Lombroso 1985; Torres and Anderson 1985).

Parmelee (1968, 1975) believed in the gradual emergence of sleep states from a rather ill-defined and disorganized stage to a more organized one near term. Dreyfus-Brisac (1970) described the appearance of typical active sleep at about thirty-five weeks and of typical quiet sleep at thirty-seven weeks. Rosen *et al.* (1969, 1970) also used the terms of active and quiet sleep for the fetus, but this terminology has been recently refuted by Prechtl and his co-workers (Nijhuis *et al.* 1982). A good review and discussion of the previous literature can be found in Mancia (1980, 1981).

Most recently with the aid of ultrasounds Timor-Tritsch *et al.* (1978) and Nijhuis *et al.* (1982) have concluded that human fetuses exhibit *behavioural states* that may correspond to the four recognized sleep–wake states of the human neonate. Fetal eye movements were used together with fetal movements, fetal mouth movements, and fetal heart rate for the identification and classification of fetal behavioural states. The emergence of clearly identifiable behavioural states was seen to start between thirty-five and thirty-seven weeks. Fetal behavioural states recur cyclically, but no circadian rhythm has been found to exist in the fetus. Maternal sleep seems to have no influence at all on the fetus (de Vries *et al.* 1987).

Fetal behavioural states have an influence on fetal reactiveness to various kinds of stimulation. For instance, external factors such as palpation or vigorous shaking of the uterus during the second half of pregnancy are not always followed by fetal movements (Richardson *et al.* 1981).

Fetal sensory-functions

Fetal sensory-functions were considered to be practically dormant, if not completely nonexistent, till the beginning of the last century. The famous physician Bichat, writing about the fetus towards the turn of the century, described it as living in a world totally devoid of any stimulation (Lecanuet *et al.* 1989). In 1882 Preyer considered that the fetus received some kind of minimal stimulation in an otherwise rather secluded environment. Some forty years later this perspective was completely reversed. Writing in 1920, the physiologist Feldman maintained that all fetal senses, save vision, were subjected to stimulation *in utero*. Yet till the seventies many distinguished scientists still believed that the fetus could be reached only by tactile stimulations.

Recent research has proved all human senses to be 'operative' at least by some time during the second trimester of pregnancy (Chamberlain 1983), and therefore by that time the fetus responds to tactile, pressory, kinaesthetic, thermic, vestibular, gustatory, and painful stimuli.

Responsiveness of the fetus to *cutaneous tactile stimulation* and to *proprioceptive stimulation* was first recognized in the classic researches on fetal reflexology during the 1920s and 1930s, and has been observed during the study of exteriorized fetuses (Hooker 1952; Humphrey 1978). The timing of the earliest evoked responses was seen to correspond closely to the first spontaneous movements at 7.5 weeks gestational age. Therefore by that time the fetus begins to respond to stimuli coming both from the inside and the outside of its body. During pregnancy the fetus seems to have many and varied opportunities of tactile contact and tactile stimulation with the uterine environment and with different parts of its body (Lecanuet *et al.* 1989).

The same timing seems to apply to *pain* (Humphrey 1978), though pain has been investigated only in exteriorized fetuses or in premature infants who seem to present the same behavioural reactions as the newborn. Reflex reactions *in utero* have been observed occasionally after accidental puncture during amniocentesis.

Since 1925 (Peiper), human fetal *reactiveness to sound* has been investigated with loud external stimulations. Fetuses respond to acoustic stimulations by twenty-two to twenty-four weeks gestational age (Birnholz and Benacerraf 1983; Geubelle 1984). These were seen to induce mostly an acceleration in fetal heart rate and a fast motor response. The responses were obtained when mothers were unable to hear the stimulus, and therefore the fetal response to it was direct and not mediated by placental transfer of chemical substances produced by the mother.

The fetal environment is rich with acoustic stimulation coming from the inside of the mother's body (through her eating, drinking, breathing, and cardiovascular and gastrointestinal activity), from her vocalizations, and from the attenuated environmental noise (Walker *et al.* 1971; Armitage *et al.* 1980). The most frequent sound heard by the fetus is that of the pulsation from the womb's main artery (Salk 1973), and the second most frequent one is that of the mother's voice. The relevance of pre-natal auditory experience in the infant has been demonstrated by the well-known studies of DeCasper and his co-workers (DeCasper and Fifer 1980; DeCasper and Sigafoos 1983; Panneton and DeCasper 1984) who proved the infant's liking for the familiar voice of its mother, the soothing effect of exposure to the sound of the mother's heartbeat after birth and the preference shown by the infant for listening to the sound of familiar stories which had been read to them by their mother before birth. Feijo (1981), in studying *fetal conditioning*, noted the consequences of the association of a piece of music presented for twelve seconds (Prokofiev's bassoon 'Peter and the Wolf') with deep maternal relaxation. This same piece was played at various intervals during pregnancy. In a subsequent test performed at eight months pregnancy Feijo noted that the fetus responded much earlier to such familiar stimulation and he interpreted this reaction as an anticipation of the state of comfort induced by maternal stimulation. Some authors have also observed a *habituation* after repeated acoustic stimulations (Bench *et al.* 1967; Smyth 1965; Goodlin and Schmidt 1972).

Vibration is the most potent stimulus capable of inducing changes in fetal motility as well as in fetal heart rate. Birnholz and Benacerraf (1983) applied a so-called 'electrolarynx' producing *vibroacoustic stimuli* on the maternal abdomen overlying a fetal ear. Such stimulation produced aversive reactions similar to those induced in the neonate by pain after twenty-eight weeks of gestation.

Visual stimulations in utero seem to be very limited. However, some light can probably cross maternal abdominal tissues (Liley 1972a), and therefore the intra-uterine environment is not completely dark (Lecanuet *et al.* 1989). The light reaching the womb can reach the fetal retina particularly after twenty weeks' gestation, when the fetus can open and close its lids (Humphrey 1964). In some late third-trimester examinations an orientating response to a bright light source applied to the lower maternal abdomen can be demonstrated (Birnholz 1989).

Vestibular perception, though already present in the fetus, according to some authors seems to be very little used or inhibited during pre-natal life. Prechtl (1984) believes the capacity to respond to vestibular stimulation to be suppressed in the fetus even at a gestational age when such responses occur in the pre-term infant. Other authors, on the contrary, believe vestibular sensitivity to be operative in the fetus (Lecanuet *et al.* 1989).

Chemoreception develops early in gestation in most mammals including man (Bradley and Mistretta 1973; Mistretta and Bradley 1986). The fetus develops within a rich chemical environment and many potentially important chemical cues readily cross the placenta. Therefore, as Smotherman and Robinson (1988) postulate, 'novel chemosensory stimuli derived from the maternal diet and transported to the fetus across the placenta may play a role in the control and development of normal fetal behaviour'.

Taste buds appear in the fetus at about eight to nine weeks (Bradley and Stern 1967; Bradley 1972) and by twelve weeks of gestation such taste buds are well developed and can receive information from the external oral environment. Fetuses daily swallow large quantities of amniotic fluid (210–760 ml) (Pritchard 1965) and may therefore pick up many chemical clues about changes in their environment. De Snoo (1937) showed that the human fetus responds to flavoured amniotic fluid by swallowing larger volumes. Liley (1972b) noted a diminution of swallowing after the injection of a bitter compound.

Olfaction too seems to develop very early in gestation, and olfactory pathways may be functionally active *in utero* and subject to constant stimulation (Pedersen *et al.* 1983).

The fetus seems to have largely passive responses to environmental *temperature changes*, its thermal stability being ensured by that of the mother through heat exchange with the mother's blood at the intervillous space. Yet variations of maternal body temperature can and do occur even under normal circumstances, and these are likely to be perceived by it. Vigorous responses can be noted when cold is applied either *in utero* (Gluckman *et al.* 1983) or to the exteriorized fetus (Dawes 1968).

The intra–uterine environment

The traditional and widespread vision of the intra–uterine environment as a dark, warm, and silent place secluded from the outside world and protected from the impingement of almost any stimulation and the implicit idea therein of constancy, homogeneity, comfort, and security have now been revolutionized by numerous and varied empirical studies.

We now know that the intra-uterine world, far from being a static universe, is subject to many changes and can show innumerable individual variations even within its main constant components: the placenta, the umbilical cord, and the extra-embryonic membranes. Innumerable also are the individual variations that we may encounter in each single pregnancy.

The *umbilical cord* increases steadily in length, most probably in response to tensile forces exerted by the fetus, and shows noticeable and consistent differences in size, length, type, and point of insertion in the placenta, and so on, amongst individual fetuses. No other explanation has been found for its numerous yet very variable windings than that they are due to fetal movement (Moessinger *et al.* 1982).

Placentae too are of different sizes and shapes and show an enormous variety of micro and macro differences for each individual fetus. These differences can be of enormous importance, as, for instance, restriction of placental growth limits umbilical and uterine blood flow and flow-limited placental transfer and so limits fetal growth (Smotherman and Robinson 1988).

As the fetus grows during pregnancy the *uterus* itself undergoes changes in shape and is subject to thinning and distension. Several parameters in the uterine environment also vary among mothers and in successive pregnancies, as well as during the course of gestation.

Amniotic fluid is dynamic, reflecting the mother's hormonal state and, as a plasma filtrate, also the mother's diet. Moreover, during the last trimester of gestation fetuses swallow and excrete amniotic fluid, thereby further altering its composition (Lev and Orlic 1972; Alberts and Cramer 1988). As amniotic fluid is an odorous substance and it changes constantly as a consequence of the mother's physiological state and as a result of fetal swallowing and excreting *in utero*, it may provide a rich source of chemosensory stimulation for the fetus (Pedersen *et al.* 1983).

Fetuses develop in different locations within the uterus, and micro-environmental conditions may vary systematically among different uterine positions. This is particularly important in the case of twins where one finds a marked variation in the chemical micro-environments of fetuses in different uterine positions.

Therefore not only the environment of the uterus changes continuously during gestation, but each fetus also inhabits a different, though broadly speaking similar, environment and thus is subject to different experiences and stimulations. Differences in position entailing different stimulations and differences in capacity to move more or less freely within the womb may seem trifles from our adult point of view, but are certainly relevant for the fetus, whose environment and experiences are constituted and derived from them.

2

Singleton pregnancies

This chapter deals mainly with a detailed description of three singleton pregnancies and therefore of three children observed within their natural environment in the pre-natal and post-natal stages.

The presentation of my research findings poses a considerable problem. If I were to present unedited transcripts of all the observations even for one case, the amount of material would run into hundreds of pages and would be intolerably repetitive, even boring. But to edit and select material makes one even more vulnerable to the criticism I have described above: namely, that I found what I wished to find and furthermore selected material to prove my thesis that there is marked continuity between pre- and post-natal behaviour. However, in spite of its defects, this second alternative is the only reasonable course to follow.

Having to choose from large quantities of material, therefore, I decided to include for each case two verbatim transcripts of the comments accompanying ultrasonographic sessions and one detailed transcript of the last observation when the children were four years old, or in the case of Pina (see Observation no. 3) three (her age at the time of my writing this book). The background of each observation as well as a summary of the events taking place both between the pre-natal observations and up to the last one will also be included for each case, followed by a short summary at the end.

Giulia (see Observation no. 1) is the only exception to this rule, as the fact of having witnessed her delivery as well as having treated her psychotherapeutically later in life rendered her an exceptional case indeed.

The account of the pre-natal and perinatal stages may seem unduly long compared to the richness of happenings and details usually to be found in observations taking place after birth. It is only fairly recently

39

that we have had the opportunity of witnessing the secret events of pre-natal life, and while I know of several observations of the post-natal stages, pre-natal ones are only now beginning.

The role of the obstetricians, as can be seen, was of crucial importance in the ultrasonographic observations. Indeed, it was thanks to them that I have detailed verbal records of fetal movements; it was my impression that the obstetricians were accurate and precise in their descriptions of such movements. As the reader will soon become aware, they varied considerably in sensitivity to the mother's situation and anxieties. They were not trained in psychoanalysis or psychiatry, and their central interest in participating in the research was to examine Prechtl's findings.

Unfortunately, the written account of the ultrasonographic sessions does not give nearly an accurate enough picture either of the emotions pervading the room or of the real rhythm of each observation, with its silences, pauses, and moments of excitement and intense action. Nothing can replace a direct experience of the events recorded in a verbal transcription and even if one were able to show the images recorded on the tapes, these would be just images, devoid of much of their original emotional impact. This is always a problem when working with 'scientifically' accurate, but emotionally blank recorders and videotapes. I hope that my attempts to describe the emotional atmosphere of the observation and its impact on me each time will help to recapture part of this vital, yet unmeasurable, parameter of the observations.

OBSERVATION NO. 1 – GIULIA

Background

Mrs A, a woman in her early thirties, came accompanied by her husband for her first ultrasonographic observation. Even before they were introduced to me I had been struck by the aspect of both future parents when I passed them in the corridor. Though she was only thirteen weeks pregnant, Mrs A looked enormous in her wide maternity dress. Being also a rather tall woman she made her husband, a short man in his early forties, look even shorter next to her. On that day Mrs A was also rather heavily but somehow clumsily made up, with bright red lipstick emphasizing her already fleshy lips, and bright blue eyeshadow and silvery pink blush smeared carelessly on her lids and cheeks. Her old-fashioned yet rather vamp-looking, low-necked, black velvety dress, together with her smeared and bright make-up, made her look quite 'whorish', though in an outdated and clumsy way, like a character out of a Fellini film.

Her 'whorishness' disappeared completely in all the following observations, when she came back looking pale and washed out, wearing a modest and childishly innocent-looking tartan dress, as if somehow maternity had changed her into an ageless and innocent child. Till now, almost six years later, I have only seen this 'whorishness' of hers again when pathetically reflected in her daughter's face, after she had been brought to me for treatment following her brother's birth.

On the day of the first observation Mr A looked provocatively comfortable showing off his grotesque-looking wife. Being so short he too looked like a caricature; his sporty leather jacket, his baggy corduroy trousers, his checked deerstalker hat and his pointed pepper-and-salt beard made him look like a malicious gnome. His attitude, too, during each observation was that of an apparently cynical and mischievous aloofness, laughing at our 'fantasy' in decoding the projected images and commenting on the general ugliness of babies as well as his total uninvolvement with his daughter, 'that thing', whose limited movements we were all so interested in following on the screen. Yet, right from the very beginning I could sense something both tender and tragic under this apparent bravado. And as I have come to know him over the years and have seen him take tender and loving care of his wife and daughter whilst he knew all along that he could, at any moment, be condemned to death by his extremely high blood pressure and his increasing renal failure caused by a rare malformation of his kidneys, this first impression of fragile bravado has proved to be quite accurate.

Giulia: the first four ultrasonographic observations – summary

During that first meeting Mrs A was rather silent and showed no signs of anxiety. As the obstetricians asked her to take her clothes off, whilst commenting rather derogatorily on her fatness and on the difficulties posed by it – 'with so many layers of fat interposed between the probe and the uterine wall it is much more difficult to get a clear picture of the child . . . ' – Mrs A lost all of her sinful allure and just looked clumsy and pathetic in her enormous shapelessness. She lay on the bed keeping her arms behind her head with her face turned towards the screen. She made almost no comment, nor let out any exclamation, and one had the impression of just hearing the rhythm of her calm and regular breathing. She smiled though at her husband's remarks and occasionally responded to his cynical comments saying, 'But come on . . . what are you saying . . . ', whilst seeming amused by them. His comments were pretty frequent and along these lines: 'You must all have a lot of imagination . . . where can you see that? . . . I can't see anything of what you are describing . . . ', 'I much prefer my beloved computers', 'That thing is not my child . . . how can I feel anything for it? . . . '. Yet each time the 'thing' moved even slightly (and it moved very little and very slightly) he seemed immediately interested in it: he sat on a chair and stared intently at the screen, looking both fascinated and surprised. Mostly Giulia (the name subsequently chosen for the girl) just floated in the amniotic fluid following the rhythm of her mother's breathing, as if lulled by it, seeming totally in tune and at one with it. When the observation time was over one of the obstetricians, probably alarmed by her lack of movement, stimulated her rather violently by shaking her mother's abdominal wall and by pushing the probe against it forcefully. Giulia reacted with a couple of jumps and a few uncoordinated movements, before plunging back to the lulling of the regular rhythm of her mother's breath. The only activities that were noted during that observation were some slight movements of her fingers, which were often kept between her legs, and some equally slight in and out movements of her tongue.

At the following observation Mrs A came with her husband again (in fact she always came accompanied by him). When she lay on the couch, she again breathed calmly and regularly while staring rather blankly at the screen. Again she smiled at her husband's remarks, and the only question she asked was when she would feel her child move. Her husband still continued to make cynical remarks, but could not conceal his interest in the activities of 'the thing', though he said he was only interested in its measurements (each fetus was measured and the integrity of its organs was checked each time before the actual observation began). Giulia seemed again to move only passively, lulled by her mother's regular and drowsy breathing. She was also seen a few times rocking herself into what appeared to be sleep. Her general passiveness was in contrast, though, with the almost incessant activity of her tongue, moving in and out of her lips and rolling as if she were sucking it, together with frequent opening and closing of her mouth. Such closing, though, even when her tongue was not in the way, was always incomplete, and since the image of the umbilical cord, when visualized, was adjacent to her mouth, presumably Giulia often kept the cord in her mouth and licked it too. The same patterns were repeated during the third and the fourth ultrasonographic observations with an added and ever-increasing interest in licking the placenta and the almost constant presence of her hands between her legs.

I can read from the notes I took at the time that 'While I was observing Giulia, she gave me the impression of being of a placid nature, well at ease in her intra-uterine world, but somehow she also conveyed the impression of being quite a sensuous creature, in allowing herself to be peacefully lulled, in rocking herself to sleep, in keeping her hands between her legs and particularly in her constant and seemingly voluptuous use of her tongue.'

I will now report in detail the transcription of the recordings of the fifth and the sixth ultrasonographic observations. During these observations Giulia's floating in tune with her mother's breathing is less evident than before as it is now impossible to visualize her entire body. Therefore the focus of these observations revolves mainly around her head.

Giulia: fifth ultrasonographic observation (thirtieth week) – transcript

Mrs A arrives a few minutes early accompanied by her husband. She looks enormous and tired. They both smile at me, then she hands over her obstetric file to the nurse and she goes and gets ready for the observation. She lies down on the couch. The obstetrician comes in, takes the file from the nurse and goes up to Mrs A and sits down ready to start the observation. The nurse goes out and another obstetrician comes in.

MR A (laughing):   I would like to know its sex . . . if it is a boy I will call him Agilulfus . . .
MRS A: How can you call him Agilulfus! . . . come on . . . if it is a boy he wants to call him Agilulfus . . . well I hope it is a girl! . . . (Everybody is laughing now.)
FIRST OBSTET: (She is also visibly pregnant.) I don't know why, but my husband last night was also thinking about names . . . he was choosing them from a television programme . . . a serial . . . one character was called Odoacer . . . (She laughs.) . . . he decided on that . . . (Laughs.)
MR A: That was precisely my second choice!..
MRS A: My God! . . . poor little thing! . . .
SECOND OBSTET: I am sure she will be a girl . . . at least to avoid these names . . .

43

MRS A: In fact my husband refuses to choose its name until he knows what it is . . . I am afraid we will end up doing what my sister did with her son . . . he was nameless for at least four to five days . . .

FIRST OBSTET: (who seemed rather lost in thought) What! You mean four or five days without moving! . . .

MRS A: No, I meant without a name . . .

FIRST OBSTET: Sorry, I understood without moving . . . well, I think S. (another obstetrician who is often in charge of the observation) is not coming . . . let's start with its measurements . . . and let's look for its sex! . . . (She starts operating the probe.)

MR A: His name is Agilulfus, I told you . . .

MRS A: Come on, poor little thing! . . .

FIRST OBSTET: Well . . . (She laughs.) . . . we can see its sex . . . she didn't like any of those masculine names . . .

MRS A: (sounding rather thrilled)   You mean it is a girl . . .

SECOND OBSTET: Yes, it's a girl . . . '

MR A: It's Theodolinda then . . . (Laughs.)

MRS A: Is it really a girl? . . .

FIRST OBSTET: These are her buttocks . . . whilst this is the genital area . . . you see . . . it's typical of a girl . . . now she is moving her legs slightly . . . you can see it even better . . .

MR A: My! . . . you are full of imagination! . . . how can you see all this? . . .

SECOND OBSTET: It's a matter of experience . . .

FIRST OBSTET: Look, you can see it clearly . . . this is the rima vaginalis . . . this image is typical of the female . . . let's start measuring her now . . .   (She measures head, femur, and abdomen, and her colleague writes them down. Then she says, 'We are ready to start with the observation now . . . look at the time – this is said to me) . . . I have started . . . these are her eyes . . . her nose . . . her mouth . . . her hand is near her mouth . . . it could even be inside it . . . the mouth is open . . .

MRS A: It's so complicated to understand . . .

FIRST OBSTET: The other hand is here . . . on her knee . . . now she is bringing it between her legs . . . she is stretching both legs slightly . . .

MR A: But where is her head? . . .

SECOND OBSTET: Down here . . . but we are looking at a section now . . . so we are not visualizing it . . .

MR A: How is it possible that we can't see the head . . .

FIRST OBSTET: It's down here . . . you can see it now . . . before we were looking at another section which included buttocks and legs . . . so it was not on the same plane and therefore you couldn't see it . . .

MR A: Now I get it . . . I just wanted to understand . . .

SECOND OBSTET: You see she is still holding her hand between her legs . . . she is not moving at the moment, just floating . . .

MR A: I have heard that you are also planning to observe some twins . . . how do you do that? . . .

FIRST OBSTET: We enlarge the field . . . look . . . now we are looking at her head . . . you can clearly see her eyes and her nose . . . she is opening and closing her mouth . . . again . . . again . . . again . . . she is chewing all the time . . . her tongue is there . . . she is sucking it . . . non-stop . . .

MR A: How can you call that amorphous mass a head? . . . (Exclamations of protest from Mrs A and the obstetricians.)

SECOND OBSTET: If I were you I would feel offended, poor little one! . . .

MR A: All these doctors read science fiction at night . . .

FIRST OBSTET: Look now she's opened her hand . . . it's still near her face . . . look, she is licking it . . . you can see her tongue sticking out . . .

MR A: Yes, now I can see it . . . the fact is that I am an engineer . . .

SECOND OBSTET: Everyone has his problems . . . I am sure I could never understand all your mathematical formulae . . .

FIRST OBSTET: The tongue . . . look at the tongue . . . how she is sucking it . . . and now she is even yawning . . . with her tongue sticking out of her mouth . . .

SECOND OBSTET: Look at her tongue . . . what she is doing with it! . . . I have never seen such a big tongue . . . of course she must be a female! . . .

MRS A: She keeps her hand in her mouth too . . .

FIRST OBSTET: Yes, she is licking the palm of her hand, not her fingers . . . her fingers are sticking out . . . her tongue . . . she is moving it again . . . she is also moving her fingers slightly . . . again her mouth . . . and her tongue . . . these images are really beautiful . . . we should take a picture of them . . .

SECOND OBSTET: They look like pictures from the moon . . . you know from another world . . . they have such an extraordinary quality . . .

MR A: I want a picture . . .

FIRST OBSTET: Her tongue again . . . now she is moving it in and out of her lips . . . she has removed her hand . . . her tongue again . . . now she is breathing . . .

MR A: Are these her lungs? . . .

FIRST OBSTET: No, it's all her chest . . . you can see it . . . she is raising and lowering it . . . now she has turned herself round . . . my God, what a big open mouth! . . . she is incredible . . . completely agape . . .

look at her tongue . . . she is sucking it . . . now . . . wait . . . she is swallowing . . . you can see it from her neck . . . look here . . . it is moving up and down . . . again . . . again . . . again . . . again . . . again (This activity goes on for about ten minutes.) . . . she is drinking a lot . . . look, she is gulping enormous quantities of amniotic fluid.

MR A: Once they are out, I mean they are babies they are really horrible . . . one must be objective . . . I have seen many babies in my life . . .

MRS A: Don't be silly, come on . . .

SECOND OBSTET: How come an engineer has seen many babies in his life . . .

MR A: My nephews . . . I have six nephews . . .

SECOND OBSTET: It's not true . . . they are just wonderful . . . I can tell you, they are really marvellous . . .

FIRST OBSTET: With your daughter you will feel completely different, you will see . . .

MR A: Women always lack any objectivity . . .

MRS A: (sounding slightly embarrassed and annoyed) Come on, stop it now . . . poor child . . .

MR A: How can you talk about objectivity . . . until they are at least six to seven months old they look terrible . . .

FIRST OBSTET: Your voice . . . be careful, you know that she can hear your voice . . . all babies are beautiful . . . look at her . . . her profile . . . her tongue . . . again her tongue . . . she is licking something . . . her head is slightly bent backwards . . . she is probably licking the placenta now . . .

SECOND OBSTET: She is moving her tongue all the time . . .

FIRST OBSTET: Here is her mouth again . . . she has opened it again . . . she is opening and closing it . . . and sucking her tongue . . . you can see her chin moving up and down all the time . . . look . . . you can also see her teeth-sockets . . . this fragmented image . . . she is opening her mouth again . . . now she has brought her hand in front of her mouth . . . she is sucking her palm . . . now she is sucking her thumb! . . . let's look at what she is doing with her other hand . . . it is still there right in between her legs . . . she is still opening and closing her mouth . . . swallowing . . . she must be hungry . . . she is swallowing the amniotic fluid non-stop . . . again . . . again . . . gulping enormous quantities of it . . . plus she also sucks her tongue . . . as many babies do . . .

MRS A: I used to suck my tongue too when I was a child . . .

SECOND OBSTET: Babies do that frequently . . .

MRS A: I went on doing it till I was at least five . . . (then, after a pause, talking to her husband) Your father will be happy that she is a girl . . .

I wonder about my nephews though . . . they are all boys . . . six boys . . . we are all sisters . . . five sisters . . .

SECOND OBSTET: So, what are you complaining about? . . . This Theodolinda is a real rarity . . . look now she is opening and closing her hand . . .

MR A: Yes, I can see it . . . after a while one gets a bit used to all this . . .

FIRST OBSTET: Now she is moving her fingers . . . very fine movements . . . can you feel her? . . .

MRS A: Not at this moment . . . usually when she moves, she moves completely . . . she turns herself round . . . she moves much more during the night . . . I don't know whether it is really so or whether it is because I pay less attention during the day . . . probably because I am also moving about during the day . . . I hope she will move more during the day, once she's born . . .

FIRST OBSTET: They realize when their mother is active or resting . . . this is something that they certainly realize . . . they can feel it from the different state of contraction of the womb . . . when the mother is resting, the womb is extremely relaxed . . . whilst when you move . . .

MR A: But inside the amniotic fluid they should not feel a different contraction . . .

FIRST OBSTET: Inside the amniotic fluid certainly the pressure is evenly distributed all over the body . . . but they feel contractions all the same . . . plus the utero-placental flow is different according to whether you are standing or are in a resting position . . . look what she is doing now . . . licking the placenta again . . . my God . . . she is really wild this time . . . look . . . it just goes on and on . . .

The wild licking of the placenta goes on till the observation is over. Then Mrs A stands up and cleans herself from the jelly on her stomach. The first obstetrician asks her if she is on a diet and Mrs A says that she is on a very low-calorie diet.

FIRST OBSTET: I am afraid you will have to continue with the diet . . . as your daughter has a tendency to put on too much weight . . . just like you . . . she has never been small . . .

MR A: The funny thing is that she was undergoing a series of tests when we found out . . . she was in hospital . . . she even mentioned it to her doctor: perhaps I am pregnant, she said . . . He said: Impossible! . . . They decided she was not . . . they were studying God only knows what . . . lots of all sorts of tests . . . they wanted to find out why she was so fat . . . certainly there is no relationship between her intake of calories and her increase in weight . . .

MRS A: I continue to put on weight . . .

MR A: Then the hormonal counts put a stop to all the enquiries: she was pregnant! . . .

MRS A: All the hormonal counts were wrong . . . obviously . . . I was pregnant . . . certainly it was a messy start . . .

By now Mrs A has put on all her clothes. The first obstetrician makes another appointment with her and they leave saying goodbye to all of us.

The general atmosphere of the following observation is quite different from the rather manic one of the previous session. Mrs A begins to voice her worries about the delivery and her fear that her child might not be able to come out of the womb. Giulia in fact is becoming increasingly bigger and instead of descending gradually towards its opening seems to have retreated higher up in the womb. The wild motions of Giulia's tongue are a constant and almost monotonous element of this observation.

Giulia: sixth ultrasonographic observation (thirty-fifth week) – transcript

OBSTET: So let's start . . . we measure it first . . . do you already know its sex? . . . (She was present at the last observation, but she probably forgot.)

MRS A: Yes, it's a girl . . .

MR A: She will become stupid poor girl . . . with all these rays . . . I am sure she will . . . on the other hand it may not be the fault of the rays . . . look at her parents! . . .

OBSTET: (ignoring him) Have you put on more weight? . . .

MRS A: Well, yes . . .

OBSTET: How much since last time? . . .

MRS A: Well, perhaps a couple of kilos . . .

OBSTET: The girl too is fat . . .

MRS A: I hope not too fat . . . I hope she can come out . . . they say it is dangerous when they are too big . . . they can remain stuck inside . . . in the last three . . . well actually, two weeks I have been weighing myself systematically every morning . . . I am very careful now . . . I got such a fright when I realized I had put on three kilos in a fortnight . . .

OBSTET: Another victim of Easter! . . .

MRS A: No, this happened before . . . I hope she is not too big . . . I hope she will be able to come out . . .

OBSTET: (not paying attention to Mrs A's worries, writes down the child's measurements, then says) Let's start with the observation now . . . here is her head . . . it is down here . . . her position is all right . . . you can see her eyes . . . her mouth . . . both her legs are bent . . .

MRS A: Is this the right position? . . . I am sure she was in the transversal position last week . . . she was hurting me on the side . . . Now I worry frequently about the delivery . . . I have only a little more than a month left . . . How can she come out when she is so big and I am so fat? . . .

OBSTET: (again not listening to her worries) She is opening her mouth . . . her tongue . . . again . . . again . . . she is moving her tongue . . . again . . . her tongue . . . she sucks it and moves it in and out . . .

Another obstetrician comes in a moment. She says hello to Mrs A, then asks her, 'Do you feel her moving a lot?'

MRS A: Not really . . . this daughter seems rather inert . . .

SECOND OBSTET: Yet she moves . . . what worries me is that she is so big . . . We might have to do a Caesarean . . .

Mrs A hugs her husband and says, ' Well, I hope not . . . '

SECOND OBSTET: We shall see . . . she is also still very high . . . but in any case we shall talk about it later . . . (and she goes out).

The other obstetrician continues to describe monotonously the same activities.

OBSTET: Her tongue . . . again her tongue . . . sucking it . . . now she is swallowing the amniotic fluid . . . again . . . again . . . her tongue . . . she is stretching her head backwards . . . she is licking the placenta now . . .

MR A: How disgusting!

OBSTET: Look how she licks it! . . . we can almost hear the noise . . . look . . . she is pulling it down towards her mouth . . . my God! . . . her tongue is really strong . . . look she is doing it again . . . and again . . . and again . . .

(Some exclamations followed by a rather long silence)

OBSTET: Now she is breathing . . . rather vigorously . . . you can see her chest . . .

(Again a rather long silence)

OBSTET: Her tongue . . . she is sucking it . . . now she is bringing her hands near her mouth . . . making some slight movements with her fingers . . . crossing them . . . her tongue . . . she is licking her fingers now . . . the back of her hand . . . she seems to be licking it . . . she is back to the placenta now . . . licking it . . .

Apart from some more breathing movements the rest of the observation continues to register just licking movements and no other comments.

At the end of the observation Mrs A again expresses her worries about the child being able to come out. She says, 'She is too comfortable there . . . ' The observation is now over. Mrs A needs to be helped down from the couch. She thanks me and then gives me the address of her mother saying that she will be spending the next fortnight there as her husband will be away. She says, 'I hope he will be here for the delivery . . . ' We agree to meet in about a fortnight to make all the arrangements for the observations after the delivery. Then she picks up her file and leaves rather hurriedly.

Giulia: up to the delivery – summary

After this session and before the delivery I visited Mrs A once at her mother's home in order to make arrangements for the observations after birth. Her husband was away for a few days and Mrs A was staying with her parents. On that day her clothes looked freshly ironed and immaculately clean, and she said that she was looked after by her mother like a baby. 'When I stay at my mother's I just do nothing all day . . . I allow her to cuddle and fondle and feed me like a baby . . . ' Her mother's meals had certainly left a mark on her as Mrs A now weighed over 100 kilograms. Mrs A then introduced me to her mother, a tall, solid woman with a nice warm smile on her face. I was immediately offered coffee and a cake and we all sat down round the table with Mrs A and her mother talking almost non-stop. Mrs A complained of being very tired and unable to sleep at night. She was quite terrified of the delivery as she feared she would almost certainly have to have a Caesarean. Again, 'I am too fat . . . she will never come out . . . ' She also told me that she was afraid of losing her freedom: she and her husband had been married for over nine years and were used to coming and going and eating as and when they pleased. As a child she had constantly hung on to her mother and was afraid that Giulia might be the same. She had known her husband since they were children; he was at school with one of her sisters and had been practically adopted by all of them. All the children of their village loved her mother and during the war she had taken in and adopted two young cousins as well. Whilst she was telling me this her mother blushed with pride and handed me some more cake, making me feel that I had been adopted as well, though at the same time reduced to a child. During all these years they have almost never asked about myself,

50

my work, my husband, my children, and so on, and each time I went to visit Mrs A at her mother's place I had the pleasant but disquieting feeling of being brought back in time to some improbable childhood age. Both Mrs A and her mother loved talking to me, and each time my visits were the occasion for endless conversations which sounded to me like verbal feasts.

On that day as they accompanied me to the door Mrs A told me, 'Now my mother will take me out shopping . . . she is spoiling me . . . ', and then hugged her mother, looking like an enormously overgrown little girl.

I will now report on the delivery.

Giulia: the delivery – detailed report

After several phone calls from Mr A and Dr R (the obstetrician on duty that night, whom I had never met before), finally at 2.30 a.m. Dr R phones me saying, 'So now you can come . . . ' By the time I get to the hospital it is about 3 a.m. All the corridors are dark and when I reach the obstetric ward nobody seems to be around. I walk along the main corridor and I notice a woman wearing a green overall sitting at a desk at the end of it. As soon as she hears my steps she comes towards me smiling. She introduces herself to me saying that she is Dr R, then she asks me to hang up my clothes (I have my theatre-gown with me) and then accompanies me into the delivery room.

Mrs A is lying in the obstetric chair, with her legs up in the obstetric position. A phleboclysis is inserted in her arm and several electrodes are inserted in her vagina. A midwife is sitting next to her and is reading the intensity and the length of her contractions on a small monitor. Mr A and Dr P, the friend of the family, are also in the room, both wearing green theatre-gowns. I go near the couch and Mrs A turns her head towards me and smiles at me with a big smile. She is very pale and looks very tired and is all covered in sweat. She says, 'I am very tired . . . I can't stand this any longer . . . ', but then smiles at me again and says, 'But I am sure that you will bring me luck . . . now that you are here she will be born soon . . . '

As soon as she finishes saying this a strong contraction intervenes followed by a violent push. Mrs A moans, and says, 'It hurts . . . it's too much . . . it hurts too much . . . ' The midwife tries to encourage her saying, 'Come on, push now . . . stronger . . . stronger . . . a stronger push . . . ' Contractions and pushes now follow one another at very short intervals, and Mrs A looks totally exhausted. I am standing next to her and find myself putting my hand on her forehead. She smiles at me saying, 'Whose hand is this? . . . it is so nice and cool . . . ' As her pushes increase in frequency so does her pain. Mrs A moans, then starts to scream 'I can't stand this any longer . . . can't you do something about it? . . . ', then indicating her pubis, 'I feel a terrible pain here . . . ' Dr R is now back in the room and she explains to Mrs A that often during the delivery pubic tissues become loose causing much pain. Mrs A says, 'Yes, it is causing much pain . . . but even before, I was already suffering from pubic pain . . . can't you do something about it? . . . ' Dr R tells her that she can't do anything about it. The only way to combat pain is to try and push even more strongly. The pushes start again and Mrs A screams, 'I can't do it . . . it's too much . . . it hurts too much . . . ' Dr R and the midwife try to encourage her. Her husband paces the room looking as pale as a ghost in his enormously outsized green theatre-gown. Mrs A screams, 'I can't do it . . . I can't push . . . I am holding it back . . . I am inhibiting it . . . she will never come out . . . ' In between contractions and pushes she looks more and more tired and covered in sweat. She says frequently, 'She will never come out . . . ', and her screams progressively take on a more despairing and terrified tone.

The midwife puts a rubber glove on. She whispers something to Dr R and then tells Mrs A that she is going to examine her. She inserts a finger in her vagina and Mrs A screams, 'No . . . it hurts too much . . . what are you doing? . . . take your hand away . . . ' The midwife tells her to be patient and then also Dr R intervenes saying that it is important to feel if the head is lower. The midwife takes her finger out and shakes her head, saying, 'She is still quite high . . . ' and Dr R adds 'And no blood mark yet . . . ' The midwife in a whisper to Dr R: 'She is even higher now . . . ' Mrs A: 'Come on, my little one . . . come on, please come out . . . or we will both die . . . ' Her husband and their doctor friend have now left the room. Violent contractions and pushes start again and Mrs A's screams sound even more desperate now. I put my hand on her forehead again, and she says, 'What a nice cool hand . . . how nice . . . ', then, 'If at least I could have some rest . . . ' Then suddenly during a particularly strong push she complains, screaming, that she feels an unbearable pain in her side. She seems very frightened and screams, 'But what is this? . . . I don't know what it is . . . it's unbearable . . . what's happening to me? . . . ' Dr R tries to comfort her and says that now she will examine her too. As she inserts her finger inside the vagina, Mrs A starts screaming, 'It hurts too much . . . stop it! . . . you are hurting me! . . . ' Dr R looks worried and says whispering to the midwife, 'She is still high . . . actually she has retreated even higher and the contractions seem weaker now . . . ' The midwife continues to encourage Mrs A as soon as a contraction intervenes: 'Come on . . . push . . . come on Margareta [Mrs A's name] . . . stronger . . . push stronger . . . again . . . again.' As soon as each contraction stops Mrs A says, 'Please come out, my little one', 'This is too much', 'I am too tired', 'I am in a sweat', then as the contractions start again she screams. Dr R goes out of the room and goes and talks to the husband and the family doctor. From what I can hear she is saying that she is considering a Caesarean. She comes back a moment and says, 'Now we shall have to do some blood tests and an electrocardiogram . . . ' Mrs A complains, 'I am all in a sweat . . . ' Dr R says, almost absent-mindedly, 'If you like I can give you something to drink . . . ', but then probably thinking about the Caesarean, 'No, better not . . . '

A nurse arrives holding a big syringe for the blood tests. She inserts the needle in Mrs A's arm saying, 'Don't push now, please . . . ' Mrs A: 'How can I do that . . . it's not up to me whether I push or not . . . ' In fact, during the blood abstraction several pushes intervene and each time the nurse says, 'Don't push, please don't push now . . . ' Then when she has collected sufficient blood she goes out. Dr R tries to encourage Mrs A while the midwife takes a handkerchief, soaks it, and then puts it on Mrs A's forehead.

Dr R goes out of the room and asks me to follow her. Mr A and the family doctor are sitting on a desk in the room next door and they both look exhausted and dismayed. A technician arrives with the electrocardiographic machine. She goes into the delivery room and from time to time we can hear Mrs A screaming with pain. The technician often tells her not to move. Dr R says, 'It's terrible to have to think of a Caesarean after all this pain . . . ' Mr A looks terribly sad and depressed, and says, 'I would hate to be in her place . . . ' Dr R: 'Now in any case we shall have to see what the Professor has to say . . . it will be up to him to decide . . . ' The screams continue, 'Help, please help me . . . I am going to die . . . ' Dr R asks their doctor if Mrs A suffers from allergies and he says no. She looks at her file. The technician comes out with the electrocardiographic machine. The family doctor looks at the electrocardiogram and says that everything seems to be going well. Dr R goes back to the delivery room and I follow her too. Mrs A is now screaming practically non-stop and looks both terrified and in terrible pain. Then, after screaming 'Please help me . . . I am going to die . . . she will never come out . . . ', she begins to feel sick and makes loud vomiting noises. The midwife lowers the light that had been put on during the various tests and then puts a towel under Mrs A's chin. Mrs A continues to feel sick for a while. She also belches twice and seems to feel rather ashamed. She says, 'I don't understand why this . . . I have not eaten anything since last night . . .'

A few minutes later the Professor arrives. He is a man in his sixties who must have been quite attractive once and looks very arrogant and snobbish. I move aside. He listens to what Dr R has to say with an air of subtle contempt. Then he moves towards Mrs A and I have the impression that he is going to examine her. I go out as I feel slightly embarrassed and I am afraid that he might ask who I am (he has been glancing at me in a rather inquisitive way) and might object to my presence there. Mr A is still sitting in the room next door and is looking more and more depressed. He says to me, 'It's terrible to have to have a Caesarean after all this pain . . . ' Just then the Professor comes out followed by Dr R, and he is saying to her, 'It's not necessary . . . you will have to try with the step-ladder first, – at this point I really don't understand what he is talking about; I have never heard of a step-ladder being used in obstetrics – . . . and then use the vacuum-extractor . . . ' Dr R looks rather sceptical and annoyed. The Professor goes away and she goes back to the delivery room.

Mr A says to me, 'I am afraid she will not make it . . . how can she make it? . . . ' We go back together into the delivery room. The family doctor follows us too. Dr R tells the midwife that now they will try with the step-ladder. In fact I notice a small step-ladder in a corner of the room. The midwife brings it to Mrs A's side. Dr R climbs on it and as soon as she notices that Mrs A is pushing she too pushes with all her strength by practically lying across her stomach. Mr A goes out shaking his head. The family doctor remains and after each push raises Mrs A's head. She looks too pale, frightened, and exhausted to even scream. A few minutes later the Professor comes back followed by an assistant who says 'Hello' to Dr R. The Professor looks at Mrs A and without examining her says, 'It is coming down . . . ', then goes out again. Dr R, continuing to look rather annoyed, tells the midwife to start incising Mrs A's perineum.

Mrs A looks slightly reinvigorated. She says, 'She is coming down . . . please do come out, my little one . . . I am tired, you know . . . ' The midwife gives her some local anaesthetic and she screams, 'What are you doing? . . . you are hurting me! . . . ' Dr R explains to her what the midwife is doing. Mrs A shouts, 'But why all these people? . . . [she is referring to the assistant who has remained in the room] . . . please send my husband away . . . ' Her husband is already in the room next door and Dr R points this out to her. The midwife starts cutting. Mrs A says, 'What are you doing! . . . leave me alone! . . . take your hands away . . . why do you still want to torture me? . . . '

The midwife looks rather annoyed. She cleans Mrs A's perineum with some wet cotton-wool and Mrs A screams, 'It's too cold . . . my God it is so cold . . . you could have at least used warm water . . . ' She starts pushing again with Dr R lying across her stomach. The Professor comes back. He gives a nod to the assistant and they both practically jump on her stomach. Dr R is pushed aside. I can't see Mrs A's face at this point. Her pushes are almost continuous now and the Professor urges her in an authoritative manner, 'Come on . . . push now . . . hard . . . ' He is using his foot and sometimes his knee to push against her stomach. His assistant does the same. Dr R looks on silently angry and quite horrified. The midwife, who is now sitting between Mrs A's legs, says, 'She is beginning to come out now . . . I can see her hair . . . it's black . . . ' Mrs A screams non-stop, sounding both terrified and in pain, and practically everybody is now on her stomach. The Professor almost jumps on it. Dr R says, 'The head is swollen . . . ' The Professor nods and continues to urge Mrs A. He says, 'The vacuum-extractor now . . . ' and Dr R gives it to him. I can see almost nothing of what is happening now as they are all over Mrs A who continues to scream. The scene is really quite barbaric.

Then they all move slightly aside and the Professor says, 'Come on now . . . she is coming out . . . ' I stand in front of Mrs A and I see the head of the child emerging from Mrs A's vagina. The midwife turns and pulls it, then pulls out the shoulders. A lot of blood comes out too, then all the body together with the umbilical cord. The midwife clamps the cord. Giulia is rather cyanotic, her head is terribly swollen and all bruised, but her eyes are closed and she looks completely unperturbed, as if she didn't realize all that had happened or feel the transition to another world. The midwife turns her upside-down and she starts breathing without screaming and without opening her eyes, again apparently unperturbed.

The Professor and his assistant go out. Mr A comes in. The family doctor says 'Congratulations!' to him. Then I hear him saying that he must go home now as tomorrow he has to start work early and he wants to try to get a couple of hours sleep. (It is now 4 a.m.) The midwife, still holding Giulia by her legs, puts her in a cot under an almost painfully bright light. A paediatrician is also there now. (I hadn't noticed her come in.)

Giulia doesn't cry or open her eyes and her expression is completely unchanged. Two nurses poke a small pipe inside her nose and her throat and she cries, clenching her fists up to her face, as if trying to protect it from the intrusion, then she turns her head away. Her eyes are still closed. As the pipes are removed she stops crying and moves her head from side to side. She opens her eyes and wanders with her gaze, seeming at ease. Dr R comes near me and looks at her. Giulia's head is very tumefied. The nurse wipes it with some wet cotton-wool, trying to clean the blood from it. Giulia makes some grimaces and seems on the verge of crying, but then quickly resumes her unperturbed expression.

We hear Mrs A complaining loudly: the midwife says that she has to examine her again to make sure that the placenta has been completely expelled. Mrs A starts shivering all over with cold and Dr R tells her, 'Don't worry it's quite normal to shiver like that . . . ' Mrs A turns her head towards me and asks, 'How is she? . . . ', and I say that she is well. The nurse now cuts Giulia's cord. She doesn't react to it. Then she wraps her in a warm blanket and brings her near her mother. Mrs A looks at her saying, 'Hello my little one . . . you have your father's nose . . . ' The nurse puts Giulia on Mrs A's stomach, but she objects to that, saying, 'She is not comfortable like that . . . I am still shivering all over . . . perhaps later . . . ' The midwife asks her if she has already decided upon a name. Mrs A says 'No', smiling at me. The nurse picks Giulia up again and goes into a small room next door, followed by me and by the paediatrician. She removes the blanket and puts her on the presumably cold surface of a scale. Giulia starts screaming, keeping her clenched fists near her face. Then she moves her head from side to side. The nurse picks her up almost immediately, goes near the sink, opens the tap and puts Giulia's back under the running water. Giulia stops screaming immediately. She looks calm. Her eyes are still closed. The nurse makes sure that the plastic bracelet with her name and number is well tied to her wrist, then wraps her again and quickly disappears along the corridor.

I go back to the delivery room and tell Mrs A that the child is really nice, as in fact she is. Mrs A smiles at me. Mr A says, 'How can you say that she is nice . . . they all look like little monsters . . . ', and while saying this he laughs, holding his wife's hand. I say that I have to go. Mrs A thanks me for coming and says, 'I shall see you soon . . . ' I say goodbye to Mr A and again congratulate him on his child.

Dr R accompanies me to pick up my coat and then walks with me along the corridor. She says, 'I can't stand seeing women treated like that . . . these things only happen in Italy I am afraid . . . luckily things are changing a bit now . . . that was a scene from the Deep South . . . a woman literally stamped upon! . . . and it's not different with the children either . . . ' We have reached the door. It is still dark outside and nobody is around. She shows me the way out. I thank her very much and say goodbye to her.

The following observation takes place when Giulia is two days old.

Giulia: first observation (two days old) – detailed report

As I reach the ward I ask a nurse if she knows where I can find Mrs A. She says, 'I don't know . . . try over there . . . ', and she indicates three rooms where the puerperae are supposed to be. I look inside each of the rooms and in the last one I see Mrs A propped up in the middle bed between two other mothers. They are all breast-feeding. As she sees me, she smiles and seems very pleased to see me. She says, 'Good morning! . . . how are you? . . . ' I say that I hope I am not interrupting or disturbing her. She says, 'Absolutely not . . . please do come in . . . come and sit near us . . . ' Then, looking at Giulia, 'She was present at your birth, you know . . . she saw you coming into this world . . . ' I take a chair and sit next to her. I ask her how she is this morning and if she is feeling better. She says, 'Yes, I feel much better today . . . I had some rest . . . it was terrible the other night . . . I must have behaved awfully . . . what a scene I made! . . . but the pain was unbearable . . . it was intolerable . . . and I was so tired . . . I had been in such pain since the previous day . . . I was in pain for more than a day . . . but what a poor figure! . . . ' I smile at her, and say that she really must have been exhausted and in terrible pain.

Mrs A now looks at her baby and says, 'Her name is Giulia . . . her father chose this name for her . . . ' Giulia is leaning against her mother's left breast, with her cheek close to the nipple. Her eyes are closed and she seems completely immobile. Mrs A forces the nipple inside her mouth, but she doesn't react and doesn't suck. Gradually the nipple slips out of her mouth. Mrs A says, 'She seems to be calm . . . she has a quiet temperament . . . I was very worried that she might have been nervy or anxious . . . I was afraid of influencing her . . . I tried to be as calm as possible while I was pregnant . . . but she seems calm . . . ', then, looking at her, 'Now she is sleepy . . . hey, you, aren't you hungry? . . . '

She fastens her nightgown and lays Giulia in between her legs, with her face turned towards her. Giulia seems to wake up and looks at her mother with an expressionless face, then closes her eyes again and continues for a while to open and close them, without moving and with an expressionless look on her face. Her mother holds her hands and I notice that Giulia holds on very tightly to her mother's thumbs. After a moment she starts sucking her tongue, moving it almost continuously in and out of her mouth. She makes no noise with it.

Mrs A says, 'All my right side is in pain . . . ', and she indicates her thigh and her leg. She says, 'They told me that it is due to compression of the nerves . . . not to worry . . . it can happen, but it will pass . . . yesterday in any case I asked for an injection against the pain . . . and

57

after that I slept a lot . . . I really needed that . . . I must find the right position, otherwise it hurts . . . ' She turns slightly on her side, then looks at the child. She says, 'Her forehead is low . . . and her ears are different one from the other . . . just like my husband . . . [then looking at Giulia] . . . Your forehead is really low . . . I like teasing children . . . ' She stares at her rather blankly for a while, then she seems to notice the constant movement of her tongue, and says, 'But perhaps you are still hungry . . . she definitely prefers the other breast . . . ' While saying this she picks her up and brings her close to her left breast. Now Giulia's face is out of sight, but I can see the profile of her cheek and whether she is moving it, and therefore sucking, or not. Giulia is still holding on tightly to one of her mother's fingers and with her other hand is clutching the edge of her nightgown. Mrs A says, 'She clenches my fingers so tightly . . . look . . . her grip is so strong that her fingers become almost white . . . ' Giulia makes two or three weak sucking movements, then stops. Then I hear a noise, as if she were licking the breast. Her mother says, 'What are you doing? . . . you are not sucking it, you are playing . . . she is not sucking it . . . she is licking it! . . . just on one side . . . ' She takes the nipple out of her mouth and shows me how Giulia's tongue has deformed it on one side. Giulia now closes her eyes. Mrs A says, 'I don't think she is hungry . . . she loves leaning on here . . . ', and points at her chest.

Then she leans Giulia with her face against her chest. While still keeping her eyes closed, Giulia immediately starts licking her mother's chest vigorously with the same wild motions I had previously noticed when she licked the placenta. She makes a lot of noise. Her head is slightly turned to one side, towards me. Her mother looks at her for a while, smiling, then says, 'Perhaps she is still hungry . . . I can't make out what it is . . . ' She doesn't seem at all worried, as other mothers in the ward are, about the fact that Giulia is not sucking. During the entire observation, in fact, Giulia seems to be just licking.

Mrs A puts her back at her left breast. Again I cannot see her face and therefore I don't know if her eyes are still closed. I notice, though, that she immediately brings her hands to her mouth and starts licking one of them. With the other one she holds on tightly to the edge of her mother's nightgown. Judging by the noise, she goes on licking her hand for quite a while. Mrs A looks at me, and says, 'She didn't want to come out from the womb . . . she liked it too much in there . . . I was scared . . . I was afraid she was never going to come out . . . I felt trapped . . . I felt really helpless . . . I was afraid I was never going to make it . . . we would have both died . . . you were too comfortable in there, weren't you? . . . You liked it too much . . . you were too comfortable inside the womb . . . ', and she looks at her. She says, looking lost in thought, 'It is difficult to get used to all this . . . she was inside before . . . now suddenly she is outside . . . I am sure it will take her a while before getting used to this world . . . ', then after a pause, 'I hope she will be quiet . . . not screaming all the time . . . she has been very quiet up to now . . . '

Giulia now seems asleep. Her mother picks her up and again lays her between her legs facing her. Giulia puts her tongue out several times, then moves her head from side to side, makes some grimaces keeping her eyes tightly closed, then starts whimpering. Her mother says, 'It's the first time I've heard your voice, you know! . . . perhaps she is still hungry . . . ', and she puts her back at the breast. I hear some licking noises, then silence. Her mother says, 'She must have fallen asleep . . . ' She takes the nipple out of her mouth and Giulia sucks her tongue keeping her eyes closed. Mrs A cleans her nipple again (during the entire observation she cleans her nipple carefully each time before giving it to Giulia), and says, 'I am doing it for her . . . I am afraid that she may catch some infection . . . '

When back at the breast, Giulia doesn't suck and doesn't move. Her mother looks at her and says, 'I wonder whether we shall be able to make it . . . you and I together . . . ' She looks lost in thought, then says smiling, 'We shall have to tell daddy to come home early . . . at seven o'clock . . . not at nine as he usually does . . . (then talking to me) . . . I haven't yet looked for a daily help . . . my mother will be helping me now . . . then we shall see . . . but I can't ask her to come to my house every day . . . nor can she stay with us . . . nor can I move in with them . . . if it is necessary, I can . . . but otherwise I prefer not to . . . I can't ask anything of my father . . . '

She remains silent for a moment, looking rather lost in thought, then says, 'Today in any case I feel better . . . rested . . . the pain was terrible . . . particularly after they began to induce labour . . . I had been told before that the pain was not constant . . . and it stopped in between contractions . . . but I was in constant pain . . . perhaps I was tired . . . the membranes were ruptured at 4 a.m. the previous day . . . therefore I was in labour for 24 hours . . . another woman who was with me in the ward delivered her child in three hours . . . [then looking at Giulia] . . . but you didn't want to come out . . . she weighs almost 4 kilograms . . . I was afraid that she might be born small because I was on a diet . . . just think of it! . . . '

A nurse comes in and starts picking up the babies. Mrs A says, 'They leave her with me only for half an hour . . . ' The nurse comes over to her. Mrs A looks at Giulia saying, 'Goodbye my little one . . . ' and then hands her to the nurse. Giulia doesn't seem to react to the transition and continues to sleep. Mrs A looks rather pale and worn out now. I point this out to her, saying that she seems to need some rest now and that in any case I have to go. She smiles at me, saying, 'I shall phone you then . . . as soon as I am a bit settled . . . ', then she gives me instructions about how to reach her village. She thanks me warmly and I thank her too. She waves at me, smiling, till I am out in the corridor.

Giulia: post-natal observations until age three – summary

The next time, I went to visit Mrs A at her house and I was impressed both by the great chaos, with piles of empty bottles and unemptied ash-trays, and by the amount of food on display. Rather than a house with a new baby it felt like a gargantuan cellar with tins, spaghetti, biscuits, jam, sauces, and salami everywhere. This time Giulia sucked her tongue even before opening her eyes, then licked her blanket, and her licking continued throughout. Her mother told me that she was very voracious, ate in five minutes and spent the rest of the time playing with her tongue. She also told me that Giulia seemed a placid baby who liked looking around, hearing voices and sounds, and licking her mother's chest.

What happened in the following months seemed to form a continuum with what I had observed before. Giulia continued to be a rather voracious baby who 'ate in five minutes' and spent the rest of her time licking with her tongue. She also licked any surface or fabric which came into contact with her face. I saw her licking her mother's chest, her shoulders, her chin, her arms and the clothes covering them. Any pleasure she derived from sucking the breast and the amount of time she spent in contact with it seemed short and less strong than the pleasure she seemed to derive from licking any of these things.

It was only when Giulia was introduced to solids, when she was about four months old, that food seemed to become almost an obsession for her. According to her mother, Giulia now gulped enormous amounts of baby food and was attracted by anything she saw on her mother's plate or entering other people's mouths. Each time I visited Mrs A I was offered coffee, and a dish full of biscuits always came with it. Each time Giulia saw the biscuits or noticed the sugar, she started screaming and stretching her arms frantically towards it, till eventually she was given a biscuit and then another and another, all of which she licked and gulped noisily and voraciously. Not surprisingly she also began to put on weight and at the age of ten months she already weighed as much as a child of two.

Nor did food seem to be the only source of pleasure for her. Giulia seemed to derive pleasure from the use of almost all her other senses.

She seemed to find it extremely pleasurable to let her eyes wander. As her mother said, 'She loves looking', and her gaze didn't seem to reflect much curiosity or inquisitiveness. She seemed rather to have a 'big feast' with her eyes. Her grandmother's face seemed as attractive as the sight of her scarf or of her huge baroque lamp. Her mother told me that Giulia also 'loved hearing', so much so that she often left the radio on for her all day long. She certainly listened with pleasure to the sound of her mother's or her grandmother's voice talking to me. According to her mother, Giulia went 'wild' whenever she heard the sound of a man's voice and I was rather inclined to believe this given the reactions that I witnessed to her grandfather's talking. As her mother said, 'She is really a little whore . . . she is mad about men . . . '

A bit later she also seemed to enjoy her own sounds and at times she could be heard babbling non-stop and emitting all sorts of sounds while her mother spoke to me. Giulia also seemed to love touching and stroking and feeling the texture of things, particularly of any soft and velvety object. Except when it came to food, smell was probably the least visibly used of her senses. When she was a bit older Giulia also seemed to derive a sensuous pleasure from rather masturbatory activities such as endlessly rocking herself. Her grandmother seemed to have well understood her inclination as she told me that Giulia, when picked up, loved to have someone's arm between her legs. Yet Giulia was far from being dull and when one year old she seemed more the portrait of a *bonne vivante*, who seemed absolutely at ease with her surroundings and was determined to derive the maximum of pleasure rather indiscriminately from any source at hand. Though food still ranked higher – and as her mother told me, 'I have seen her licking the floor . . . ' – looking, listening, talking, touching, and so on, all seemed extremely pleasurable for her.

As with her senses, her attachment to people seemed also rather indiscriminate: I never saw her look back at her mother provided someone else's arms were at hand. As time passed Giulia became rather skilful in mastering her motor functions. From the very beginning she showed that same skill in moving her hands that I had observed in the womb. She was very soon able to suck her thumb while at the same time stroking her hair and her face. She grasped objects readily and by nine months she was able to crawl. When ten months old she could stand and by eleven months she began to take her first steps. Not surprisingly, her locomotion became yet another aid in her constant hunt for pleasure and for food. Gurgling too came easily to her, and by eleven months I heard her repeat a few simple words.

When two years old Giulia appeared to be a rather precocious and skilled child. She could walk securely and was already talking quite fluently. She seemed well at ease with her surroundings and was treated by everybody like a little queen. At first glance, by many standards she could have been defined as a perfectly happy and well-adapted child. Yet to me her obesity was already very noticeable and her constant search for food very disquieting. Giulia always had to have something in her mouth – a biscuit, an apple, a sweet, some sugar, some bread, and so forth, and her mother and her grandmother constantly either spontaneously supplied her with something to eat or else gave in to her insistent demands. But at that stage her insatiable appetite was, for the people surrounding her, something to be made fun of with perhaps more than a tinge of pride.

People surrounding Giulia seemed in fact to be either similar to her or at least inclined to foster her tendencies. Except for the second observation, all the following ones took place at Giulia's grandmother's home (Mrs A's mother). Mrs A found this more convenient and she said that she was going to be there anyway on the day we had agreed to meet and resisted any subsequent attempt to bring her back to her home. There, she said, she could be 'fed and cuddled like a baby' and she certainly was. Mrs A's mother was a 'Mother', always dispensing food and gentle opinions on child rearing, her real 'specialization'. Mrs A behaved like a child with her. All her life seemed to be centred on her mother, and she lived and behaved as if she were still physically tied to her. Though she worked part-time, such excursions into the outside world were also I think sheltered by her knowledge of this constant link with her mother who would be waiting for her at home, and the outside was probably felt as an extension of her mother's protective shield. All her numerous elder sisters, though married or living far away, were also in constant touch with one another and with their mother, and all spent their savings in paying enormous telephone bills. All their husbands were also somehow related to one another and had been known by the family since childhood. Anyway, men, including Mr A, were kept rather in the background.

The impression all this made on me was that Mrs A was too comfortable and too sheltered inside the niche created by her own mother and by her family to be properly living in the outside. Her mother took over with Giulia, and Mrs A did not seem to mind. Every observation took place around the table with biscuits and coffee, with Mrs A eating non-stop and both she and her mother also talking non-stop. Giulia soon joined in with her gurgling. In this respect Mrs A seemed rather similar to Giulia. She seemed rather addicted to food, and for her and for her mother talking seemed as pleasurable as Giulia's licking feasts.

Giulia was certainly given a lot of attention, though of a rather sensuous and wandering type, and at least apparently, seemed to be slightly more adventurous and enterprising than her mother. But, particularly looking back in retrospect, one could notice how her own adventures always took place inside the narrow space of her grandmother's home and never took her farther than a few steps from her mother's and her grandmother's watchful eyes. Giulia seemed to be the centre of their attention and a constant source of delight. Very little was shown to her of the outside world and anyway, for her too, the family circle seemed to provide such a pleasurable and comforting experience as to render it difficult to envisage any other source of pleasure.

At the age of two, apart from the pleasure derived from her mother's and her grandmother's presence and from the constant gulping of enormous amounts of food, Giulia also seemed by now to be addicted to all her other sources of sensuous enjoyment. Each of her senses seemed to be used constantly and in a sensuous way to feed her with unending pleasure. Giulia seemed to be living at the time in a kind of continuous 'orgy' of sensuality. Her 'whorishness' was also beginning to be more noticeable, and Giulia went wild whenever a man was around and immediately ended up between his legs. As previously when responding to her grandfather's voice, her mother used to say that she was 'a little whore'. But all this was before her apparent security was shattered by another event derived from sex: the birth of her little brother. When Giulia was just turning two, her mother became pregnant again. This pregnancy had not been planned either, and we see its rather devastating effects on Giulia nine months later when her mother phones me in despair asking for a consultation.

Giulia is now almost three. Her mother phones me saying that she is worried about her and requesting a consultation. Mrs A has recently had another baby, a boy, and apparently his birth has precipitated 'terrible regression' (Mrs A's words) in his sister. Giulia now refuses to go out of the house, 'Not even to buy bread, the shop is just round the corner from where we live . . . as we approach the door to go out, she screams as if terrified and goes back to her room . . . actually she spends most of her time confined to her room . . . she refuses to see people and whenever someone comes to visit us she runs back to her room and often falls deeply asleep . . . also she wants me there all the time . . . she is always holding on to me . . . she clings to me in a morbid way . . . even during the night she can only sleep in my bed and constantly holds on to my hair and keeps her lips in contact with my chin, sometimes even licking it . . . ' Not surprisingly, Mrs A then complains of being very tired and asks me for an appointment. I see her the following week.

Consultation with Giulia (three years old) – detailed report

Giulia arrives rather late accompanied by her mother, her grandmother, and her baby brother. Mrs A is carrying the baby turned towards her chest in a kind of sling pouch and Giulia is holding her hand. Giulia looks enormous. She is quite tall and terribly fat. Her obesity is rendered even more evident by her tight purple trousers and by the glossy embroidery of her equally purple blouse that somehow also gives her a rather whorish and vulgar appearance. Mrs A apologizes for the delay saying that it was impossible to pull Giulia out of her room.

After exchanging a few words with her mother and her grandmother and showing them into another room, I ask Giulia if she would like to come with me and see the toys I have prepared for her. She looks back at her mother and doesn't seem to want to let go. I am quite prepared to see her with her mother, but tell her that her mother will wait for her in this room while she plays with me. Should she want to see her, she can always go back to her. Giulia takes my hand and follows me inside the playroom. I notice that her face is intensely flushed and she looks rather tense. She will hardly look at me during the whole consultation.

I show her the drawer with the toys. She gives them a quick glance and immediately picks up the fence saying, 'What is this? . . . this is useful . . . one can use it to shut oneself up . . . ' (Her vocabulary is quite precise, but she talks almost in a whisper and with a sort of dreamy, absorbed look on her face.) She takes the ambulance and says, 'It is closed . . . one cannot open it . . . ' In fact the ambulance has a very large and evident opening at the back. As she looks at it, two small figures that were inside it fall on the floor. She says, 'They can't come out . . . they can't get out . . . ' She explores the back of the ambulance and says, 'It has no opening . . . one cannot open it . . . ' She seems to ignore completely the opening, even when she touches and explores it.

She leaves the ambulance and takes the two balls, brings them near her mouth, looks at them disgustedly, and then throws them away. She sucks her thumb for a moment, then picks up all the animals and the figures one by one. Each time she tries to pull off its head saying, 'This is useless . . . ', then she discards them on the floor saying, 'They are all the same'. She takes the ambulance again and says, 'It has no opening . . . ' Her expression is still very serious.

Now she takes the smaller animals and suddenly her eyes brighten and she says with a smile, 'These are tiny . . . how nice . . . they can stay inside! . . . ' But then as she takes them out of the drawer and puts them on the floor, she loses her smile and looks again serious and absorbed. We hear the voice of a child coming from the outside. She smiles cunningly and says, 'He is outside!'

Then we hear some other noises and, though barely audible, the voice of a man. She looks suddenly worried and says, 'What is that? . . . what is that noise? . . . ' She looks around (previously she had concentrated totally on the drawer) and notices the pencils on the small table. She goes near them and takes one. She says, 'It is too short . . . here is the pencil-sharpener . . . now I will make it grow long . . . ' She puts the pencil inside the pencil-sharpener and says, 'Now it is big . . . it is all right now . . . ' She puts the shavings inside the bin and says worriedly, 'Why is there so little in it? . . . why is it not full? . . . ' Then she does the same with some other pencils, and each time she says, 'Now it is longer and bigger . . . it is all right . . . ' She still looks worried because the bin is almost totally empty. She notices a hole on the table and puts all her pencils, one after the other, into it. Then she puts all the pencils back inside the box saying, 'This is better . . . ' She takes some Sellotape and seals the box with it (she is quite skilled in the use of her hands). She says, 'Now we have to close it well . . . to seal it . . . otherwise they will fall out . . . ' When all the pencils are back inside the box she says, 'Now they are all well shut . . . ', then suddenly she looks anxious and says, 'Now I want to go . . . I want to be cuddled by mummy . . . '

She opens the door and runs back inside the waiting room. Her mother is sitting in an armchair. Her grandmother is sitting on another less comfortable chair and is rocking the baby. Giulia throws herself on to her mother's lap and hugs her, taking up all her stomach while at the same time noisily sucking her thumb. Her mother says, 'You want to be with me', then she asks Giulia, 'Why don't we go back together to the playroom? . . . ' Giulia clings to her mother as she walks. She is still sucking her thumb. As her mother sits on the couch, Giulia again throws herself on to her lap. She carries on sucking her thumb and holds her mother's hair with her other hand.

Mrs A says, 'Have you told her what you do now? . . . she always holds my hair . . . she even puts it in her nose! . . . ' Giulia with a smile shows me how she puts some of her mother's hair inside her nose. Then she clings to her more and more. She is now cheek to cheek with her mother. Mrs A says, 'Now during the night she comes to our room . . . she puts herself between us . . . she sticks to me and holds my hair as well . . . don't you, Giulia? . . . ', then she looks at her and notices that her face is flushed. She says, 'Your face is all red . . . it's so hot in here! . . . also I think that she must be a bit upset . . . she is holding on to her thumb . . . now she is also on a diet . . . she was too fat . . . and her blood pressure was found to be alarmingly high . . . I was so scared . . . and the doctor told me to put her on a diet immediately . . . no more sweets . . . no more cakes . . . no more soft drinks . . . but I decided to start it gradually . . . she was used to going into the kitchen and helping herself to what she wanted . . . I can't stop her abruptly . . . she was used to eating all the time . . . now she is only allowed to eat at meals . . . the problem is that she eats nothing for breakfast . . . then of course she is hungry . . . not even a drop of milk . . . she absolutely refuses milk . . .'

Giulia now looks rather sleepy. Her mother says, 'I hope you are not going to fall asleep! . . . You see, this is what she does now when something upsets her . . . or if someone comes to our flat . . . she goes to sleep . . . she locks herself in her room and falls asleep . . . just like that! . . .'

I tell her that anyway now we have to finish. Mrs A says, 'We have to go home now . . . I am sure you must be starving . . .' Giulia points at the drawer and says, 'Let's put it back in . . .', then she goes and takes some elastic bands and puts one on her mother's wrist, then another one around her wrist. She insists, pointing at the drawer, 'Put it back in . . . and lock it . . .'

Mrs A is still sitting and seems unable to go. Now she hoists herself up and we go back to the waiting room. Giulia holds her hand while at the same time keeping hold of several of the rubber bands. As soon as she sees her brother in her grandmother's arms, she flings herself against him, tries to strangle him with a rubber band while at the same time trying to hit and push him back. He starts crying. Her grandmother scolds her and says, 'She is terrible . . . you cannot leave her alone with him . . .'

Mrs A flops back into the armchair. Giulia goes and takes her mother's bag. Mrs A says weakly, 'No', but Giulia pulls out a small make-up bag. Mrs A wrings her hands and says, 'No . . . you see what she does . . . she takes the lipstick and smears it all over her face . . . she looks like a mask . . .' Giulia smears the lipstick all around her lips. Now she really looks like a whore.

Mrs A says, 'Let's go now . . . I'll buy you some chips . . .' Giulia smiles at her and says, 'Yes'. Mrs A says, 'You should see her when she walks along the High Street . . . all made up . . . everybody stares at her . . . you can imagine . . . in such a small town! . . .'

Then they start putting on their coats, but it takes them a while to leave. Mrs A in the meantime keeps repeating, 'You must be starving . . . I'll buy you some chips . . .', then they all say goodbye to me.

We shall meet Giulia again in the chapter dedicated to the treatment of young children, but this observation is already worthy of several comments.

Consultation with Giulia (three years old) – comments

Had Giulia already been in treatment, I would have probably interpreted her wish to remain tied to her mother (her clinging to her, her holding on to her hair, her tying her with the elastic band, and so on) as if still living inside her womb, denying any opening ('It is closed . . . one cannot open it . . . ') or coming 'out' at birth ('They can't come out . . . they can't get out . . . '). Everything has to be tightly and securely locked in (like the drawer and the pencils that have to be securely locked in or, as her mother says, 'She locks herself in her room').

I would have probably also linked all this with the fact that her physical space inside her mother's womb had recently been occupied by another intruder, her little brother, a fact that she cannot deny, though she hates and tries to obliterate it (see her trying to push back her brother while at the same time trying to hurt and strangle him).

All her defences, which probably include sleep ('She locks herself in her room and falls asleep'), seem to be mobilized to recreate an illusion of non-birth, as if she were still living locked inside ('The fence is useful . . . one can shut oneself up . . . '). Being inside seems to be her ideal condition ('They are tiny . . . how nice . . . they can stay inside! . . . '), and what Giulia seems to be looking for in people is just this kind of physical link. Emotional ties with them (their heads) are 'useless' and they can be got rid of as a disturbing element. What should remain is just their centre, the womb, with no openings and only one occupier, herself, inside (see Giulia's triumph at hearing a child's voice from the outside: 'He is outside!').

The breast too (the two balls) seems to be a despicable object belonging to life in the outside ('Not even a drop of milk . . . she absolutely refuses milk . . . '). The constant presence of her thumb which she can simply help herself to seems to be much superior. Her striking fatness and her constant search for food also seem probably linked with this and her mother with her constant reminding her of food ('You must be starving') and with her offers of it ('I will buy you some chips') undoubtedly seems to foster Giulia's already prominent tendencies. Her mother during this consultation appears rather similar to Giulia. She too is still tied to her own mother; is constantly preoccupied with food; and seems to be experiencing great difficulty in parting from me.

In this observation there are certainly many other elements that would need discussing, all simply as hypotheses to be kept in mind and tested in the future during the treatment of the child. We shall come back later to Giulia and her problems as seen in the different and unique light of the interchanges taking place in her therapy (see Chapter 4).

OBSERVATION NO. 2 – GIANNI

Background

Even before I met Mrs B, she was described to me by her obstetrician as a very anxious woman. She already had a child of seven, a girl, but another recent pregnancy had ended in still birth due to *abruptio placentae*. Her anxiety was certainly increased by that, but as the obstetrician said, 'She is frightfully anxious . . . she is perfect for you . . . she phones me every minute . . . including at night . . . the other evening she even phoned me to say that she had just had intercourse and had lost some blood . . . and she was worried about that . . . imagine, phoning me just after intercourse! . . . ', and whilst saying this she raised her eyes to the ceiling. In fact all the obstetricians seemed to know Mrs B and they all tried to avoid her, describing her as a 'pain in the neck'. Yet in the course of the years, as my knowledge of her vulnerabilities as well as of her intelligence increased, I have grown fond of her and her family too, and particularly now that Gianni seems to have improved, I find myself looking forward to visiting her.

On the day of the first ultrasonographic observation, when she was fourteen weeks pregnant, Mrs B arrived punctually, accompanied by her husband. Mrs B is a rather slim, not very tall woman in her mid-thirties. Her medium-length brown hair with gold highlights appeared rather unnaturally styled with a great deal of lacquer keeping it perfectly in place. Her rather pretty face was heavily made up, with layers of foundation, well-contoured lips, and silvery olive-green eyeshadow matching the rather striking colour of her eyes. She certainly looked attractive, though in a rather mask-like way. She was also wearing a black and white paisley woollen dress, very light, almost white tights, and a very heavy and ornate gold choker that made her appear somehow out of place in the bareness, if not squalor, of the recording room. But her most evident feature was her all-pervasive anxiety, almost tangibly invading the space of the room. Her husband looked slightly younger than she did. Not very tall, but rather attractive, with dark hair, dark beard, and dark eyes, he always kept his hands in his pockets and stood rather silently aside. His few questions and his general stiffness seemed to foster and to match the anxiety of his wife.

A verbatim report of the first and the third ultrasonographic observations will now follow.

Gianni: first ultrasonographic observation (fourteenth week) – transcript

FIRST OBSTET: Here we are . . . it's perfect now . . . (then talking to Mr B) . . . you can come nearer if you like . . . so you can see better . . . you can also sit down if you like, we have a chair for you . . .

MR B: (almost in a whisper) Thank you, but I'd rather stand . . .

FIRST OBSTET: Here we are now . . . the bladder . . . the vagina . . . the anterior wall of the womb . . . the placenta . . . the gestational sac . . .

MRS B: (immediately) Is it already possible to see the placenta? . . .

FIRST OBSTET: It is anterior . . . but at this gestational age the placenta takes up an extensive area of the internal wall of the womb . . .

MRS B: But anterior means normal or not? . . .

FIRST OBSTET: Anterior is normal . . . these are now the two legs of the child . . . and this is one foot . . .

MRS B: Is that its foot? . . .

FIRST OBSTET: This is the body . . . the head . . . the arms . . .

MR B: Is it possible to see enlargements of the details? . . .

SECOND OBSTET: Well . . . this is the maximum enlargement . . .

MRS B: The fetus is moving, isn't it? . . .

FIRST OBSTET: Look, now I will show you . . . this is its heart . . . you can see it beat . . .

MRS B: Oh, yes . . . now I can see it . . .

FIRST OBSTET: Under the heart you can see the stomach . . . now the child is not moving . . . one of his arms is on its head . . . covering it . . . the other hand is kept at the side of its head . . . you see, this is the hand . . . both his legs are bent . . . crossed . . . it is difficult to visualize it well when it is in this position . . .

MRS B: And how is my womb now? . . . is it in the right position now? . . . last time you told me that it was retroflexed . . .

FIRST OBSTET: Yes, now it is anteflexed . . . in a normal position . . . it is all curled up . . . you can see its spine . . . here is its heart again . . .

MRS B: Are all its measurements all right . . . I mean normal for its week . . .

FIRST OBSTET: We shall measure it at the end this time . . .

MR B: When is it possible to see its sex? . . .

SECOND OBSTET: Around the twenty-eighth to twenty-ninth week . . . that is around the seventh month . . . look, it is perhaps moving slightly . . . its legs are still crossed . . . its head is covered by its arms . . . the head is turned slightly towards one side . . . in fact you can see the spine here . . .

MRS B: But is it already possible to see whether it is normal or not? . . .

SECOND OBSTET: Well, we can see many things . . . first of all we can see the bladder . . . and therefore we can check that its kidneys are functioning . . . then two arms, two legs . . . a normally shaped head . . . the heart is beating . . . the stomach . . . which means that so far its gastrointestinal tract shows no alterations . . .

MRS B: Is it immobile now? . . . or is it sleeping? . . .

FIRST OBSTET: Look, this is its hand . . . covering its face . . . this is the arm . . . these are the legs . . . they are still too . . . flexed . . . crossed . . . this lighter image is part of its face . . . its upper and its lower jaw . . .

MRS B: But then what is this weight I can always feel down here? . . .

SECOND OBSTET: The weight you feel down there is just due to pregnancy itself . . .

MRS B: I mean, it's not something to worry about . . . since I lost that child . . . I always worry about the placenta . . . I had an *abruptio placentae* at that time . . .

SECOND OBSTET: How far in your pregnancy were you? . . .

MRS B: I was in the fifth month of pregnancy . . . then I stayed in hospital for another three months . . . they say that nobody knows why it happens . . . sometimes it may be even due to too violent a gynaecological examination . . .

FIRST OBSTET: Look, now it is moving . . . he moved his body slightly and his legs . . .

MRS B: He's woken up . . .

FIRST OBSTET: Yes, it should be awake now . . . look it is moving its hand . . . again . . . again . . . sort of rubbing his face . . .

MRS B: I can see it better now . . .

FIRST OBSTET: It turned slightly on its side . . . its head too . . . it is all curled up . . . touching its knees with its hands . . . stretching its legs slightly . . . now crossing them again . . . its hands are still on its knees . . . now it's brought its hands over its face . . . he's covered it with them . . .

MRS B: Has it turned round? . . .

FIRST OBSTET: Yes, now it is facing us . . . its hands are in front of its face . . . it is kicking like mad . . . it has stopped now . . . it is immobile again . . . its hands are still in front of its face . . . we can see its breathing movements now . . .

MRS B: We didn't see all this before, did we? . . .

FIRST OBSTET: What you mean by before? . . .

MRS B: When I had ultrasounds before . . . without looking at movements . . .

SECOND OBSTET: Yes, in fact we are also doing a research on movements now . . .

MRS B: Yes, now I understand . . . I understand . . .

SECOND OBSTET: Besides what Dr Piontelli is looking at, we are observing what movements the fetus does within a certain amount of time . . .

FIRST OBSTET: Always its arm . . . covering its face . . . now it's turned on its side . . . it keeps changing side . . . he can't find the right position . . . it is not peaceful this one . . . it is either restless or completely immobile . . .

MR B: Is that its heart? . . .

FIRST OBSTET: Yes, it's its heart . . .

MRS B: When will I start feeling its movements? . . .

SECOND OBSTET: In a little over a month . . . it has turned again on the other side . . . its hand . . . its hand . . . in front of the face . . .

FIRST OBSTET: It tends to curl up in a corner of the womb . . . though there is still quite a bit of space . . .

MRS B: Is this normal or not? . . .

FIRST OBSTET: Its hand and the other arm are now in front of its face . . . look it is covering its mouth with its hand . . .

MR B: It's true that it is all curled up . . . I thought it had more space at this stage . . .

FIRST OBSTET: It's turned completely . . . very restless . . . it's very difficult to see its face . . . its hand and arm are still covering it . . .

MR B: Is that dark area on the left its skull? . . .

SECOND OBSTET: This is its head . . . this light line is its outline . . . the dark area is the amniotic fliud . . . this is a hand . . . above its head . . . the other hand is now at the side of its face covering its ear and eye . . .

MRS B: (laughing) It is scratching its ear! . . .

FIRST OBSTET: It touches its face a lot . . . but we can't see it well . . . for instance we can't see if it is swallowing or not . . . '

MRS B: 'Why is it more important to see it swallowing? . . .

FIRST OBSTET: It's not more important . . . only it is easier to observe it if it can be seen in profile because it moves its chin . . . it turned round again . . . therefore you see, even if it is all curled up in a corner, it means that it still has a lot of space . . . otherwise it wouldn't be able

71

to turn round like that . . . its hand is still there . . . the other arm is still raised with the hand behind its head . . . you will never see a young baby doing that . . .

MR B: Has it kept it there all the time? . . .

SECOND OBSTET: No, it moved it quite a bit . . . but always in front of its face . . . now both its hands are in front of its face . . . covering it . . . it is not giving itself away very much this child! . . . it is completely still now . . .

MRS B: And the placenta? . . . how is the placenta? . . . that's what worries me most . . .

FIRST OBSTET: The placenta for the moment is all right . . .

MRS B: I hope it will continue to be all right . . .

FIRST OBSTET: But in any case an *abruptio placentae* is always a sudden event . . . most often there is no way of predicting it . . . it is actually one of the least predictable happenings in obstetrics . . . let's measure it now . . .

SECOND OBSTET: The placenta is anterior . . . marginal and rather low . . .

MRS B: What do you mean by rather low! . . .

FIRST OBSTET: Look, it means nothing . . . there are many pregnancies that proceed absolutely normally with a low placenta till the end . . . and nothing at all happens . . . it's meaningless . . . on the other hand there are women with a placenta inserted very high in the womb and it can happen to them . . . now you are fourteen weeks pregnant . . . the placenta will be in a different place by say twenty weeks . . . as the womb stretching pulls the placenta with it . . . so please, don't worry about it! . . . your child moves well . . . it is well . . . the placenta is well inserted and all is going well . . . and we shall see you soon . . . next month . . . you can wipe the jelly off now . . .

MRS B: And what about the pains I feel down here? . . .

FIRST OBSTET: If they are just mild pains, they are absolutely normal as they are due to the physiological adaptation of the womb to pregnancy . . . if they are strong . . . like, say, periodic pains, then it is a different matter . . .

MRS B: Sometimes they feel just like periodic pains . . .

FIRST OBSTET: Are you sure you are not working too much? . . .

MRS B: No, I am resting . . .

FIRST OBSTET: Your womb was not contracted when I visited you . . . in any case it is better if you try to forget about those pains . . . the more you think about them, the more you are bound to feel them . . .

She says goodbye to everybody and goes out. Mrs B now gets dressed. The Second Obstetrician goes near her and says, 'Your next appointment is on the 28th of March . . . I have written it here . . . come with your bladder rather full . . . I have written it here for you . . . '

MRS B: Can I move? . . . I mean can I go out? . . . because we would like to go to the mountains for a few days . . . I would like to know if it is dangerous . . .

SECOND OBSTET: How long does it take for you to go to the mountains? . . . are you staying in your house there? . . .

MR AND MRS B: (together) About two hours . . . perhaps a bit less . . . an hour and a half . . .

SECOND OBSTET: But then will you be staying at home? . . .

MRS B: Yes . . . but then what worries me is the trip . . .

SECOND OBSTET: There is no problem about the trip . . . unless of course you go terribly fast and take every bend at 100 miles per hour . . . or drive over every possible hole in the road . . . and it is also important to stop for a while whenever you feel like it . . . I mean don't take it all in one go . . .

MRS B: But it is always a mountain road . . . I always have this fear . . . and then going up . . .

SECOND OBSTET: If the road is well paved, it's almost like sitting on a chair, right? . . .

MR B: Yes, well, the road is not well paved . . . there are a few holes . . . that is the main problem . . .

SECOND OBSTET: (looking rather annoyed) The most important thing for her is not to feel anxious and to take it easy . . .

MR B: Well . . . and in any case before we go Dr W will examine her . . .

SECOND OBSTET: That is a good idea . . . next week you will see how she is . . . and before deciding you can speak to Dr W . . .

MRS B: And isn't Professor T? . . .

SECOND OBSTET: No, he is in Rome . . . he will be back on Monday . . .

MRS B: Then if I need anything I can phone him then . . .

SECOND OBSTET: Yes, you can phone him too if you like . . .

MRS B: (collecting her file) So everything is all right . . .

SECOND OBSTET: Yes, everything is all right . . .

MRS B: All my tests are all right? . . .

SECOND OBSTET: Yes, they are . . .

Mr and Mrs B say goodbye and go out, and the second obstetrician says to me, 'These two are a real pain in the neck! . . . '

Gianni: second ultrasonograpic observation (twenty-first week) – summary

The second observation was almost a repetition of the first, with Mrs B constantly asking questions about the placenta, its insertion, its general normality, and its shape and with the obstetricians answering her questions with a mixture of annoyance and derision. Gianni, the name given to him later, on the other hand seemed to do very little, still curled up as he was in a corner of the womb, mostly immobile and covering his face with his hands and his arms. His legs too were so tightly folded and crossed so as almost to cover his face. As the first obstetrician had remarked in the first scan, Gianni continued to be ' . . . not peaceful this one . . . it is either restless or completely immobile'.

On the third observation (reported below), Mrs B came accompanied by Mavi, her seven-year-old daughter. Mavi is a rather unattractive child, she is quite fat and with none of her mother's pretty features. Both she and her mother now seem obsessed by another question: sex. Though by now it is possible to tell clearly that it is a boy, the question is repeated over and over again: What is its sex? Is it a boy or a girl? Is that the penis? Are those its 'balls'? and so on. Mrs B seems to react with a mixture of annoyance and amusement to her daughter's endless questioning about sex. As the obstetrician remarks, 'You must be talking a lot about sex at home! . . . ' Gianni seems particularly immobile, and as the obstetrician remarks, 'double wrapped', 'all curled up', and protected by the (uterine) wall like a 'second skin', 'as if the womb feels too big for him'. Gianni's arms are mostly kept above his head, covering his face 'as if he had a weight there . . . like when someone is worried or in despair'. He is also seen to hang on to the umbilical cord like a rope and the obstetrician comments that 'he always seems to be looking for something to hang on to'. His immobility, in fact, is rather disquieting and conveys none of the placidity of Giulia's floating, as if it seems born out of tension, if not terror.

Gianni: third ultrasonographic observation (twenty-fifth week) – transcript

DR B: Let's look at your womb first . . . since I have been told that you are always worried to be on the verge of delivery . . . this is your bladder . . . look we can see even the neck of your womb . . . the placenta . . . slightly low . . .

MAVI: What is she doing, mummy? . . .

DR B: I will show you in a minute . . . look, this is its head . . . that black hole is its eye . . .

MRS B: Is it possible to know its sex? . . . I am pretty sure it is a girl . . .

DR B: So, your mother thinks it is a girl . . . we can try and see if it is true . . . first we measure it . . . then we shall see . . .

MAVI: Yes, I want to know its sex . . .

Dr B dictates the measurements to the second obstetrician, who writes them on the obstetric file. Then the second obstetrician takes over the observation.

SECOND OBSTET: Now let's see if it is a boy or a girl . . . he looks like a boy . . . testicles . . . scrotum . . .

MRS B: Are you sure about that? . . . I mean is it possible to be mistaken about sex? . . . are you really sure it is a boy . . .

SECOND OBSTET: (teasing her) Are you sure about everything . . . are you sure everything is all right? . . . are you sure I am not going to deliver it now? . . . are you sure it is really a boy? . . .

MAVI: (looking at her mother's pubic hair) How hairy you are! . . .

MRS B: (laughing) You are just incredible (then sounding worried, to Dr B) You made me feel anxious again . . . you said that the placenta was lower . . . last time apparently it had moved up again . . . it's better not to know these things . . . otherwise I feel anxious all the time . . .

Both Dr B and the second obstetrician pretend not to listen to her.

MAVI: But why couldn't I understand anything before? . . .

SECOND OBSTET: You have to get used to the images . . .

MAVI: (singing and whistling and talking to the microphone) I am touching you, mummy . . . your tummy . . . how nice . . . you are hairy! . . . and what is this? . . . is it jelly? . . .

MRS B: Yes, it is jelly . . .

MAVI: Can I eat it then? . . .

MRS B: No, why are you talking about silly things! . . .

MAVI: When can I eat it then? . . .

MRS B: You never eat this kind of jelly . . . stop being silly now . . .

At this point I realize that the cassette is not inserted in the video-recorder. I tell this to the obstetricians. There are a few minutes of confusion, till they find the right cassette. Mrs B in the meantime speaks to me.

MRS B: So they think it is a boy . . . his penis was clearly visible . . . and his balls . . . one can't be mistaken about that . . . daddy will be happy about that . . .

MAVI: I am happy too . . . was that the penis? . . . were those its balls? . . . daddy was right . . . but why are we not switching off the light now? . . .

DR B: In a minute, when we start recording . . .

MAVI: But why? . . .

DR B: Because if the light is on we cannot see properly . . . we are ready now . . . we can switch off the light . . .

MAVI: I can't see anything now . . . now I can see . . . can you tell me its sex . . . is it a boy or a girl? . . .

SECOND OBSTET: I already said . . . it is a boy . . .

DR B: Let's start now . . .

SECOND OBSTET: He is not moving now . . . his arms . . . here above his head . . . his legs . . . his legs are flexed . . .

MAVI: When does he move? . . .

SECOND OBSTET: He is all curled up . . . totally still . . . his legs on his stomach . . .

MAVI: Where are his balls? . . .

SECOND OBSTET: His face is covered by his arms . . . his legs are folded . . . he is crouched in a corner of the womb . . . his arms are in contact with the uterine wall . . . double wrapped . . . all curled up and protected by the wall . . . like a second skin . . .

DR B: Look . . . you can see the cord there . . . in front of his face . . . he is moving his hands . . . he seems to be doing something with it . . . I think he is hanging on to it . . . yes, he is definitely doing that . . .

MRS B: But where is his sex? . . .

SECOND OBSTET: He is immobile now . . . his arms over his face . . . he is covering his face . . .

MAVI: And his face? . . .

DR B: It's covered by his hands . . .

MAVI: Is he hiccuping or is he breathing now? . . .

SECOND OBSTET: He is breathing now . . . his hands are covering his ears now . . .

MAVI: He is sticking his elbows against something . . . what is it? . . .

SECOND OBSTET: It's the placenta . . .

MRS B: Can you tell me if it is inserted high or low? . . .

SECOND OBSTET: (not paying any attention to her) Now the cord is slightly lateral . . . I think he is holding on to it again . . .

MAVI: Can he pee? . . .

SECOND OBSTET: Yes, but like an angel . . . I mean his pee doesn't yet stain or smell . . . all infants have a little concentrated urine . . .

MRS B: It's not true their urine smells . . .

SECOND OBSTET: Only gradually . . .

MRS B: Only when they begin to eat . . .

DR B: Look . . . his hands are at the side of his head . . . he is holding his ear with one . . . the other one is covering his eye . . .

MRS B: Has your colleague already had her baby? . . . was the delivery all right? . . . what is the child called? . . .

SECOND OBSTET: Yes, everything went all right . . . her name is Bruna . . . look, now he is covering both ears with his hands . . . you can see the fingers well . . . now he is covering all his face . . . and now both hands are above his head . . . he is covering his face with his arms . . . just here . . . in front . . . now he is sort of moving his hands slightly in the narrow space between the uterine wall and his face . . . he is inserting them there . . .

MRS B: But why is he doing this?

SECOND OBSTET: Well, some of them like to thrust themselves into holes . . . just look at him . . . he is all curled up in a corner . . . yet the womb is narrow now . . . but it looks as if it feels too big for him . . . he is not doing much . . . just moving his hands and arms over his face . . .

MAVI: I want to see the sex . . .

SECOND OBSTET: You shouldn't be interested in his sex now . . .

MAVI: I don't understand . . . is that his sex . . . I want to know . . .

SECOND OBSTET: Now he is completely stuck to the uterine wall . . .

MAVI: Where do you put babies once they are born? . . .

SECOND OBSTET: In a cot . . . upstairs we have a ward . . . and in the ward there are all the cots . . . he is still hiding his face . . . covering it . . . one hand is in front of it . . .

MAVI: He put it there . . .

SECOND OBSTET: It is in front of his mouth . . . but he is not sucking it . . . it looks as if he is scratching himself . . . his legs are still all curled up . . . bent . . .

MAVI: But where is his sex? . . . (Everybody laughs now.)

DR B: When we have finished we will show it to you . . .

SECOND OBSTET: Now the hands are back over his ears . . . look at his fingers . . . they are almost inside his ears . . .

MAVI: (yawning) Again with his hands! . . . but where is his sex? . . .

(A nurse comes in. She talks to Dr B and makes a lot of noise.)

SECOND OBSTET: (sounding rather annoyed) Stop making all that noise! (then she starts describing the images again). His hands . . . he's raised them . . . marvellous . . . he really likes keeping his arms above his head, covering it . . . and keeping his hands in front of his face . . .

MRS B: He is all tightly crouched . . .

MAVI: Mummy, how can I see his sex? . . .

77

SECOND OBSTET: He moves very little . . . funny how he keeps his arms above his head . . . as if he had a weight there . . . like when someone is worried or in despair . . .

MAVI: Why that?

SECOND OBSTET: He is already thinking about you . . . when he will meet you . . . that worries him a lot . . .

MAVI: I want to look at his sex . . .

SECOND OBSTET: It's not always easy to see it . . . he is touching his face . . . he is creeping along the wall . . . these images are wonderful . . . he is surrounding all his head with his other arm . . .

MAVI: (pointing at a dark spot) It's his sex! . . . the sex! . . . the sex! . . .

SECOND OBSTET: You must be talking a lot about sex at home! . . .

MRS B: She is terribly curious . . .

MAVI: (triumphant) I have seen his sex! . . .

SECOND OBSTET: Now I shall try to show it to you . . . his legs are all folded up . . .

MAVI: Here it is . . .

SECOND OBSTET: This is his testicle . . .

MRS B: (sounding worried) Which one? . . . that . . . has he got just one? . . .

SECOND OBSTET: No, Mrs B . . . look here, he's got two . . .

MAVI: The penis! . . . I can see his penis! . . .

MRS B: It is very small . . .

SECOND OBSTET: Of course it is! . . .

MAVI: (more and more excited) I have seen his balls! . . .

SECOND OBSTET: In any case we shall see it even better next time . . .

MRS B: And what about the placenta? . . .

SECOND OBSTET: The placenta is anterior and slightly low . . . he brought back his hand between the placenta and his head . . . he remains there in his hole . . .

MAVI: Which hole? . . . he is a boy . . .

SECOND OBSTET: He moves very little . . . he has a tendency to remain curled up all the time . . . everybody has different tastes . . . he likes to stick tightly to the uterine wall . . . with all his limbs . . . just following the outline and the anfractuosities of the wall . . .

MRS B: (to Mavi, sounding rather annoyed) Stop eating all those sweets! . . .

SECOND OBSTET: Now the cord is there . . . he seems to be pulling it . . . he is hanging on to it . . . like to a rope! . . . now back with his hand over his head . . . he always seems to be looking for something to hold on to . . . his cord . . . or his head . . . always looking for an anchor . . .

MRS B: Could this be dangerous for the placenta . . . I mean him pulling the cord? . . .

SECOND OBSTET: We have finished now . . . I think he was always awake . . . very small movements . . . but restless . . . not finding any peace . . .

MRS B: About his sex, are we 100 per cent sure? . . . and about the placenta . . . can I also be 100 per cent sure?

The obstetrician doesn't seem to pay any attention to her. Mrs B gets dressed again, then she says goodbye to all of us and we hear her in the corridor discussing with Mavi about sex.

Gianni: the last ultrasonographic observations and the delivery – summary

During the following observations Gianni seemed to do little or nothing at all. Only occasionally did he seem to show some of his initial restlessness, but otherwise he remained immobile, tightly crouched in a corner of the womb, with his hands and arms screening his eyes and face and with his legs so tightly folded and crossed as to completely cover his face. Even the narrow space of the womb seemed to be too big a space for him. The umbilical cord was often seen between his arms and his legs, but it was impossible to tell whether he did something with it other than holding on to it. The only clearly visible thing continued to be his sex.

When the term approached he had not yet turned and was still tightly crouched in a corner of the womb in the transversal position. In the meantime Mrs B's blood pressure was found to be slightly raised and she was sent into hospital. Since the child gave no sign of wanting to turn round and Mrs B's blood pressure continued to rise, a Caesarean was decided upon. I could not be present on that day, but the obstetrician later told me that the child was so crumpled up into a corner of the womb that she had considerable difficulty in pulling him out. She said, 'He would never have been born.' One of his feet, due to his position *in utero*, was found to be crooked and therefore had to be put in plaster for three months. Once she pulled him out the obstetrician was also struck by his immobility and by his fixed and sad look. 'He looked old . . . a hundred years old . . . it was somehow frightening to see the immobility of his face . . . '

Gianni: post-natal observations up to the age of four – summary

During the next two months Gianni continued to be practically immobile. Whenever I saw him, his arms were kept at his sides, his head was bent backwards, his eyes were closed and he seemed immersed in a deep sleep. When his mother put him at the breast, he sucked slowly, frowning, with his eyes tightly closed and his arms at his sides, but he also clung to the breast for hours on end. As his mother said, 'He doesn't want to let go . . . he is using me as a dummy . . . he doesn't care about the rest of me . . . ', but Gianni, frowning and tense as he was, did not seem to derive much pleasure from the breast, only perhaps some security, as he seemed to hold on to it like a rope. His mother on the other hand, though apparently resenting it and often saying, 'When he grasps it, he kills me . . . ', kept feeding him for hours on end and found the breast convenient as it required no effort and seemed to stop any other request from the child.

Though totally immobile and apparently asleep, Gianni seemed very sensitive to any kind of unexpected or sudden noise, each time reacting with a start and a frightened expression on his face. While feeding him, his mother never looked at him and spoke relentlessly with me. Now that the placenta was a problem of the past, her attention and curiosity shifted to other areas connected with genitality and sex. She wanted to know all the details of my gynaecological history and tried to find out details about the intimate life of each member of the obstetric ward. She spoke repeatedly of abortions and contraception. She seemed to know all the details of her friends' pregnancies and seemed obsessed by anything even remotely connected with reproduction and sex. She continued to wear rather 'sexy' clothes, and often when I visited her in the early afternoon the atmosphere in the house was embarrassingly redolent of sex, with lowered shutters, transparent or pink silk négligés and her husband disappearing into the toilet and then waving goodbye looking all ruffled and rather dishevelled.

Apart from sex, and anything related to it, Mrs B seemed to find any other subject intolerable and suffocating. Though she certainly liked my presence, she managed to keep me at a distance by cancelling my visits regularly every other week. She found it oppressive being at home with her child and longed to go back to work and so on. Gianni too did not seem to thrive on the endless contact with his mother's breast. During an observation when he was forty days old, whenever he clung to it while frowning and closing his eyes he began to give out a prolonged, desolate moaning sound. Then when he was three months old he began to wake. Though still immobile, he began to whimper non-stop, with his eyes wide open staring fixedly and blankly into space. Mrs B always attributed his crying to colic and wind.

Now that his muscular strength had increased, at times I also saw Gianni bringing his arms near his head and his face very much as I had seen him do before birth. But the most striking feature was still the immobility of his body, his eyes, and his face. In order to placate him now his mother spent hours walking about with Gianni turned against her chest while tapping his back mechanically. Gianni was often ill and he continued to be so with colds, bronchitis, earaches, and still had problems with his left foot and leg. Mrs B, on the other hand, kept saying that she couldn't stand being with him all day and was afraid of 'going mad' if she had to be stuck at home. Proximity seemed distasteful to them both. Whenever she put Gianni down in his push-chair in order to smoke a cigarette, though still immobile, he suddenly looked somehow more relaxed and often stopped his desolate whimpering. Mrs B also told me that the best way to keep him quiet was to go out for walks with him. 'He loves going out and he soon falls asleep . . . '

When Gianni was about five months old, Mrs B began to make plans to go back to work. She found a 'young and not very intelligent' baby-sitter. On the few occasions I saw her, though she talked non-stop, she seemed kind and gentle to him. Christmas was also approaching and the family went away for a short holiday in the mountains. I was told that Mr B, otherwise very busy at work, had looked after Gianni a lot. When they came back from their holidays, Mrs B went back to work. I saw Gianni again and though he was still quite immobile, he looked more relaxed. Mrs B too said that she felt better now that she was back at work. 'I feel as if I am breathing again . . . he seems better too . . . ', and funnily enough while she was saying this Gianni let out two heavy sighs which sounded like relief. Though his gaze still continued to be rather fixed and vacant, Gianni sometimes looked at me and smiled. He also accompanied his mother's endless inquiries about gynaecology and sex with constant long sounds which reminded me in their tone of the endless talk of the au pair. His main contact with his mother was still the breast, and Mrs B continued breast-feeding him till he was ten months old.

At one year of age Gianni looked rather backward in his development. Though he could certainly sit and apparently crawl, he preferred to sit in a corner holding the same toy all the time and almost never moved about. By then I had heard only sounds and no words. But what seemed most disquieting to me was his almost absolute rigidity and immobility as well as his blank and fixed stare. Any animation soon turned into a restless irritation and nothing seemed to soothe him. As the obstetrician had said, 'He is not peaceful, this one . . . it is either restless or completely immobile.' His mother was now considering sending him to a kindergarten.

Such distancing from his mother seemed to have a beneficial effect on him. Gianni began to walk and to talk like any other child and what I feared could have become an almost total autistic closure became more a kind of fixity and rigidity of character covering an extreme nakedness and vulnerability reminiscent somehow of his search for a double wrapping inside the womb. In his extreme vulnerability Gianni still continued to look for 'anchors' in the outside world and showed a marked tendency to cling to people and to objects.

In the following observation Gianni is four years old. As his grandmother and then his mother say, 'He is better now . . . his character has softened a bit . . . ' Yet his unfolding has been very slow and careful. His immobility and fixed stare, his search for anchors, and for covering and protection, are all still very evident.

Gianni: observation at four years old – detailed report

I have not seen Mrs B since before the summer (it is the beginning of October now). When I phone her and ask her how she is, she says, 'Pretty much as usual . . . but one can't complain . . . it could be worse . . . ' Then we arrange to meet as usual on the following Thursday.

I arrive on time and call on the interphone. Mavi replies. Her voice sounds much more grown-up and she carefully explains which corridor and which floor I have to go to, though I know my way around the building quite well. As I arrive at their flat, Mrs B is there near the open door and as she sees me she kisses me on both cheeks. She is very heavily made up and is wearing a flowery silken blouse and a skirt with a deep vent. I give her a small box of chocolates, and she says, 'You are ever so kind . . . you always remember to bring us something . . . but now forgive me a moment . . . I am on the phone . . . ' Gianni is there near her and stares at me rather fixedly, with his usual serious expression on his face. Then, as his mother goes to the phone, he takes my box of chocolates and tries to open it, but then gives it back to me saying, 'It's too heavy . . . ', then covers his face with his hands and stares at me from between his fingers. Mavi comes and says hello to me. She is wearing a very short miniskirt which renders even more pathetically evident her clumsiness and her plumpness and the over-ripeness of her body. She moves and acts just like a woman now. She takes the chocolates and starts eating them.

Gianni also eats one after taking its wrapping off very carefully and very slowly.

Mrs B's mother also comes in from the kitchen and says hello to me, saying, 'We see each other from time to time . . . we have been here for a while . . . but we'll go back on Sunday . . . my husband is busy . . . he is resting now . . . ' She has the usual shabby and myopic look I have noticed each time I have seen her. She asks me to sit down and she sits down too. Gianni is now standing near me and I ask him about his nursery school. He nods when I ask whether he likes it. Then he tells me a list of names. His grandmother says, 'He is telling you all the names of his teachers and friends . . . he is skinny [in fact he is not] . . . while she [Mavi] is fat . . . he eats nothing and she eats all the time . . . but he is better now . . . his character has softened a bit . . . but he tends to cling to people . . . he really holds on to them . . . he glues to them . . . as if he were frightened to let go . . . then occasionally he has sudden outbursts of rage . . . without any particular cause . . . just pure restlessness and irritation . . . '

Gianni now takes my hand and pulls it. I follow him. He continues to hold my hand and we go into the kitchen. He shows me a cake. Mrs B finishes phoning and comes into the kitchen too. She says, 'Oh my God! . . . he has already seized you . . . you remember he did the same last time . . . he holds on to people . . . and allows them no breathing space . . . I desperately need a breathing space . . . ' Gianni in fact is holding on to my hand very tightly. He doesn't look at his mother while she is talking to me, but keeps his head slightly bent down.

We go back to the sitting room. Mavi is still sitting there and is eating more chocolates. Mrs B tells her, 'Go and do your homework now . . . all she thinks of is eating . . . come on go now . . . ' Mavi stands up and moves rather reluctantly towards her room. But then Mrs B calls her back and says, 'Offer something to drink to Dr Piontelli . . . would you like some coffee, or perhaps some fruit juice? . . . ' I thank her and say that I'd rather have a fruit juice. Mavi brightens up and goes in the kitchen.

Mrs B says, 'She eats all the time . . . she is fat . . . and now her periods have started . . . she is sort of ashamed of it . . . she doesn't want to tell anyone . . . they say that after that you stop growing . . . I hope not . . . she is only eleven and quite short . . . at what age did you start? . . . ', and I tell her. She says, 'I started at thirteen . . . eleven is quite early . . . and since she doesn't want to tell anyone, I don't know about her school-friends . . . I will have to make some inquiries with the mothers of her friends . . . perhaps these generations start earlier . . . so I will have to inquire into that . . . '

We are still standing and now Gianni pulls my hand. I follow him inside the kitchen and we find Mavi there secretly eating mouthfuls of cake. She looks slightly embarrassed when she sees me, but then swallows what she is eating and goes back into the sitting room with a tray with a glass and a fruit juice. We follow her.

Mrs B says to Gianni, 'Let her go now . . . [then to me] please, sit down . . . let her have her drink in peace . . . ' The grandmother says, 'Go and get your dog . . . you can show it to her . . . ' After a moment's hesitation, Gianni releases my hand and runs towards his room. Mrs B says, 'It's in the study . . . don't go in there . . . your grandfather is sleeping . . . don't disturb him . . . you know that his siesta is sacred for him . . . ' (it's 5 p.m.).

Gianni goes in the study and comes back with a rather big battery-operated dog. He stands next to me. He shows me the tail of the dog and says, 'Its hair is all gone . . . it is naked . . . I don't like it naked like that . . . it feels terrible . . . but nobody can repair it now . . . it was not my fault . . . ' Then he sits next to me on the sofa and shows me its batteries, saying, 'Look . . . they are here . . . all tight inside . . . ' While showing them to me, the batteries fall down and he picks them up and asks me to put them back, saying, 'They must be in there . . . all wrapped up . . . otherwise they don't work . . . ' His grandmother tells him to show me how his dog can walk, but Gianni leaves it next to me and goes and gets another dog. He comes back almost running and again sits down next to me. He shows me another dog. His grandmother says, 'This one barks if you whistle to it . . . ' Mrs B, who is sitting in an armchair opposite me and is smoking a cigarette looking rather annoyed, says, 'Try to whistle . . . ' He looks rather lost. I try and the dog barks. Gianni shows me its collar, and says, 'He must have this . . . all around his neck . . . otherwise he will get lost . . . ' Mrs B says, 'Leave her in peace . . . [then to me] . . . how frequently do you have a pap-test? . . . ' I tell her. She asks, 'And have you ever had a mammograph? . . . ' I say yes. She says, 'I should too . . . one of my friends has just been told that she has a cancer of the womb . . . another one recently had an ovarian cyst . . . '

While she is talking Gianni holds my hand and sits next to me. His head is slightly bent down, his back is curved and he looks almost all curled up. Mrs B continues, 'Any news about Dr B? . . . I am sure that by now she must have at least four more children (she laughs) . . . she will go on until she can (she laughs) . . . ' She lights a cigarette, and says, 'I have lost some weight . . . I feel much better . . . I decided to go on a diet . . . but it was enough not to eat any bread for a while . . . '

The grandmother stands up and goes towards the bedrooms. Mrs B says, 'My father is here too . . . he went to see a specialist for his eyes

. . . his sight is very poor now as he suffers both from detachment of the retina and cataracts . . . they came directly from Sicily without us . . . during the summer we were not there . . . so they wanted to see the children again . . . we went to Sardinia . . . just when the fires started . . . we didn't know anything as we went by boat . . . we arrived in the evening and when we reached our village everything was on fire . . . it was already past midnight and we were all exhausted . . . luckily someone was there and he told us to go back to Olbia . . . we were put up for the night in a small room in a pensione . . . it was very crowded there . . . people were coming from all over the island . . . but then the following day we were told that the situation was back to normal again . . . we went back to the village and in fact we had no more trouble . . . the fire struck mainly the northern part of Sardinia, therefore we were all right . . . '

Gianni, after being immobile for a while, now leaves my hand and goes into the study and gets yet another dog whose body can be pushed or pulled so that its size changes from short to long. He shows it to me. Mrs B laughs very loudly (I think because of the possible sexual associations with its changing from short to long). She says, 'Look at that . . . short and long! . . . his grandmother must have given it to him . . . he is all interested in it . . . ' Gianni seems to ignore his mother's remarks and keeps staring at me while changing the size of his dog. Then he puts it in my lap and sits back next to me holding my hand.

Mavi comes back with a plate and a huge slice of cake. Mrs B looks at her, and says, 'All she can think of is food . . . her friends are all very careful about their diets and they are all slim . . . but she can't stop eating . . . ', then looking at Gianni, 'Stop sticking to her . . . show her something if you like . . . '

He goes and gets a colouring book and some pencils and starts colouring some figures on it. He shows me some robots and sits next to me. He colours them carefully and meticulously, but then realizes that his hands are rather dirty now. He looks rather upset, and says, 'I go and wash them . . . ' Mrs B is now smoking another cigarette, and says, 'He is always very orderly . . . everything has to be in its place . . . the same with his room . . . he is very tidy . . . all the objects are kept carefully in their place . . . '

Gianni comes back and shows me his hands that are still slightly stained. He says, 'They are no longer black now . . . they are purple . . . ' (in fact the black has changed into a slightly purplish colour). Mavi comes near us too, and she shows me that she has been drawing a cat. Gianni holds on to her arm while she is showing it to me. Mrs B says, 'He is always holding on to someone . . . he is always looking for some anchor . . . as if it were his last hope . . . ' (She laughs.)

Gianni says, 'I want to draw something too . . . but not on her paper . . . I want some other paper . . . ' Mrs B stands up and goes and gets some paper and brings it back to him. Again he sits next to me and draws a rather shapeless and worm-like figure, and says, 'It is a child . . . ', then adds eyes and mouth to it, saying, 'These are its eyes and this is its mouth . . . now we need to draw something else . . . something he can hold on to . . . ', and he draws a kind of rudimentary cord attached to the middle of it. He seems very intent in drawing all this.

Mrs B says, 'He won't let you go . . . he always does that . . . he is four now . . . he was four in August . . . I think he is better now on the whole . . . do you remember when I was so worried because he still wasn't talking . . . we had even considered having him helped . . . you remember, you suggested that . . . but then things improved . . . and I think he is much better now . . . he talks . . . his teachers at the nursery are very pleased with him . . . of course he has to hold on to something or someone all the time . . . he is sticky . . . and very often he hides . . . when nobody is around I often find him in some dark corner . . . all protected and covered . . . and all curled up . . . then sometimes he falls to pieces . . . he just screams . . . uncontrollable screams . . . he goes as far as trembling all over . . . just falling to bits . . . I wish he could say what is the matter in those moments . . . but apart from this he is quite all right . . . his teachers are very pleased with him . . . I did well to wait . . . and you are always there in any case . . . probably Mavi needs you more than him . . . well she just needs to be on a diet . . . '

While she is speaking to me, Gianni holds on tightly to my skirt. Now I say that I have to go. Mrs B says, 'I will take you to the lift . . .' I say that I would like to say goodbye to her mother, but even before finishing my sentence she appears from the corridor. She shakes hands with me, and says, 'I hope to see you again soon . . . we pop up here from time to time . . . ' I tell her to say hello to her husband too. As I stand up, Gianni leaves my skirt and goes and holds his grandmother's hand. I say goodbye to him and he replies in a whisper, looking down at his feet.

Mrs B accompanies me to the lift and Mavi follows us. She says that she will come down with me. Her mother sighs, saying, 'Leave Dr Piontelli in peace . . . ', then she kisses me goodbye, and says, 'I hope to see you soon . . . when you can . . . you are always welcome . . . ' I say goodbye to Mavi too and I go.

Gianni – summary

Gianni, while in the womb, looked as if even this limited space was too large and uncontrollable for him, all tightly crouched as he was while hanging on to his cord like a rope, almost as if trying to protect himself with a 'second skin'. The obstetrician who commented on his tight immobility and on his being 'double wrapped . . . all curled up and protected by the wall . . . like a second skin . . . ', certainly had not read Bick or Anzieu (Bick 1968; Anzieu 1985). Yet one could notice how Gianni's 'adhesiveness' ('He likes to stick tightly to the uterine wall . . . just following the outline and the anfractuosities of the wall . . . ' and 'He always seems to be looking for something to hold on to . . . always looking for an anchor . . . ', and 'when the cord is there . . . he hangs on to it . . . like a rope!') and protective 'second skin' formation seemed, right from the early days in the womb, to have had a secondary, defensive character for him. Whenever he moved, as the obstetrician said, he looked just 'restless . . . not finding any peace . . . ' Other fetuses behaved very differently from him.

Gianni's birth was by Caesarean section, and the obstetrician had considerable difficulty in pulling him out of the womb, crumpled as he was in a corner of it. As the obstetrician commented at the time, 'He would have never been born . . . ' The same obstetrician was struck by his tight immobility and by the sad and fixed expression on his face. 'He looked old . . . a hundred years old . . . it was somehow frightening to see the immobility of his face . . . '

In his tight closure Gianni seems even now to resist any impingement from the world outside and he seems to struggle now, as he did then, not to be pulled out of his obsessively orderly routines. As his mother says, 'He is always very meticulous . . . everything has to be in its place . . . all the objects are kept carefully in their place . . . '

As his grandmother and then his mother both say, 'He is better now . . . his character has softened a bit . . . ' and 'his teachers at nursery school are very pleased with him . . . '. Yet his unfolding has been very slow and careful. See how he still covers his face with his hands when he sees me and his immobility and fixed stare are often evident. His search for anchors and for covering protection are still very evident. His grandmother and then his mother remark on it: 'He tends to cling to people . . . he really holds on to them . . . he glues to them . . . as if he were frightened to let go . . . ', and 'He is always holding on to someone . . . he is always looking for some safety anchor . . . as if it were his last hope'. His grandmother sometimes finds him 'in some dark corner . . . all protected and covered . . . all curled up . . . '. See also how he clings to me during the entire observation and how he endows the shapeless, worm-like child of his drawing with a kind of rudimentary cord as if 'He needs something to hold on to . . . '.

His mother also remarks on the meticulousness and rigidity of his character: 'He is very orderly . . . everything has to be in its place . . . the same with his room . . . he is very tidy . . . all the objects . . . are kept carefully in their place . . . '

Now at four years of age his rigidity seems to mask an extreme vulnerability and nakedness, similar to the vulnerability and nakedness of the shapeless and worm-like child in his drawing that constantly has to hold on to something for its life. His protections and wrappings are often faulty and his fragility is evident. As his mother says, Gianni sometimes 'just falls to pieces' in spite of the obsessive control of the objects populating his space. And as she says, 'He just screams . . . uncontrollable screams . . . ', 'pure restlessness and irritation'. He did not look very different in his close retreat inside the uterine space.

As Gianni says in his preoccupation with his dog's nakedness which 'feels terrible' 'and nobody can repair it now', such nakedness was not his 'fault'. Whose 'fault' it was it would be almost too easy and yet too difficult to say, and, as Gianni says, it is too late to 'repair' now. Mrs B was certainly very anxious during pregnancy, and it seems possible that severe and prolonged anxiety in pregnancy may be one of the emotions that affect the uterus and the fetus, a matter which is well worth intensive observational study.

Mrs B, too, seems fragile in her desperate need of a 'breathing space'. Her enquiries about reproduction and sex continue pretty much unchanged and her daughter's periods seem to have opened a new avenue to further inquiries. Mrs B's mother looks depressed and fragile too, and her father is sleeping at 5 p.m. like a typical man from the south who finds the sunny and hot hours of the siesta better suited for rest and for sex. Mavi too with her constant over-eating and the pathetic over-ripeness of her body seems to respond to an almost inevitable fate.

OBSERVATION NO. 3 – PINA

Background

Mrs C, a woman in her late twenties, came accompanied by her husband for the first ultrasonographic observation. She looked older than her age, with a mature expression on her rather lined face, with bright, dark black intelligent eyes, bright black rather dirty hair and noticeably decayed teeth. Her parched hands too looked as if they had been exposed to the wind and sun too much. She spoke with a strong southern accent, and when questioned she told us that she originated from a little Calabrian village and that she and her husband had recently moved to the north where she worked as a nursery-school teacher. All this information was not volunteered spontaneously, but somehow extorted bit by bit by rather intrusive questioning from the obstetricians.

Mr C, who also looked very dark and hardened by life, kept rather aloof and to himself, almost suspicious, as if we came from two different and potentially antagonistic worlds. No information was extracted from him, and even now after several years of acquaintance-ship with his family I know nothing of his various activities.

Both parents though, in spite of their general reserve, seemed very interested in all that their sixteen-week-old fetus was doing, and she was doing a lot, practically all that she could do for her age and stage of development. Apart from their keen interest, however, they kept any emotions very much to themselves. In fact, only gradually did Mrs C open up to the obstetricians and to myself in particular (I saw very little of Mr C, apart from the ultrasonographic sessions), and by the time I came to visit her and Pina at their home, she considered me one of them and included me in her wide, yet rather secluded, 'clan'.

Pina: second ultrasonographic observation (twentieth week) – transcript

DR S: Now let's look at it . . . it's down here . . . it's moving . . . sort of swinging . . . one arm . . . actually both arms are up . . . above its head . . . to be more precise, you can see the back of the fetus on the right . . . both hands are now near its cheek-bone . . . now they are moving towards the orbits . . . now back towards the ears . . . look . . . there . . . it is scratching its ears . . . now it is yawning . . . look now . . . it is turning slightly . . . you can see its profile . . . it is banging its head . . . once . . . twice . . . and again . . . you can see its eyes too now . . . the crystalline lenses . . . you see, that white spot . . . now it is swallowing . . . now the hands . . . they are back . . . it is crossing its fingers . . . now it is bringing them forwards touching its chin . . . now they are both open . . . fingers spread out . . . both still near its face . . . its heart has accelerated slightly . . . in fact it brought its feet near its face too now . . . touching them with its hands . . . now the hands are behind . . . or rather at its sides . . . parallel to its head . . . now on its eyes . . .

MRS C: They move a lot . . .

DR S: Yes, this one seems to be moving a lot . . .

MRS C: Can you see it better as time passes or not? . . .

DR S: No, because as time goes on the fetus becomes bigger and its space more limited . . .

MRS C: It's more difficult for them to move . . .

DR S: Probably they can make the same kind of movements, but it becomes more difficult to observe them . . . it is not moving now . . . it is turned feet-down . . . you can see the crystalline lens well . . .

MRS C: You mean its eye? . . .

DR S: Yes, the eye . . . the white spot . . .

MR C: (teasing) I can see the colour of its eyes! . . . they are blue . . . a nice light blue . . . (He laughs and Mrs C laughs too.)

DR S: This movement is due to your laughing . . .

A nurse comes in making a lot of noise and she asks Dr S about another patient. He gets angry and tells her to wait until after the observation is over. Then:

DR S: It is scratching its cheeks . . . with both its hands . . . symmetrically . . . I am not completely sure . . . but it looks like the same movement they do once they're born . . .

MRS C: It's true . . . once they are out they rub their eyes exactly like this one does . . .

DR S: Now its hands are back at its sides . . . it is stretching them . . . you can see them down here . . . now they are up again . . . it is touching . . . actually, perhaps scratching its chest . . . look . . . now they are up here . . . near the placenta . . . look what it's doing . . . sort of squashing the placenta . . . and then moving its head as well . . . extending and flexing it . . . now one hand is above its head . . . as if it were doffing its cap to someone . . . you see . . . now the hand is over the ear . . . look at the other one . . . what is it doing? . . . trying to pull the placenta towards itself . . . it's incredible what it is doing with it . . . sort of trying to detach the placenta with it . . . it's the typical manoeuvre of manual detachment of the placenta . . . but you be careful! . . . stop doing it! . . . it is dangerous you know . . . you could be detaching it! . . . it's still on the placenta . . . this one moves a lot . . . but you can't feel it yet I suppose . . .

MRS C: Probably I can actually feel it . . . up till now I hadn't paid any attention to it . . . probably I hadn't realized that these were its movements . . .

DR S: It's not that you hadn't realized . . . you just couldn't feel them

. . . they are very light movements . . .

MRS C: Yes, I feel something very light . . .

MR C: But what about those stitches she feels sometimes . . .

MRS C: You think they are caused by its movements? . . .

DR S: (not replying to their questions) Now it is relaxing . . . it was about time . . .

MR C: Are those the ventricles? . . .

DR S: Of the heart, yes . . . now we can try with a bigger enlargement . . . look the hand is still there trying to detach the placenta . . . the eyes are still . . .

The nurse comes in again and tries to interrupt Dr S with some more questions. He gets very angry and tells her off. Then:

DR S: Still doing the same with its hand . . . on the placenta . . . (He yawns.) I hope it won't go on like this for another twenty minutes . . . it's making me sleepy . . . continuing to watch that hand . . .

MRS C: (laughing) It is probably a comfortable position . . .

DR S: It's like being between two pillows . . . here it goes . . . moving again . . . a slow movement . . . but a big one . . . a so-called 'total body' movement . . .

MR C: What is that thing up there? . . .

DR S: Its head . . . and its hands . . . now both hands are between its legs . . . now on its knees . . . another big movement again . . . from podalic to transverse . . . hands between knees . . . it is moving its feet . . .

MR C: Oh, yes, I can see its feet . . .

DR S: It is playing now . . . moving its hands . . . they are always there . . . between its legs . . . now it is kicking . . . against the uterine wall . . . look . . . now one hand is over its heart as if feeling its beat . . . this child has a wide range of movements . . . it is moving a lot . . . much better than twins . . .

MRS C: Twins must have little space . . .

DR S: This is its spine . . .

MRS C: It's a straight spine isn't it? . . .

DR S: Yes, everything is all right . . . it has got all its fingers and toes . . . look, now the position has changed . . . completely turned and all curled up . . .

MRS C: It's marvellous what one can see now . . . once all this was not possible . . . one just didn't understand anything of what was going on . . . all this is very reassuring . . . and it is incredible how much they can do already . . .

DR S: Can you distinguish what it is doing?

MRS C: Yes, I am getting used to it . . .

DR S: Our women are now experts . . . at least those whose children we are studying *in utero* . . . they know everything . . .

MR C: What is that thing there? . . .

DR S: It's a foot . . . it is all curled up now . . . its feet are up here . . . its hands here . . . now one hand is holding a foot . . . now both hands are holding its feet . . . one arm moved near the head . . . you know [he is talking to me now] last night I was out for dinner with a friend of mine . . . and I told her about our observations . . . she just had a child . . . last September . . . and she just wallowed in it . . . she is a teacher . . . but I have noticed that generally women are very pleased to be observed . . .

MRS C: Yes, this is true for me . . .

DR S: Now the hand is over the other arm . . . look, it is yawning . . . and it is making some slight jerky movements with its hand . . . as if it were plucking some hair off its arm . . . yawning again . . . you can see the tongue . . . now swallowing . . . swallowing . . . chewing . . . it looks as if it is chewing . . . what a mess it is making! . . . moving everything . . . hands, feet, head! . . . sort of swinging now . . . come on, lift up . . . so we can see your profile! . . . good! . . . what a nice nose! . . . now the hand is on the forehead . . . practically this one is already doing all the movements that we will observe at birth . . . actually now we can observe more movements . . . at birth, because of the increased force of gravity, they move less . . . it takes a while before seeing some of these movements again . . . one would need to see a baby delivered in space without the force of gravity to see all this again . . . it is moving again . . . sort of jerky movements . . . I am fascinated by this mouth . . . sorry if I move the probe . . . yes, you see the stomach is full now . . . so it was not yawning, but swallowing . . . (Dr S now gives me the probe to hold.)

DR S: What I have noticed is that *in utero* they bring their hands near their face much more easily . . . these kind of gestures are lost for a while after birth . . . in the sense that babies don't have sufficient strength to perform them . . . look how it is moving . . . this one really moves a lot . . .

MRS C: I feel it now . . .

DR S: This one is definitely a lively one . . . moving a lot and exploring a lot . . . [then talking to Mrs C] . . . this is now the twentieth week . . . so it should be born towards the end of July–beginning of August . . .

MRS C: Poor me! . . .

DR S: Why don't you like that date? . . .

MRS C: It is so hot! . . .

DR S: Now it is moving again . . . it has turned itself round . . . you can see its profile very clearly . . . touching the placenta . . . sort of dipping its nose in the placenta . . . again . . . how funny! . . . pushing its nose against it . . . getting in with it . . . again . . . again . . . opens its mouth . . . lips in contact with the placenta . . . is this your first child? . . .

MRS C: Yes . . .

DR S: Now it is sort of shaking its head . . . its hand is under its chin . . . it's a constant movement . . . this is a very active child . . . I hope it won't be a pain in the ass! . . .

MRS C: (laughs) If it is like me or its father . . . it will most definitely be a pain in the ass . . .

DR S: I didn't want to upset you . . . now it is swallowing . . . again . . . again . . . again . . . it is swallowing a lot . . .

MRS C: A good appetite! . . .

DR S: At this stage it is as if they were learning to swallow . . . but they don't breathe yet . . . I mean you can't see breathing movements . . . then when they breathe usually they don't move . . . next time you will be able to see breathing movements as well . . .

MRS C: They are preparing for birth . . .

The observation time is now over and Mrs C cleans her stomach quickly and is ready to go in a few minutes. We arrange for the next appointment and she goes away followed by her husband, barely saying goodbye to the obstetricians.

Unfortunately, Pina's 'sense of excitement' in exploring nearly turned to tragedy in the following days and her trying to detach the placenta with her hand could in retrospect be read as an ominous sign. A few days after this observation Mrs C actually started bleeding rather heavily and an initial detachment of the placenta was noted. A miscarriage seemed probable and Mrs C was ordered absolute rest for a while and was put on heavy doses of tocolytic drugs. Mrs C was worried and for a time was in considerable pain. The effect on Pina was dramatic. During the third ultrasonographic observation she seemed to have lost all her 'appetite' and her movement. She had turned in the transversal position and was tightly crouched in a corner of the womb and completely immobile.

Pina: fourth ultrasonographic observation (thirtieth week) – transcript

DR S: OK, let's get started . . . now the head is up here . . . he is not cephalic . . .

MRS C: It's a he or a she?

DR S: Last time it looked like a she ... but we could always be mistaken ...

MR C: So it is not possible to tell ...

DR S: You will certainly be able to tell at birth ... or perhaps next month ... provided she turns ... she is all curled up ... in a tangle ... here is the spine ... one arm ... the head is here ... where is the other arm? ... shit! she is so tangled up ... perhaps down here ... I swear that I can't find it! bugger! ... where on earth have you put it! ... there it is! ... down there ...

MR C: Is that her right arm? ...

DR S: No, that is a foot ... you can see the sole clearly ... this is a hand ... the other hand ... she is not moving ... what the hell is this? ... buttocks ... her feet are also all tangled up ... she is all tangled up ... one hand ... one foot ... the other foot or perhaps the other hand ... she is too tangled up ... these are her feet actually ... the hand is here ... sticking out from God only knows where ... terribly tangled up ... and she is not moving ... her nose ... her eyes ... perhaps she is moving her head slightly, but very slightly ... one hand ... the other one ... here we are ... they are both on the left ... you can see her foot clearly ... her right arm ... it is not possible to see the left one ... (Long silence) ... OK ... She is not moving anything ... today she is asleep ... (Another long silence) ... she is not doing anything ... you remember the other time ... she was all over the place ... moving all the time ... not last time ... last time she was also immobile ... I mean the time before ... then of course you were not well ... you had a threat ... have the pains stopped now? ...

MRS C: Yes ...

DR S: She is very immobile ... just moving in tune with your aorta ... but I mean passively ... as a kind of lullaby ... she is just leaning with her head against the aorta ... moving synchronously ... just passive motions (Long silence) ... nothing (Long silence) ... she is not moving ... immobile ... just lulled ...

MR C: I will sing her a lullaby when she is upset ...

DR S: (yawning) What a mess ... all tangled up ... and not moving ...

MRS C: Last time too ... yet during the first two observations she moved all the time ...

Again a long silence, then Dr S asks me to hold the probe, saying, 'I feel sleepy, just looking at her ...' (Very long silence.)

A nurse comes in and makes a lot of noise. Apart from that, no comments.

DR S: Today she is just all curled up . . .
MRS C: Yes, all in a corner . . . (Very long silence)
MRS C: She is not doing anything today . . . like last time . . . but generally I feel her moving much less . . .
DR S: Does she move more in the evening? . . .
MRS C: In the evening and in the early morning she moves a bit more . . . but always very little . . .
DR S: She seems asleep . . . (Very long silence and a lot of noise coming from the room next door.)

Another obstetrician comes in and she stands near me. She says:

OBSTET: She is all curled up . . . she is not moving . . . this looks like the cord . . . but I can't be sure (Long silence) . . . it is such a tangle . . . it's impossible to see anything . . . (She takes the probe from my hands.) No way . . . it's impossible to see anything today . . . she is calm . . . still . . . (Long silence) . . . how many more minutes? . . . [I say that we have four more minutes.] It is so boring . . .
DR S: She hasn't been moving at all . . .

The time is over now and Dr S tells Mrs C that we have finished. She dresses herself again and then we arrange for the next appointment. Dr S says that he will see her in ten days. (She has to have frequent check-ups.) Before leaving, Mrs C says, 'I have stopped working altogether now . . . I am at home all day . . . but I am terrified . . . I hope the delivery will not be delayed . . . I hope everything will be all right . . .'. Then she picks up her file and goes out with her husband saying goodbye.

Very little seemed to have changed the following month. During the fifth observation Pina was still curled up and 'all in a tangle' in a corner of the womb turned in the podalic position and she seemed completely immobile. Her mother too said that she moved very little during the day.

Pina: the delivery and the first two post-natal observations – summary

Both Dr S and Dr F forgot to phone me during the delivery. One week before she was due to be born, Pina had not yet turned round in the womb. She was in the transverse position now, and Dr S decided it was too dangerous to risk a natural delivery and therefore a Caesarean was decided upon. Apparently Dr S had considerable difficulty in pulling her out of the womb and one of her feet, due to malposition *in utero*, had to be put in plaster. Dr S was struck by the fact that Pina cried at first, but then 'seemed greatly relieved to be out . . . ' and described her as a vivacious and alert child. Rules were rather strict in the hospital where Mrs C was staying, and therefore I just saw Pina very briefly. Mrs C looked rather tired and in pain, and the heat was almost unbearable on that day.

Pina was brought in for a few moments (visitors were not allowed during the feeding-times and feeds took place in the nursery), and I was immediately struck by her bright and alert black eyes. Her mother told me that she moved a lot, while she had some difficulty in eating which she attributed to the heat. She was soon going to go on holidays for about a month, back to her little village in Calabria. Her husband and her mother were going to accompany her, while all her relatives were there waiting for her. When I visited her at home the following week, Pina was asleep and all her luggage was ready. Mrs C spoke mainly about the difficulties of bringing up children in a big town. In her village everybody was ready to give a hand. Here in the North she could see almost only desolation and loneliness and I had to agree with her. Then Mrs C left for her holidays and came back rather late, so that, by the time I saw Pina again she was nearly two months old.

Pina: summary of post–natal observations up to the age of three

When I saw Pina again, when she was two months old, I was very struck by her alertness and precociousness, with her big black eyes exploring every detail of the house. Though only one month and twenty days old, Pina smiled as soon as she saw us and could already hold her head straight. Pina also moved a lot. As her mother said, 'She was just like that when she was inside, wasn't she? . . . ' Yet Pina was not always just like that when she was inside and also now that she was outside she seemed to show many fears, particularly of not being held securely and of falling. One of her feet was still in plaster because of her malposition *in utero*. She was also a rather tense child, and food was already beginning to be a problem for her.

Contrary to her original plans, Mrs C waited well into spring before resuming her regular work as she felt that Pina was too tense and therefore wanted to be with her. Mrs C waited for spring almost as a country woman, completely dependent on the changes it would bring with it, attributing to it quasi-magical powers of revealing hidden reserves and melting frozen resources. Pina would flourish once again after the winter's harsh weather had ended.

In fact Pina did have some problems during and beyond that first winter of her life, particularly when it came to eating and to food, but there were some milder problems too. Pina was an extremely alert and bright child, as her mother said, 'keeping everything under control with her eyes . . . '. One could read in her adventurous and alert look a mixture of pleasure in exploring as well as a desperate attempt to keep every detail of her world, her house, under control. Nothing seemed to escape her attention. At the same time, however, she found it difficult to 'let go' and her visual 'journeys' somehow had a tense life-and-death quality about them, like an explorer enjoying the ever-changing scenery of the trees and birds of the jungle while at the same time being constantly on the alert for potential dangers and enemies lurking everywhere. I was told repeatedly that this was true particularly within the walls of her house: once she was outside, Pina apparently really enjoyed what she saw and seemed much more relaxed and much less on the alert. Problems, according to her mother, began once she went inside any closed space.

By the age of three months Pina was in fact acutely aware of strangers and reacted to them very much as a much older child would have, particularly if strangers came to her house. 'Outside she is all right . . . she is actually very sociable . . . but once inside she has a kind of radar and is aware of every change and detail . . . ' Pina on the other hand seemed to 'love novelties' and found it intolerable to be 'locked inside four walls'. I am rather inclined to believe Mrs C, given Pina's smiles and enthusiasm each time her mother accompanied me to the lift with Pina in her arms, followed by her distant cries as I heard the door being closed again. I do not think all this had very much to do with missing me. Apparently Pina reacted with acute 'claustrophobic' anxieties whenever she was brought to visit someone like her paediatrician or some relatives or friends and therefore felt 'the walls closing in on her'. Again, as her mother once said, 'constriction and being inside equal danger for her . . . she would like to live like a gypsy in the street . . . ', 'she screams as soon as we close the door . . . '.

Pina seemed to hate any constriction in general, and her mother told me that she couldn't bear being wrapped in her nappy. 'Any constriction is fearful for her . . . ', and her coat was only accepted and even welcomed when she began to realize that it meant going out.

For quite a long while Pina also had some problems with her stools as she kept them inside for days; she seemed terrified to 'let go', and her mother had to help her while she was in the unconsciousness of deep sleep; if unconscious she could 'rid herself of her stool . . . but without realizing it . . . without even having to push . . . '.

For months Pina was also frightened of falling and of not being held securely in her mother's arms. She was frightened of having her bath: 'She doesn't like it . . . each time it's a tragedy . . . first I have to put her hands gently into the water . . . then she has to get in bit by bit . . . and mostly I have to hold her tightly . . . otherwise she screams . . . as if she were afraid of drowning or of being washed away . . . ' One of her worst fears were the stairs. 'As soon as I go down one step . . . even if I go down very slowly . . . she feels the void . . . and she gets terrified . . . she screams . . . ' Yet Pina was far from being an immobile child and she actually moved a lot, so much so that her mother had to pad her whole cot with a thick layer of pillows, because, as she said, 'She moves all the time . . . she moves so much that unless I put pillows all around her, in the morning her head is full of bumps and bruises . . . '

Pina was also frightened of being left alone 'in a void' and could not bear silence. 'Even if I am in another room, I have to talk to her . . . or else leave the radio or the television on . . . otherwise she's afraid of the emptiness . . . the silence.' Indeed, the radio or the television were on practically all the time whenever I visited them.

It was when Pina was about five months old that I noticed another behaviour of hers which was to continue for many months, well after the spring and summer were over. Pina often used to react to people or events with great, mounting excitement, but very soon her excitement seemed to turn into fear and crying and her explorations into tragedy. The border between excitement and tears was often very narrow indeed. But Pina's worst problem was probably food. Soon even the breast seemed to take on a persecutory quality for her and when it came to trying the bottle or solids she refused to eat altogether. As her mother said, 'You act as if I'm feeding you with bitter liquids, like bile . . . poisoning you . . . ', and Pina reacted to any of her mother's attempts at feeding her by using all possible strategies of counter-attack. She was soon able to close her mouth tightly and by four months old if force-fed she vomited; later she learned to spit out her food actively or to let it dribble passively and silently out of her mouth. Later still she used to push her mother away with her feet while also pulling her hair, and each time her bib was put on she almost tore it away. Mrs C tried more or less everything; putting sugar on her food; reducing its quantity while doubling the dose of cheese in it; constantly trying to introduce new tastes and foods into her diet. Pina in fact liked new tastes and foods for a while, but soon rejected these too, and the best strategy was always that of trying to distract her attention from what was being put into her mouth. Her mother sang her endless songs, made all sorts of grimaces, showed her all sorts of toys, invented all sorts of tricks and in the end, a bit like a skilled conjurer, succeeded in making some food disapppear inside Pina's otherwise tightly closed mouth, and Pina very slowly continued to put on a tiny bit of weight. She was in fact a rather skinny child with big dark eyes devouring her bony face and when it came to food, Mrs C and Pina's otherwise affectionate relationship became almost a nightmare and certainly a torment for both of them.

Mrs C seemed to feel the isolation of living in a big town acutely, surrounded by anonymity, indifference, and concrete. She spent hours on the phone with her aunts and cousins asking for advice particularly about food, and was always reassured by the fact that the little cousin born a few days before Pina remained rather backward in comparison.

Around Christmas her own mother came to stay with them and helped her with Pina during several of the winter months. Mrs C's mother was a typical peasant, toothless and dressed all in black (her husband had died several years before), speaking in a strong and (for me) almost incomprehensible dialect, yet full of warmth and generosity and a mixture of wisdom and superstition which rendered her very appealing to me, and she became very fond of me too. She filled my visits with endless village tales of abandoned and molested women, of whores attracting men 'like dogs', as well as of drought and heat and crops and pigs. When she found out that I had been married twice (something Mrs C knew through the obstetricians at the clinic), she immediately jumped to the conclusion that I had been abandoned by my first husband 'for another woman' and therefore I too was another victim of the age-old indifference of men, depicted rather like 'animals' when it came to matters of sex. In fact she couldn't stay with her daughter till the end of the spring because, not only did she have to kill her pig, but also she had to go back to keep an eye on her twenty-five-year-old son whom she was afraid would fall victim of some little hussy, totally unworthy of him, as soon as he was out of the control of her watchful eyes.

With Pina Mrs C's mother was very affectionate and warm. She spoke and played with her all day long. She held her in her arms and walked about with her, though never letting Pina's face come into contact with her black dress as this might bring 'bad luck' (in fact she always went round with two white handkerchiefs on her shoulders, so as to avoid any contact between Pina's face and her black clothes). She also made intelligent remarks about her: 'Her problem with food probably goes back a long way . . . but otherwise she likes looking at everything . . . it's her nature . . . she is just like that . . . she is both frightened and very interested in life . . . but I am sure that her fears will soon go away . . . ' Pina seemed to love her grandmother, as apparently did all the children of their village, and she, her mother, and, it would appear, her father too all fell ill with flu when it was time for the grandmother to leave to return to her village.

Pina's father, on the other hand, seemed to be left very much in the background. There were hints of quarrels, and resigned complaints, and on the whole he seemed to behave very much as a stereotype of a 'tough male'. Only much later apparently did he begin to take an active interest in Pina and from then on he seemed to treat her more like a 'woman' in competition with his wife, than like his child. Indeed, apparently, Pina always responded with great excitement to his coming home.

Yet, apart from food, many of Pina's problems seemed to fade or at least go underground with the arrival of spring and then summer, and particularly when the family returned to their village during the holidays.

Pina had always been a very precocious child who desperately seemed to want to grow fast. As her sensitive mother said, 'This is partly her nature . . . she has always looked older than her age . . . but also she seems to think that by growing up she will be less exposed to dangerous and uncontrolled falls . . . her fear since she was born . . . '

Not surprisingly Pina began to talk and to crawl by eight months. When she came back from the holidays she was thirteen months old and she could walk and was already talking like a much older child. Her newly achieved independence seemed to restore much of her lost security. Now that she could no longer be dropped or 'washed away', Pina seemed to feel on top of the world. She began exploring every corner of the house and was aware of the contents of every single room. Her mother said, 'She likes seeing everything . . . exploring everything . . . she was much more frightened before . . . I don't know why . . . but she looked like someone who had been traumatized . . . '

Soon after the holidays Pina was also dry and clean and learned to hold her spoon and her glass by herself. She still loved going out and hated being inside 'surrounded by walls', but as her mother said, 'Before she used to cry as soon as she saw her coat . . . any constriction was frightening for her . . . now she realizes that her coat means going out . . . and she smiles when she sees it . . . while she still hates bibs, strings or ribbons . . . '

In October, when Pina was fourteen months old, her mother went back to work part-time (so far she had only been working occasionally when her own mother was with her) and Pina spent her mornings in a kindergarten. She seemed to enjoy it there and all the teachers were enthusiastic about her. Food, though, was still a problem with her. Pina was certainly rather skinny, but she was also growing and was not seriously underweight. As her mother said, 'She is well now . . . she is happy . . . only she doesn't want to eat . . . ', and also, according to her, some distant nightmare had remained in the back of Pina's mind. 'She is a happy child . . . but sometimes she has nightmares . . . they have remained . . . but then as soon as she opens her eyes . . . she realizes that she is out of the nightmare . . . and her fears are gone . . . ' In order not to fall prey to her nightmares Pina apparently slept very little at night, as 'she has to keep the world under control . . . '.

Pina: post-natal observation at three years old – detailed report

In the following observation Pina's mother is about to have another child, a little boy. The new pregnancy seems to have re-awakened in Mrs C the memory of all the fears she experienced when Pina was inside her, and Pina shows in a drawing how she herself was nearly 'washed away'.

I had phoned Mrs C the week before and she had told me that she was pregnant again. She said, 'I was tempted to tell you that before the holidays (I had visited her at the beginning of June) . . . but at the very beginning you never know . . . I was afraid of having all the problems I had with her . . . but this time it seems different . . . I am seven months pregnant now . . . it's a boy this time . . . I had some slight problems . . . but nothing compared with her . . . I will stop working now . . . it's my last day on Friday . . . I am rather tired and I don't want to risk it . . . Dr S wrote a certificate for me . . . ' We had then arranged to meet the following week, when she would be at home from work.

I arrive on time and ring the interphone. Mrs C opens the door with the buzzer and I cross the courtyard and take the lift. When I reach her floor she is waiting for me in front of the door. She lets me in, shaking hands with me and with a warm smile. She is wearing a yellow track-suit. Though she hasn't put on much weight, she is visibly pregnant. Pina is sitting on the sofa. She is wearing her pyjamas and is looking sleepy and sulky. She seems to have lost quite a bit of weight. Mrs C says, 'She just woke up . . . ' I give her a small box of chocolates and she unwraps it very quickly and skilfully. She is still silent and the expression on her face is still very serious. Her mother takes the box from her and gives her a chocolate to eat. Pina eats it silently, keeping her head slightly bent forwards.

I ask Mrs C how she is. She says, 'Much better now that I am at home from work . . . I have been rather tired lately . . . but this pregnancy has been different . . . none of the problems I had with her . . . I was sick during the first three months . . . but no bleeding as with her and particularly no detachment of the placenta during the fifth month . . . I was always scared with her after that happened . . . I was scared with this one too . . . but not any more now . . . unfortunately I had some problems again with my teeth . . . in July . . . just when I had planned to go away . . . another wisdom tooth again . . . as with her . . . I had to take antibiotics . . . but then I had to wait for the swelling to disappear . . . they couldn't pull it out as it was so swollen . . . but it took ages . . . so I lost more than a fortnight waiting . . . it was really terrible with the heat . . . '

In the meantime Pina has finished eating her chocolate with small bites and looks rather sleepy and very serious again. Mrs C looks at her, and says, 'She is rather tired now . . . she has been to nursery school all day . . . she is going to nursery-school this year . . . but I have some problems with her teachers . . . they want her to be silent . . . but she talks all the time . . . it's impossible to ask a child like her to be silent . . . she talks all the time . . . and she was used to the kindergarten . . . so she is not shy . . . and they also want her to sit down . . . but that's absurd . . . at her age! . . . they complain because she tends to move from her desk . . . but she is only three . . . how can they sit down all the time at her age? . . . then to begin with they asked me to introduce her very gradually . . . so for ten days I had to take her for only two hours a day . . . from 10 to 12 . . . but she had no problems . . . she wasn't in the least upset . . . she's always been very independent . . . and she was used to kindergarten . . . but they insisted on it . . . in fact she likes going to nursery school . . . she gets on very well with other children . . . she plays . . . she is independent . . . her only problem is food . . . but that has always been her problem . . . since she was born . . . you have to stand over her . . . I told them that food was her problem . . . but they have too many children . . . twenty-eight in a class . . . they say that they cannot keep tabs on whether she eats or not . . . but it is their fault . . . they shouldn't accept so many children . . . particularly at this age . . . '

Pina starts fidgeting with her mouth and pulls out a small whitish bit (probably a bit of almond from her chocolate). Mrs C looks at her and wipes her mouth, saying, 'You are all dirty . . . ' Pina gives her the white bit, saying, 'I don't like this bit . . . ' Then she seems to wake up and gets off the sofa and stands up. Her mother says, 'She always ate very little . . . but she's well . . . and apart from that she looks and behaves as if she were older than her age . . . ' Pina smiles and goes and gets some paper that is on the table. She takes a pencil too and sits down on a small chair at a low table next to her mother's armchair, saying, 'I will draw something for you . . . ' She rather carefully and quite skilfully draws a circle, and says, 'This is an egg . . . an unlucky egg . . . it is going to be washed away by the waves of the sea . . . ' Her mother hands her some coloured pencils. She picks up the light blue one and starts colouring all around the egg. She says, 'And this is the sea . . . with all the waves . . . ', and she stands up and shows them to me.

Her mother says, 'When we were at the sea during the summer she was very frightened . . . too much water . . . and she was terrified of the waves . . . she said that they made her dizzy . . . she was afraid of being overwhelmed and washed away by the sea and all the waves . . . she said so . . . then gradually she got over it . . . and in the end she enjoyed it . . . '

Pina now is back at the low table and is drawing many little circles. She says, 'These are a lot of other eggs . . . no danger for them . . . they are lucky . . . they are firmly planted inside the ground . . . '

Mrs C says, 'The weather was good . . . not too hot this year . . . so I went to the beach too . . . my husband took us by car . . . we went almost every day . . . she was very happy there . . . all day long with my mother . . . they had so much fun together . . . out in the fields . . . weeding and digging and picking fruit . . . '

Pina stops drawing her eggs and shows me some scratches on her arms, saying, 'Look, I did these when I was out in the fields . . . they are still there . . . they left a scar . . . wounds always leave a deep scar . . . '

Mrs C says, 'Yes, you still have some scars left . . . but she is terrible . . . she touches everything . . . and with her grandmother she did whatever she liked . . . you remember how many peanuts you ate? . . . ' Then she tells her to go and put her slippers on (Pina is bare-footed). Pina takes them from the sofa and puts them on. Then she says, 'I have to go to the loo . . . ' and she goes out. Her mother says, 'She is very independent . . . she does everything by herself . . . getting dressed . . . eating . . . going to the loo . . . she seems much older than her age . . . you remember my cousin? . . . the one who had a baby just a few days before me . . . well she was worried to death this summer . . . she said that her son looked positively retarded compared to Pina . . . '

We hear Pina flushing the toilet and then she comes back into the sitting room. Mrs C says, 'Would you like a coffee? . . . Perhaps it is a bit late now . . . ' I thank her and say that it is late now. She says, 'I have put on 4 kilos during the summer . . . Dr S was cross with me . . . he said it was too much . . . but it was impossible to resist the food at home . . . with my mother cooking . . . and then I had a lot of rest as well . . . with everybody looking after her . . . '

Pina in the meantime opens a drawer full of toys and takes out two small cups and a coffee machine. She puts them on the table and pretends to be making coffee.

Mrs C says, 'She is crazy about her father now . . . whenever he is around she ignores me . . . he is crazy about her too . . . she has replaced me in his heart . . . ' Pina pretends to be giving us coffee and I thank her. Mrs C continues to talk. She says, 'Now we shall have to change house . . . this flat is too small . . . I would like to have four rooms . . . one for the children . . . this one is too small . . . she still sleeps with us as we have no room . . . but it is difficult to find another flat now . . . there was one on the market a few weeks ago, but it was on the first floor . . . I didn't like that . . . too much danger of burglars . . . anyone can just walk in . . . and too dark . . . what I liked about this flat was the light you get . . . so we are still looking . . . '

Pina pretends to be offering us some more coffee, then she pretends to wash up her cups and puts them back inside her drawer together with the coffee machine. Then she goes and gets a big doll. She comes back hugging it. She walks about pretending to be rocking it to sleep. Her mother says, 'She would like to have a little sister . . . but this one is 95 per cent a boy . . . for me it's the same . . . one or the other it doesn't matter . . . I shall see Dr S again at the end of this month . . . I would like to try and have a natural delivery this time . . . with her I had to have a Caesarean as she was in the transverse position . . . but otherwise there was no other reason for it . . . had she been in the right position the delivery would have been all right . . . this one so far is cephalic . . . so we are going to try . . . '

Pina now puts her doll down on the sofa and covers her with a small blanket, saying, 'She is asleep . . . ', then goes and gets some plastic dishes from her drawer, and says, 'Now I am going to prepare you something to eat . . . ' and she pretends to cook and puts some ingredients on the plates.

Mrs C says, 'My mother will be here for the delivery . . . and then she is going to stay with us at least until Easter . . . then everything gets easier once the winter is over . . . and I should go back to work . . . I will do the same as with her . . . anyway we shall see once he is born . . . work was tiring now . . . I was in charge of four handicapped children . . . badly handicapped . . . so it was also physically tiring . . . and not very rewarding . . . I prefer to teach normal children . . . but since I was pregnant I was given this job . . . but then Dr S told me that if I was feeling tired I had to stop . . . and he wrote a certificate for me . . . it is not worth risking . . . '

Pina in the meantime pretends to give her mother some chips to eat and then gives me some 'roast beef'. Her mother continues, 'She is terrible . . . she always was . . . she notices everything . . . and is inquisitive about everything . . . ' Pina now gives us some 'cake'. Each time her mother smiles at her. She says, 'This one is moving a lot . . . he seems to be moving all the time . . . she was like that too to begin with . . . then she stopped . . . after I had that threat . . . probably the treatment interfered with it too . . . I was given Vasosuprine [a tocolytic drug] . . . and that is poison . . . I think for the child too . . . I had to take it for such a long time . . . I think it had an effect on her too . . . '

Now Pina offers us some 'biscuits'. Her mother says, 'I wish you ate as much . . . she eats so little . . . as if food were poison for her . . . and she's so careful about what she is eating . . . the only things she would like to eat are chocolates and peanuts . . . though the doctor says that she is quite strong . . . '

Pina pretends not to hear what her mother is saying, but I think she is in fact listening very carefully to every single word. Now she goes and gets a cloth from the kitchen and wipes the plates with it.

Mrs C says, 'She is terrible . . . it is very difficult for her coming back from the holidays . . . when we are back home she is out all day . . . here she finds it difficult being locked inside . . . then she misses my mother . . . and her grandmother misses her a lot too . . . she phones her often . . . they have long conversations on the phone . . . I can hardly speak to her . . . '

It is time for me to go and I tell Mrs C. She stands up and goes into the kitchen and comes back with a bottle of olive oil, saying, 'This is for you . . . from last year's vintage . . . it was particularly good . . . luckily the olives don't have to be picked this year . . . otherwise my mother would have been unable to come . . . she says that I did it on purpose getting pregnant this year, so that she could come . . . ' I thank her very much for the oil. She says that she will give me a ring as soon as the child is born and I wish her all the best. Pina opens the door for me and waves me goodbye.

Pina – summary

At the ultrasonographic observations at the sixteenth and twentieth weeks Pina was the most active of all the fetuses we observed – so much so that the obstetrician, Dr S, said she was 'trying to detach the placenta . . . it's the typical manoeuvre of manual detachment of the

placenta . . . but you be careful! Stop doing it! It is dangerous you
know . . . you could be detaching it!'

And shortly after this observation, as described above, there was a
detachment of the placenta leading to fear of miscarriage, considerable
pain, bed rest, and large doses of tocolytic drugs.

We cannot of course know whether it was Pina's vigorous
exploratory and pulling actions that caused the detachment of the
placenta, but she certainly came close to being 'washed away' in a
miscarriage. Whether because of the drugs or the general disturbance
of the uterus, Pina became very still, 'all tangled up', had to be born by
a Caesarean section, and needed a foot in plaster for several weeks
because of its rigidly maintained, bad position in the uterus. Once
safely born, however, she seemed, as the obstetrician put it, 'greatly
relieved to be out'.

Her post-natal history showed a similar pattern: much activity and
excited exploration, high intelligence, rapid and early achievement of
all developmental accomplishments, but accompanied by many fears,
claustrophobic anxiety, eating difficulties, and retention of faeces. She
showed evident apprehension about being dropped. She was especially
afraid of the bath and Mrs C had to hold her very tightly. 'Otherwise',
Mrs C explained, 'she screams . . . as if she were afraid of drowning or
of being washed away.' Pina also seemed to regard any closed
environment or tightly adhering texture with more than a hint of
claustrophobic anxiety. She always wanted to go out and could not
bear to be shut in. She resisted being wrapped up tightly in her coat,
and only consented to it once she realized that it meant she was going
to go outside. It was as if the narrow space of the womb and its
enveloping constriction might have felt to her suffocatingly charged
with potential deadly hazards, and she treated later constricting spaces
as if they too were threatening and dangerous.

At three years of age Pina appeared to be a very bright and
adventurous child. All her teachers were enthusiastic about her. Her
mother, however, said that her nightmares had remained, and her
distant fears seemed to have surfaced again, as if they had left a deep
scar within her. She was constantly on the alert in the monitoring of
her environment. Her quasi-anorexic carefulness in taking her food
also appears to be linked to her deep suspiciousness about what she
cannot control. Her mother links this with Pina having been
'poisoned' during pregnancy by her high intake of tocolytic drugs. As
Pina said, 'Wounds always leave a deep scar . . . ' Later, Pina drew an
egg for me, and called it 'an unlucky egg' which was going to be
'washed away by the waves of the sea', while all the other eggs were
lucky as they seemed 'firmly' planted in the ground (as her yet unborn

brother, unlike her, was firmly planted in his mother's womb). Pina's mother, while looking at her drawing of the egg washed away by the sea, described Pina's terror and dizziness in front of the real waves of the sea.

Although Pina's mother had not explicitly told Pina about her near miscarriage, Pina seems to show tacit awareness of the danger she had been subjected to, and has a persisting tendency towards vigorous activity, almost hyperactivity, accompanied or followed by fear of disaster and tragedy.

Pina has been particularly fortunate in having parents and grandparents, especially her mother and grandmother, who were especially thoughtful and tolerant in helping her to come to terms with her hazardous behaviour and its accompanying fears.

Twin pregnancies

Two main types of twins are usually encountered in man: monozygotic (MZ) or uniovular, and dizygotic (DZ) or binovular twins. DZ twins are met much more frequently than MZ ones, which represent only 25.4 per cent of all twin births.

Dizygotic twins arise from the fertilization of two different eggs and are also called fraternal as their genetic endowment is no more similar than that of ordinary siblings. Only the fact of having shared the same pre-natal environment distinguishes them from ordinary siblings.

Monozygotic twins result from an early division of the same fertilized egg (zygote) and therefore are also called identical as they share the same genoma. Such divisions of a single embryo into two different ones can take place at varying stages between the first division of the zygote and the fourteenth day. If the division occurs very early on (roughly during the first day after conception), the MZ twins will have separate placentae, chorion and amniotic sacs (dichorionic diamniotic twins). If it occurs within the seventh day after conception, this will result in MZ twins sharing the same placenta and the same chorion (monochorionic), but not the same amniotic sac (diamniotic). If the division occurs still later, from the seventh until the thirteenth day after conception, the twins will be sharing not only the same placenta and chorion (monochorionic), but also the same amniotic sac (monoamniotic). If the division of the embryo takes place between the thirteenth and the fourteenth day after conception, this will result in the very rare occurrence of conjoined or Siamese twins.

The recognition of these different types of pregnancies and stages of division is not only relevant from a purely biological, medical, or even ethico-legal point of view. (The recent establishment of fourteen days after conception for the lawfulness of embryo research in England stems, amongst other considerations – principally the formation of the primitive streak and therefore the beginning of the development of the nervous system – from the fact that beyond such a date a division of the embryo does not take place and therefore continuity and individuality of development are by then established. Before that date, at least theoretically, two separate individuals could result from the potential division of the embryo.) It is also significant for the possible determination of type of twinning with ultrasounds. Pre-natal determination of zygosity with ultrasounds can only be arrived at through exclusion and can only be considered accurate in the face of two occurrences. If the sex of the observed pair is different one can state with certainity that the twins are DZ, as having a different sex clearly means not sharing the same genoma. Things become more complicated when an ultrasonographic diagnosis of same-sexed twins is made, as these could be either fraternal or identical. The fact of having separate placentae does not *per se* mean, as was and is still often believed, that the twins are DZ, as those MZ twins whose zygote has divided within the seventh day after fertilization have separate chorions. In fact only two-thirds of MZ twins will have mono-chorionic placentae (Bryan 1983). But also, when faced with an apparently monochorionic pregnancy it is not possible to diagnose with any certainty ultrasonographically if what we are observing is in fact a single placenta or two different but adjoining 'fused' placentae which could also belong to DZ twins. This distinction will only be made possible by a careful observation of the placenta and the membranes at birth. Therefore, so far, the two most common ultrasonographic findings recommended to diagnose this condition are the appearance of cord-knotting together with the carefully monitored non-visualization of a dividing membrane (Colburn and Pasquale 1982; Townsend and Filly 1988). This latter type of pregnancy, though, is very rare (1 per cent of MZ twins and 0.1–2.3 per cent of twin gestations) and is considered to be highly at risk (with a fetal mortality rate reported to be 50 per cent). This therefore greatly restricts the possibility of planning beforehand to observe pre-natal MZ twins, as in the majority of cases one will have to wait until after birth for a correct determination of the type of zygosity.

In my study I had in fact the chance of observing a pair of MZ monochorionic and monoamniotic twins (see Giorgio and Fabrizio). This type of pregnancy, though, being highly at risk, poses other problems of a more properly deontological nature; that is, of not causing too much distress to the potential parents and to the mother in particular should the pregnancy end in still birth. Many authors have pointed out how the visualization of the fetus through ultrasounds often seems to facilitate bonding, therefore the death of one or both components of the pair under observation could be even more painful if these had been strongly 'cathected' (W.E. Freud 1989) after lengthy and repeated pre-natal observations. I was very much aware of this problem when I was presented with the chance of observing this pair of MZ twins, so much so that I decided to restrict the number of my observations from the usual five to three. Whilst this certainly rendered my observations still less 'scientific', it also made them safer from a strictly human and moral point of view. In the end all went well. A similar problem, though, is common to all twin pregnancies, DZ and MZ alike.

Until recently it was generally accepted that twins occur in about one in eighty pregnancies. Recent evidence indicates that twin pregnancies occur more frequently than the number of twins observed at birth would suggest (Little and Thompson 1988). Recent data from ultrasounds screening early in gestation suggest that the death of one twin *in utero* is not infrequent. Ultrasound scanning studies increasingly provide evidence of the phenomenon known as 'the vanishing twin' (Landy *et al.* 1982), whereby early detection of twins seems to be followed, later, by the disappearance of one of the components of the pair. The only relevant complication reported in such cases seems to be vaginal bleeding – that is, diagnosed as threatened abortion – with subsequent singleton birth. Therefore the number of twin pregnancies appears to be higher than that of twin births (Bryan 1983).

The disquieting possibility therefore of coming up against a so-called 'vanishing twin' poses further deontological problems; namely, that of not causing too much disappointment or upset where an early detection of a twin pregnancy is followed a few weeks later by the disappearance of one twin.

During my study,wanting to avoid both this possibility and that of early fetal loss, I decided to delay the beginning of the observations by about two weeks (eighteenth to twentieth weeks) compared with single pregnancies.

As with single pregnancies I observed several twin pregnancies in the pre-natal stages before deciding to select a few to follow in the post-natal stages also. Again the selection was based purely on immediate availabilty.

As with single pregnancies the observations then continued at monthly intervals till the end of pregnancy. Each mother was therefore subjected to an average of five ultrasonographic observations lasting about one hour each. No stimulation was applied during the observations.

The ultrasonographic observation of twins is much more complicated than with single pregnancies. Ideally, in order to obtain a better visualization, one should use two different sets of ultra-sonographic equipment and two different probes, one for each twin. Unfortunately this was far beyond the very limited resources available for this study. Given the difficulty of concentrating simultaneously on both fetuses, it was decided first to observe each component separately and then to focus on the interrelation between the two. Given also the difficulty of observing the whole body of each fetus after the twentieth to twenty-second weeks, it was decided to focus on the cranial section of the body of each. Whenever possible these sections also included some small parts of the body of the other twin, so as to observe any possible correlation between the movements of the two. Twins were differentiated basically following four criteria: (1) whenever possible, sex, (2) presentation, (3) side and position, (4) size. With the one pair of monozygotic monoamniotic twins, size was the only possible discriminating factor. The observations were then continued at weekly intervals for the first year of life of the children, and subsequently once-a-term follow-ups have been carried out. This made it possible to study in detail not only the behaviour of each individual child and its relationship with the other twin, but also to observe the impact of the environment on their growth and development.

The first thing that struck me when I started observing twins with ultrasounds was how different the intra-uterine environmental conditions were for each member of the couple. First of all, it is well known that one twin is usually less favoured than the other, who grows almost at its expense, and in some extreme cases this can actually lead to the death of the co-twin. This is more common in the case of MZ twins, but weight discrepancies are often very evident also with DZ twins. From our adult point of view the uterus may well seem just a narrow and uninterestingly monotonous cavity, but for a fetus the womb represents its whole universe and therefore even what, for us, are small differences are presumably of major importance for it. Many are the environmental differences in the intra-uterine sojourn of twins: their position is different, they occupy a different side, their placenta is frequently different, their cord is mostly different and the majority of them are separated by a dividing membrane and hence inhabit two different amniotic sacs. Presumably therefore such sensations as noises, sounds, pulsations, or proprioceptive and tactile sensations, and so on, reaching each twin are also quite different. For this reason one could postulate that all twins, including identical twins, do have in fact, from the start, different experiences which could have a bearing on their future mental as well as physical development.

Also with twins it was possible to note clear individual tempera-mental differences between the two members of the couple from the early stages. In this respect twins seemed to behave like ordinary siblings, each with their own distinct temperamental endowment. Individual differences found their expression in various somatic manifestations, such as the choice of preferential postures, the repetition of certain activities and patterns, the higher or lesser frequency of bodily movements and their quality, and so on. As with infant observations such differences acquired a particular relevance and meaning only if they could be noted repeatedly over several ultrasonographic sessions.

What was also striking was the variety of individual reactions towards the other member of the couple. In this respect twins were far from behaving and reacting always according to a few simple patterns. Some apparently showed no reaction at all even to the strongest punches and kicks. Some seemed to perceive contact and actively reacted by withdrawing and turning away from it. Some others seemed to respond to contact. Still others not only responded to contact, but actually seemed to search actively for it. The responses, when present, to contact from the other member of the couple also varied a lot. For instance, they could be gentle, with the twins engaged in a mutual and seemingly affectionate cheek-to-cheek stroking. Or they could be violent, with each contact seeming to end up in a fight. At other times the contact could simply be characterized by an almost instantaneous counter-contact followed by an immediate withdrawal, as if the twin, during the touching, had been struck by something akin to an electric shock.

Each couple, in fact, from the early stages seemed to have its particular mode of relating, which continued throughout pregnancy and could still be noted in post-natal life. Therefore from the very early stages one could observe the emergence of both individual and couple patterns which continued to be seen in later life.

A detailed account of the four twin pregnancies (three DZ and one MZ) observed in the pre-natal and the post-natal stages now follows.

OBSERVATION NO. 1 – DELIA and MARCO

Background

Mrs D, a woman in her mid-twenties, came accompanied by her husband (also in his mid to late twenties) for the first observation. Rather tall and strongly built, she looked pale and plain, without a shadow of make-up or a hint of an even distant visit to the hairdresser.

Her clothes looked perhaps intentionally out of fashion and she conveyed an impression of inhibitions coupled with a kind of timeless respectability. She looked somehow like 'the girl next-door' of the fifties, quite untouched by the sexual revolution of the sixties, or by the happenings and social movements of the seventies or eighties: the typical image of the safe, good girl one marries as opposed to the woman one loves or has fun with. Her husband, in fact, showed no signs of affection towards her and, if anything, kept rather at a distance from her and even dropped a few derogatory remarks. He immediately managed to let me know that he was a doctor too, though a rather unemployed one, while his wife was only a nurse.

I was later to find out from the obstetrician that they had met through the religious organization they both frequented.

Mr D himself was certainly no Adonis, but seemed to use his slightly superior economic and intellectual background to look down on his wife. All this conveyed an impression of sadness and of dullness, as if life had already passed them by. A bit of flirting, though, seemed to be not totally alien to Mrs D, and whenever a man was around she certainly forgot about me. Afterwards her latent interest in men often seemed to be projected on to her daughter Delia (the name subsequently chosen for the girl), whom she declared to be fascinated by her little brother's penis and by men in general. This latent interest seemed to contribute strongly to Mrs D's rather overt preference for Marco (their little boy).

Delia and Marco: first ultrasonographic observation (eighteenth week) – transcript

DR T: All right . . . let's get started . . . If the husband would like to take a chair . . .

MR D: I don't need one . . .

MRS D: (talking to the first obstetrician) Are you pregnant too?

FIRST OBSTET: I am more than pregnant . . . I am bursting . . . it couldn't be worse . . .

DR T: We produce a lot here . . . actually we produce all the time . . . (Laughs. She is referring to the fact that either she or her colleagues are almost constantly pregnant.) . . . Let's see what they are doing now . . . let's hope they are doing nice things . . . You know (she is talking to me) that we spoke about this research . . . she (the obstetrician who is pregnant) introduced it in her thesis . . . We'll tell you later about that . . . Well . . . let's try first of all to understand their position . . . You can see the dividing membrane here . . . these are the two gestational sacs . . . now let's start with the head of this one . . . this one is below . . . therefore it is the first twin . . . probably a boy as we have seen before . . . the other one looks like a girl . . . but it is difficult to tell at this stage . . . its hand is in front of its eyes . . . it is moving its head slightly . . . opening its mouth . . . opening and closing it . . . how nice! . . . the cord is just in front of it! . . . probably it is sucking it . . .

FIRST OBSTET: How funny! . . . it looks as if it is really chewing it . . .

DR T: It is chewing . . . small up and down movements . . . it is swallowing now . . .

ME: (talking to Mrs D) Can you see it? . . . (No reply.)

DR T: I am convinced that it is licking the cord . . . it might be just an idea . . . it is difficult to distinguish its tongue clearly at this stage . . . yet something is there . . .

MR D: Yes, yes . . .

DR T: The cord is clearly there . . . they like licking it very much . . . now it is probably just holding on to it . . . it is a funny one this one . . . all curled up . . . holding on to its cord . . . resting on the placenta . . . as if it were a big pillow . . . the cord has moved now . . . something moved it . . .

FIRST OBSTET: The other twin is moving . . . up here . . . kicking a lot . . .

DR T: Yes, the cord moved . . . you can see it well . . . it is visibly pulsing now . . . the other twin kicked it . . . look, now it is covering its face . . . its hand is in front of its eyes . . . covering its eyes . . . moving its fingers a lot in front of its eyes . . . very fine slow movements . . . now it is turning its head away . . . sheltering it inside the placenta . . . (Mr D laughs.) Look . . . here it goes again . . . the other one . . . I am not sure whether the stimulus can reach it . . .

MR D: What is that? . . . is it the other twin? . . .

DR T: Yes, it's the leg of the other twin, actually this is its foot . . . just reaching the other one . . .

MR D: Aren't they separated? . . .

DR T: Yes, by a membrane . . . it is thin though . . . look what it is doing . . . trying to touch him with its foot . . . actually feet . . . both legs are extended now . . . it is pushing him . . . and this other one doesn't seem to like it . . .

MR D: I am afraid that these two will fight a lot . . .

DR T: The first one has buried himself inside the placenta . . . its back is completely turned now . . . covering its head and its ears with its arms . . . it doesn't seem to like it when it is stimulated by the other one . . . look at the other one . . . we can see it well now . . . it seems much more active . . . stretching its legs . . . moving its arms . . . you can see its arms up there . . .

MR D: It is stretching its head backwards now . . .

DR T: Yes . . . again . . . it is touching its knees with both hands now . . . look at that hand! . . . you can see it so clearly now . . . touching its knee . . . its leg . . . the wall now . . . it's not doing anything with its mouth . . . not sucking or anything . . . it is yawning now! . . . look! . . .

MR D: Yes . . . yes . . .

DR T: Now it is stretching again . . . bending its head . . . bending its legs . . . rubbing its feet! . . . turning now! . . . reaching the other one with its hand . . . it still doesn't like it . . . it moved away . . . it folds his legs tightly . . . it is screening its face with its hands . . . burying himself in the placenta . . . as if it were a pillow . . . definitely this one doesn't like to be disturbed . . . let's see the other one . . . it is still moving . . . moving its hand . . . it's near its mouth . . . spreading its fingers . . . moving them finely . . . sort of fidgeting . . . it is just eighteen weeks old . . . incredible! . . . now it is stretching it towards the other one . . . look how it reacted . . . kicking back! . . . this one has withdrawn . . . the kick must have been quite strong! . . .

MR D: What a kick! . . .

DR T: A real kick . . . pushing it back . . . it doesn't want to be disturbed . . . it is so funny this one . . . over the placenta as a pillow . . . here comes the other one again . . . with its feet and its arms . . . look at the other one . . . it turned completely . . . it can't find any peace . . .

MR D: It turned round again . . . completely . . .

DR T: But look at the other one . . . moving everything . . . hands . . . feet . . . the feet are together now . . . moving them closer . . . moving them away . . . flexing them . . . extending them . . . again . . . together . . .

MR D: It is impossible to follow all it is doing . . .

DR T: Look! . . . hop! . . . hop! . . . hop! . . . three small hops . . . they like doing that sometimes . . . look at its feet . . . they are up now . . . down again . . . touching its knees . . . hands back again . . . moving them up and down . . . extending its head . . . this one is really lively . . .

MR D: Poor us! . . . let's hope it will calm down after birth . . . otherwise poor woman (his wife) . . . the other one seems more congenial to me . . .

DR T: The other one is also moving . . . sort of pushing this one back . . . this one, it's crossing its feet . . . it must have disturbed the other one . . . look what movement . . . sort of pushing its feet down as if it were pressing the accelerator . . . let's look at its face now . . . the hand is always there . . . near its face . . . we can also see the crystalline lens . . .

MR D: Are they stimulated by ultrasounds? . . . or I mean by the probe? . . .

DR T: It is rather controversial . . . most authors think not . . . but even if they were, habituation would soon set in . . . look it is opening and closing its mouth . . . opened it again . . . something is inside the mouth now . . . a finger . . . certainly a finger . . . it is sucking . . . it is certainly its thumb or at least another finger in its mouth . . . now the finger is out . . . opened its mouth . . . again . . . extending its arms . . . opening and closing its hands . . . well-coordinated movements . . . not jerky . . . the other one seems to be calm . . . over its pillow . . . all curled up . . .

FIRST OBSTET: The time is over now . . .

DR T: One could go on looking at them for hours . . .

Mrs D wipes her stomach and gets dressed. Dr T hands her her file and we arrange for an appointment in a month's time. Mr D says, 'We knew we were going to have twins . . . they run in her family . . . we were told when she was eight weeks pregnant . . .', then they say goodbye to everybody and go out.

The same patterns seemed to continue in the following observations: Marco buried himself more and more inside his placental pillow while Delia continued to be active and added new movements to her already wide repertoire. She also continued trying to make contact with him and again each time he withdrew and often punched her back to her place. During the second observation Mrs D came accompanied by an aunt and both spoke about children and family events. Mrs D said laughingly that she was hoping to produce more twins soon as she liked traditional large families and since twins ran in her family she was pretty sure to achieve her aim.

Delia and Marco: third ultrasonographic observation (twenty-fifth week) – transcript

DR T: Let's begin now . . . though I must be out of my mind today . . . I am feeling terrible . . . I was not even on duty today . . . and yet I knew I had something in the back of my mind . . . then I remembered suddenly that it was the observation . . . it was in my subconscious . . . I knew I couldn't be resting . . . well, let's have a look now . . . here is the first one . . . the boy . . . his head is on the

placenta . . . as usual . . . on his pillow! . . . he is all curled up . . .
something else is showing up there . . . it must be the second one . . .
the girl . . .

FIRST OBSTET: Yes, it is the head of the girl . . .

DR T: He is lying on his stomach . . . his bottom is slightly raised and
he covers all the placenta . . . his legs are here . . . here you can see the
dividing membrane . . . his feet are just near it . . . and her feet too . . .

FIRST OBSTET: She is moving . . . sort of touching him with her
feet . . . but he isn't reacting . . .

DR T: She is sort of pushing her feet . . . as if she were pushing him
with her feet . . . he doesn't react. . . . his face is buried inside the
placenta . . . now he brought a hand on his head . . . sort of protecting
it . . . but his position is always the same . . . the other hand is there
too . . . covering his ear . . . moving his fingers slightly . . . let's try and
move the probe . . . I want to try and see his face . . . slightly
better . . . he has nothing in front of his mouth . . . the cord is near his
face . . . he is covering both ears with his hands . . . he is immobile . . .
his crystalline lens is immobile too . . . Look at the other one! . . . how
she is moving! . . . she is touching and kicking him . . . look, he
reacted . . . turning himself . . . burying himself inside his placenta
even more . . . this is his response to her stimulation . . . turning even
more on his side . . . turning away . . . annoyed . . . her foot is always
there . . . she keeps trying . . . he is turning again . . . if possible more
inside . . . inside the placenta, I mean . . . his only reaction is turning
away . . . as if he were saying . . . leave me alone . . . all I want is
sleep . . .

MRS D: He sleeps all the time . . . during the night too . . . he never
moves . . . all the movement comes from his sister's side . . .

DR T: His hands are still over his ears . . . his fingers are slightly spread
now . . . he is moving them delicately . . .

FIRST OBSTET: His legs are folded . . . he is all curled up . . .

DR T: His arms are above his head now . . . you can see the hand of
the other one . . . she is reaching out towards him . . . he has curled up
even more tightly . . .

FIRST OBSTET: The girl is definitely more active . . . he is always lying
on the placenta . . . like on a pillow . . .

DR T: Now let's have a look at the second one . . . you can see her
well! . . . she is not all curled up . . . her nose . . . her eyes . . . her
mouth . . . she brought her hand to her mouth . . . she is opening it
slightly . . . you can also see her crystalline lens well . . . she is moving
it! . . . she is stretching her hand towards the placenta . . . sort of
reaching out for it . . . she is folding her legs . . . moving her lips . . .
her knee is up now . . . touching her face . . . she is not moving the

other leg . . . now she moved backwards . . . she is quite a handful this one! . . . she moves a lot . . .

MR D: I can't see anything of what you are describing! . . .

DR T: She is yawning! . . . fantastic . . . she was really yawning! . . . you can distinguish clearly a yawn from a swallowing movement . . . swallowing is a fast movement . . . she is stretching her head backwards . . . touching her forehead . . . trying to reach out to him . . . he pulls back . . . their feet are very close . . . she is moving them a lot . . . he is not moving . . . his bottom is sticking up . . . his head is bent down . . . immobile . . .

FIRST OBSTET: He never moves . . . she is holding her foot now . . . he is withdrawing . . . all he does is withdraw . . .

MR D: Yes, all he does is withdraw . . .

DR T: His heel is leaning on the placenta . . . the cord is just there . . . in front of his face . . . it's impossible to see his face . . . it is always buried inside the placenta . . . look! . . . she is reaching towards him . . . a good stroke! . . . this time he got annoyed . . . he kicked her back into her place! . . . he is back to his placenta . . . immobile . . . always in the transversal position . . . he likes it a lot . . . let's have just a last look at her face, then we can stop . . . she is moving it . . . look! . . . very fine movements . . . mimic movements . . .

Then Dr T measures both twins. The girl is smaller than the boy. Mrs D doesn't react to anything. She wipes her stomach. Dr T gives her her file and we arrange to meet again in a month's time.

Delia and Marco: up to the delivery – summary

When Mrs D was twenty-seven weeks pregnant she was taken into hospital as she had felt some rather strong contractions and her cervix was found to be already slightly dilated. She was administered tocolytic drugs and was bedridden practically till the end of her pregnancy. She endured the first few days in hospital with resignation, but then became increasingly anxious and restless. I visited her a few times and she told me that she couldn't stand being in hospital, out of the familiar surroundings of her home. At first she was very anxious about the children, aiming at reaching at least the thirty-fourth week of pregnancy for their survival, but as time passed her anxiety seemed to become all-pervasive and she was afraid of going out of her mind.

When I visited her she kept saying, 'I can't stand this any longer . . . I don't even care about them any more . . . I will go mad if I stay here any longer . . . ', and she really seemed on the verge of some breakdown. Her husband was no support to her, worried as he was exclusively about what his colleagues thought of her. I spoke to the obstetricians and they also got worried about her mental state and, since she was now thirty-four weeks pregnant, her contractions had eased and dilation had remained virtually the same, she was allowed to continue her treatment at home. Mrs D was later to worry many times about the effect that her stay in hospital and her mental condition at the time might have had on her children. 'They say that your mental state during pregnancy affects the child . . . I was so anxious . . . I am afraid that they suffered a lot . . .'

During the ultrasonographic observations while she was staying in hospital, however, the behaviour of the two children was practically unchanged. Only, perhaps, they moved a bit less, but probably because they were also less free to move. Marco continued to bury his head inside the placenta and to screen his face with his hands. Sometimes he could also be seen hanging on to the cord like an anchor and once he was seen licking it. Delia, now that she could move less, began moving the muscles of her face a lot and many and varied expressions could be detected: smiles, yawns, sucking movements, frowns, movements of her tongue and her lips, and so on, together with an intense ocular activity.

This same activity seemed almost continuous in the last observation before the delivery when Mrs D was almost thirty-eight weeks pregnant. During that observation, though, Delia was found to have ceased growing and it was decided to induce labour soon. Two days later the obstetrician phoned me to say that the children were born and well. She was sorry not to have phoned me before, so that I could have been present at the delivery, but it had all happened rather precipitously.

Delia and Marco: first post-natal observation (one day old) – summary

The first observation took place in hospital, when the children were just one day old. Mrs D seemed very pleased to see me, and she immediately and proudly announced, 'In a minute they will bring the boy!' She then told me about the delivery, saying that she 'didn't even realize what was happening . . .', 'I felt something warm between my legs . . . I thought it was still the amniotic fluid . . . while it was the child . . . the boy . . .'.

Delia was not there during the observation, nor did she seem to be present much in her mother's thoughts. As Mrs D adds, 'I almost forgot about her . . . but she too, she had to be pushed out . . . ' She also told me that Delia had to remain in hospital for a while, but that she was 'quite happy to go home with just him . . . '.

She then described their characters as being quite different: 'She is a nervy type; he is very quiet . . . you forget that he is there . . . ' When she showed me Marco she said proudly, 'He looks just like his father . . . ' Marco, in fact, looked very much like his father, with his black hair, small eyes, and rather pointed nose. He kept his eyes half-closed and his forehead was permanently wrinkled in a frown; somehow he looked permanently tired and old. He screened his face constantly with his hands and was otherwise completely immobile.

Mrs D explained to me that he seemed not to have yet realized what the breast was: 'He has no idea of the breast . . . ' She tried to force the nipple inside his mouth, but he withdrew immediately and cried, covering his face and his mouth even more. She tried again two or three times and again he cried, withdrew and covered his face. She tried with the other breast. He leant his face against it. She said, 'He is not sucking . . . he is leaning against it . . . it's not a pillow you know!' Then she gave up trying, and said, 'Probably it is useless . . . ' and she sat him in between her legs. Again he covered his eyes with his hands with a pained expression on his face, as if noise, light, movement, breast, were all too much for him. Delia practically remained unmentioned till the end.

Delia and Marco: post-natal observations up to the age of four – summary

I met Delia the following time when I visited Mrs D at home. Mrs D opened the door with Delia in her arms and I was immediately struck by Delia's intense and interested stare. Her eyes were wide open and she looked around. She looked much more lively and pretty than Marco. Mrs D said, 'He is still asleep . . . it takes him a very long time to wake up . . . he goes on yawning and stretching and turning for hours . . . waking is a painful process for him . . . she is different . . . she is much more alert . . . she moves a lot and likes looking around . . . . he always looks sad and forlorn . . . he just wants to be in my arms . . . but I don't think he can discriminate . . . I don't think he realizes it's me or anybody else's arms . . . provided he can bury his head inside someone's chest he is all right . . . '

Marco's painful difficulty in waking to this world continued during the following months. As his mother often said, 'He hates waking up . . . he sleeps for hours on end . . . thirty-six hours a day . . . he likes to be inside . . . in his cot or in my arms . . . all wrapped and covered up . . . while she is just the opposite . . . she hates being inside . . . she can't even stand the walls of her pram as they don't allow her to have a good look at the outside . . . he would like to sleep all day . . . even light disturbs him . . . going out of the house, as you can imagine, is an ordeal . . . the light disturbs him and the noise upsets him . . . ' Therefore she kept the children inside. She also bought a sling to carry him in which she called his 'marsupial' and carried him around the house, often saying, 'I am his pillow . . . '. After returning home Mrs D had given up breastfeeding him (with Delia she had never tried) and now Marco ate quite well and continued to put on weight. His feeding time, though, had a monotonous, almost hypnotic quality. He clung to the bottle, his eyes out of focus or completely closed, and sucked for hours on end always making the same slow monotonous sound. As his mother used to say, 'When I feed him, I fall asleep . . . '

Mrs D, though, seemed to like him much more than Delia whom she found too alert and demanding (though, at least while I was there, she never actually made any demands). She seemed to find Delia's alert stare rather disquieting, and, as Delia was soon able to raise her head, she often said that she looked like a 'periscope' and was always 'trying to see what's going on in the world'.

Mrs D endured in silence and with missionary patience the hardships of looking after twins. Her mother and mother-in-law helped her with her spotless house and Delia was picked up almost exclusively by them. I think that the fact that Delia was a female also added a lot to her mother's rather distant behaviour towards her. Mrs D's behaviour always changed whenever any man was around, and all her attention was directed immediately towards him, while Delia and I were completely left out. Delia, in spite of all this, seemed to show little or no jealousy towards her brother and she often looked at him smilingly. As time passed she began trying to touch him, as if searching for a contact with him as she had done in the womb. But he always reacted by turning away, or else, as Mrs D said, 'He doesn't discriminate . . . she touches him . . . and he licks her hand . . . he probably thinks it is his hand . . . '

After the first three months Marco began opening his eyes a bit more, but his stare was always blank and out of focus and his expression always had the same sad and pained quality. He frequently squinted and his mother often commented on it, saying laughingly, 'His vision is very narrow indeed!' Mrs D now told me how Marco could not stand any strong emotion: 'Whenever he laughs . . . or something excites him . . . he vomits . . . ', but she did not seem concerned about this. Marco in fact, with his 'dead' personality, seemed to fit in well with the rest of the household, much more than his livelier sister. Mrs D seemed more and more devoid of life. Her house, in its spotless tidiness and with its dark heavy furniture, looked gloomy and totally uninhabited. The people who came to the house either belonged to her numerous and close-knit family or to her equally close religious circle. She seemed afraid and disturbed by anything else. All her liveliness and repressed excitement seemed to be projected on to Delia, whom she often called 'a little whore' because she smiled at people and liked looking outside. She also attributed to her an enormous interest in her brother's penis. To me she seemed more interested in his face.

Mrs D in fact lived almost confined to her house. She once told me that she had never ventured as far as the city where I lived, though it was only a few miles away from her village. The big city, with all its novelties, stimulations, and perhaps temptations, was probably too much for her, something that she could not take in. When the summer approached, Mrs D also gave up making projects about possible holidays and preferred to spend the summer at home. Her husband appeared on the scene less and less and took on more and more work. His choice, though, fell on geriatric hospitals and old people's homes. He envied his younger brother who seemed to be disapproved of by everyone for having numerous affairs and behaving like a Don Juan, but he seemed totally incapable of even thinking of living a less dead life himself. As he said one day, pointing to his wife, 'I am stuck with that forever!'

Delia somehow seemed to be out of place in her family. When eight months old, she began to stand and walk. Marco was much slower in his motor development, though he was still considerably stronger than her. Delia often approached him, but almost inevitably he pushed her away and later often even knocked her down. But Delia seemed quite resilient and continued to come out on top.

At one year old Delia was interested in moving from room to room and touching and exploring new things and new toys, while Marco, though he could by now walk, as his mother said, 'Always holds on stubbornly to the same toy . . . and to me . . . but I am just like his pillow . . . if I am not there he immediately finds another one . . . '.

In the following observation Delia and Marco are now four years old and not much seems to have changed other than, of course, their verbal development and physical growth.

Delia and Marco: observation at four years old – detailed report

I arrive punctually (or perhaps half a minute early) and meet Mrs D in the entrance-hall with the children. She is holding a bin and several rubbish-bags. She says hello to me looking slightly embarrassed, and goes and puts the rubbish in the collection area. She is wearing a white and blue track suit.

The children look taller and seem to have lost quite a bit of weight. Delia is wearing a pink track suit and Marco a light blue one. Delia comes near me and asks me, 'What is your name? . . . ' I say 'Sandra' and she smiles at me. Then she runs around in the entrance-hall. Marco has a sort of fixed smile on his face and looks at me squinting slightly. He doesn't move.

Mrs D comes back, and says, 'Come on children, let's go inside . . .' She opens the door of her flat and both children run towards it. Upon reaching the door they collide. Marco tries to knock Delia over, but she manages to get through first. He trips over. Mrs D says, 'They always have to collide to get in . . . as if there was no space for two . . .'

She closes the door. I give her a small cake for the children. She goes and puts it in the kitchen and I take my coat off.

Marco and Delia are in the sitting room. I go in there too. Marco shows me a robot made of Lego, and says, 'It is a robot . . . I have built it . . . I like robots . . . they feel nothing . . . ' Mrs D looks at him smilingly and says, 'The house is full of robots and guns now . . . the guns are for shooting Delia . . . ' Marco goes towards his bedroom. Delia shows me a pink smurf. She says, 'Someone cut off a bit . . . a pig cut off this bit . . . '

Her mother smiles and says, 'But what are you talking about? . . . Marco did it . . . you are full of imagination . . . ' Then she tells me to sit down.

Delia takes my hand and says that she would like to show me her room and her toys. Mrs D says, 'Come on, leave her in peace . . . '

Marco comes back holding a small house and shows it to me, putting it on my lap. Mrs D says, 'He goes around all the time holding his house . . . wherever we go he takes it with him . . . the fact is that he hates going out . . . he would like to stay in all the time . . . while she is just the opposite . . . she enjoys meeting new people and seeing new places . . . '

The telephone rings and Mrs D goes and answers it. It must be one of her numerous friends from her religious association, as they talk about meeting in church. She stops talking for a moment, and tells Delia, 'You can show her your room and your toys . . . '

Delia takes my hand and guides me to her room. Marco follows us holding his house tightly. The room is slightly different from the way it was before and there are now two beds in it. I comment on that. Delia says, 'I am five years old . . . ' and Marco, 'I am only two . . . ', looking rather lost in thought. Delia shows me a box full of smurfs. She says, 'They could all be living peacefully together . . . and enjoy each other's company . . . but there is too little space . . . they are too crowded in there . . . so they fight and fight . . . ' Then she shows me a teddy bear with a rather prominent kind of navel, and says, 'This is its penis . . . he's got one . . . '

Marco shows me his school bag. He opens it and shows me a quilted pencil-case shaped like a pillow and covered with a soft, flowery material. He says, 'This is my pillow . . . I take it to nursery-school . . . ' Mrs D comes back and smiles saying, 'He needs to have a pillow all the time . . . I even had to find a pillow-pencil-case . . . '

Delia shows me a bunch of dried flowers. Mrs D says, 'She bought them with her grandmother . . . they went out to a charity bazaar . . . he was sleeping . . . he hates going out . . . ' Delia shows me many pink flowers, saying, 'You see, they are not just pale blue . . . ' Then she says again, 'I am five years old . . . ' and Marco promptly replies, 'And I am just two . . . ' Mrs D laughs, saying, 'It is so typical of them . . . she would like to grow fast . . . to be bigger . . . he would like to remain small and not grow . . . '

Delia shows me some drawings, saying, 'I did these at the nursery-school . . . these are fishes . . . these are balloons . . . and these are children, many many children . . . '

Mrs D picks Marco up and says, 'He is a cuddly child . . . he doesn't like it at the nursery-school . . . he sleeps all the time . . . she never sleeps . . . he sleeps at home too . . . this morning it took me hours to wake him . . . sleep is all he wants in life . . . ', and she kisses him. Then, looking at Delia who is showing me her pictures, 'We saw some fishes going to nursery-school, in a pond . . . ', then, after a minute's pause, 'Have you heard about Dr T? . . . she has six children now . . . the last two were twins . . . I wonder how she can manage . . . I wonder whether she wanted them or whether it just happened . . . this time she had to have a Caesarean . . . five days later she was already at work . . . but she has many au pairs helping her . . . Dr B is pregnant too . . . it must be her third child now . . . and she is very young . . . '

Delia shows me some more fishes. Mrs D says, 'Last month we bought them two small terrapins . . . we kept them in a kind of little pond . . . and Marco simply disintegrated them! . . . he poured all his antibiotic on them . . . and they disintegrated . . . Delia was frightened

124

. . . he seemed pleased . . . he said that they would feel nothing now . . . '

Marco says, 'I want some cake . . . ' Mrs D says, 'All right, let's go in the kitchen now . . . ' We go towards the kitchen and again Delia and Marco collide trying to get through the door. Mrs D sits them next to each other and Marco starts trying to push his sister away, saying, 'I have no space . . . I want to be left in peace . . . there is no peace with her . . . ' Mrs D picks him up and cuddles him. Then she starts cutting the cake. He screams, 'Her piece is bigger than mine . . . ', and cries in despair. Delia says, 'You can have some of mine . . . ', but Marco continues screaming. She sits him down again and he pushes Delia's plate away. His mother cuts another, much bigger piece for him and he stops crying. Delia is not eating her cake, she just picks out all the raisins one by one and puts them on her plate. Marco starts doing the same thing.

Mrs D says, 'I wish my husband were here . . . they behave properly when he is around . . . ' I ask her about her husband's work, and she says, 'He is doing well now . . . he is terribly busy . . . we hardly see him these days . . . last night he came back at 4 o'clock . . . we are hoping to see him for a week at Easter . . . but he is always so busy with his elderly people . . . he works in three geriatric hospitals now . . . '

Marco pushes his dish away, saying, 'I don't want any more cake . . . ' (he has hardly eaten any).

Mrs D continues, 'When he is at nursery-school he likes being with her . . . he feels more secure when she is there . . . she had flu once and he went on his own . . . he felt completely lost . . . she is different . . . she is much more sociable . . . she looks for the company of other children . . . '

Marco complains again about his cake. Mrs D says, 'All right, let's go and play now . . . ' We all go in the sitting room. Marco says, 'I want to play Snap . . . ' Mrs D says, 'It's a game they play with their grandad . . . they have to find the matching pairs in a pack of cards . . . their greatgrandmother died last month . . . she flew up in the sky . . . ' She tells the children to sit down at two small desks. They sit down. The two desks are next to each other. Marco starts trying to push his sister away, saying, 'I have too little space . . . ' He seems very annoyed and tries to push her away several times.

Mrs D intervenes, saying, 'Come on, stop that now . . . here are your cards . . . ' Delia asks me to help them find the pairs. Each time she finds one, Marco tries to grab it from her. Mrs D says, 'They love any kind of game with pairs or couples . . . ' Marco is becoming rather aggressive and Mrs D takes away the cards, saying, 'Let's do something else now . . . ' She turns their desks so that now they are sitting one in front of the other. She gives them some paper and pencils. With great care Delia draws a 'giraffe'. She says, 'It has a long neck . . . like a periscope . . . it's lucky because it can see so much from above . . . ' Marco draws a rather shapeless circle, and says, 'This is a fish . . . without any eyes . . . so it can sleep . . . ', then he scribbles something and says, 'And this is a truck . . . a windowless one . . . you can't look outside . . . ' Mrs D says, 'They are much easier to manage now . . . before I was busy all the time . . . I don't know how Dr T can manage with six . . . '. Delia is still carefully drawing her giraffe. Marco is rather careless and scribbles more than draws. He produces another scribble, saying, 'And this is a robot . . . ', and then another one, saying, 'And this is a baby inside the tummy . . . he is alone . . . '

Mrs D continues, 'I work till about three o'clock, then pick them up from nursery-school . . . he sleeps and is tired when he comes home . . . she doesn't sleep . . . perhaps just on Sundays a bit more . . . '

I say that it is time for me to go. Delia gives me her giraffe saying, 'You can keep it . . . ' and Marco gives me all his drawings too, saying, 'You can have these too . . . ' Delia waves to me, saying, 'See you soon, Sandra . . . ' Marco stares fixedly at his desk. Then they continue drawing while Mrs D accompanies me to the door.

Delia and Marco: summary

Delia and Marco behaved very differently from each other in the womb. When Marco was *in utero* I had the impression that any stimulus disturbed him. As one of the obstetricians commented: 'He seems in search of an impossible inanimate peace . . . ' He kept burying his head inside the placenta and the obstetricians commented repeatedly that he used the placenta 'like a pillow . . . Look how he keeps trying to bury himself in it.'

Delia, on the other hand, seemed very active. In my notes on her pre-natal days I wrote that she seemed lively and looked like someone 'who might become quite interested in her surroundings and in life'. She seemed rather 'interested' in her brother too and kept attempting to make contact with him, by rather gentle motions of her feet and her hands, but as the obstetrician said, 'All he does is withdraw' and 'his only reaction is turning away', or else he responded by pushing and kicking her back to her place as 'definitely this one doesn't like to be disturbed . . . '.

Yet Marco, compared to Delia, did have much more space inside the womb environment. He was physically much more favoured before and at birth. His same lack of liveliness together with the fact that he was a boy even attracted special attention, once he was born, from what was a rather narrow-minded, lifeless, already 'old' post-natal environment.

Delia's liveliness from her early pre-natal days seemed to pose a threat to her parents, who reacted to her rapid motions inside the womb by saying, 'Let's hope she will calm down after birth . . . the other one seems more congenial to me . . . ' Yet Delia was much less favoured inside the narrow space of her mother's womb and in her post-natal environment she also met with very little space. The fact of being a girl, together with her continued interest in life, was certainly an added factor to her 'inferior condition' in life after birth.

But Delia's nature seemed very resilient. Her same alertness and interest in life helped her in reaching out towards any object that was available to her. In spite of her mother's rather evident lack of interest in her, she seemed able to attract the attention of other people surrounding her, such as her teachers or her parents' numerous relatives and friends.

Marco, in spite of having undoubtedly received more from his mother since his pre-natal past, seemed much more jealous and hateful towards her than she was towards him. Delia, regardless of the overcrowding within her mother's intra-uterine space, reached out tentatively towards him and still seems to reach out for him now in spite of his continued attempts to push her back to her place.

At four years of age Marco's tenuous interest in life is still quite evident. His fear of any strong emotion seems well portrayed in his liking for robots who 'feel nothing', while his dislike of stimulation and his hatred of going out seem well depicted by his almost constant holding of a small house. As Mrs D says, 'He hates going out' and 'sleep is all he wants in life'. But I am simply astounded when Marco shows me his quilted pillow-pencil-case! His need for a pillow seems to have very deep and very remote roots indeed. Growing and waking up both seem to be too painful a process for him. His 'disintegrated' terrapins are said to be lucky as they were past the pains of living and 'they would feel nothing now . . . ', and when asked about his age, contrary to his sister, he seems to want to go back in time to when he was smaller and less confronted with life, when he did not have to go to nursery-school. His ideal seems to be well expressed in his drawing of an eyeless fish and a windowless truck, from where 'one cannot look outside . . . '. His peace, though, seems to be perpetually disturbed by the presence of his sister, as 'there is no peace with her', and throughout the observation he complains of having too little space. Again his drawing of the baby inside the tummy 'alone' seems to express his wish to have had the chance of a solitary life right from the start.

Delia, on the other hand, seems to be very lively indeed. She inquires about me, she likes going out, enjoys nursery-school, and clearly expresses a wish to grow quickly. Her drawing of a giraffe with a long neck like 'a periscope' also seems to reflect an attitude that has been present in her from a very distant past. Delia so far seems to have survived all the attacks from her brother who goes around 'shooting' her, as well as the lack of attention from her mother. Mrs D probably has never had 'space for two'. Yet Delia seems very determined to find her own space in life, as when she beats her brother through the door despite her apparent frailty. The chauvinistic attitude of her family seems to have affected her, as when she calls her brother 'pig' or when she shows me her teddy bear and says that its navel is 'its penis . . . he's got one . . . ', while on the other hand showing me that her flowers are also pink and not 'just pale blue . . . '. Yet later she seems to be generous towards her brother as, for instance, when she offers him her cake, and she is often remarkably kind and outgoing towards him.

Both children, though, in their constant talking about overcrowding and lack of space, as in their preference for playing games connected with pairs and couples, seem to be forever linked by the fact of having once been together as a pair inside too narrow a space.

OBSERVATION NO. 2 – ALICE and LUCA

Background

I met Mrs E, a woman in her late twenties, a few days before the first ultrasonographic session, as she had asked the obstetricians to meet me in order to get a more detailed explanation about our study. She came to the appointment dressed and made up in a rather unfashionable manner that seemed to indicate a more humble social origin than the quasi-ideological statement which Mrs D and her husband had made. Mrs E, with her short green coat, her long ear-rings, her small patent bag, and her pointed high-heeled shoes, conveyed a totally different impression from the dull shyness of Mrs D. One was immediately conquered by her warm, open smile, by her bright and tender big green eyes and by the intelligence and directness of her remarks. First of all she wanted to be sure that the ultrasounds were not going to be dangerous for the children and then seemed very interested in my study, as she said, 'Babies are all different . . . you can see it from the start . . . I don't see why fetuses shouldn't be different too . . . even with identical twins, I am sure there are some differences . . . we all have different selves . . . '

She was very relieved when I told her I was going to visit her at her home, once the children were born. 'It is so much better for me . . . I am sure I will be pretty busy with two . . . and this is also the first time for me . . . ' Then she told me how she had been married for six years and 'tasted a bit of freedom' before deciding to have children. She and her husband loved travelling and had visited many countries in Europe 'always with another couple of friends and our motorbike . . . you know we don't have all that much money . . . but it was such fun travelling and seeing new countries and meeting new people . . . but I am going to be thirty soon . . . and they say that it is better to have children before then . . . so we decided to settle . . . we had planned to have two children . . . so here we are . . . this will be enough now . . . we couldn't believe it when they told us we were expecting twins . . . at first we were shocked . . . but then we were actually pleased . . . perhaps we were also a bit nervous . . . and we laughed and laughed . . . '.

Alice and Luca: first ultrasonographic observation (twentieth week) – summary

Mrs E came back the following week for the first ultrasonographic observation. She was twenty weeks pregnant and was on her own. She seemed very pleased to see me and was very relieved to know that the children seemed to be growing well, though the boy was certainly smaller than the girl (we could already tell their sex). She participated throughout the observation with keen interest and with intelligent remarks. The little boy (Luca) seemed much more active than the girl. He kept turning and kicking and changing position and stretching his legs against the uterine wall, showing none of the restlessness and withdrawal that had characterized all of Marco's observations. As his mother remarked, 'Oh, my God! . . . look at him . . . he is so small and he already seems fed up with being in there . . . ' He conveyed the same impression to me, and I wrote in my notes, 'Watching him is more like watching a few months' old baby or even a little adult . . . one almost forgets he is a fetus . . . he seems to have a strong and interesting personality . . . '

From time to time Luca would interrupt his motor activities and seemed to turn his attention towards his sister. He reached out with his hands and through the dividing membrane he touched her face gently, and when she responded by turning her face towards him, he engaged with her for a while in a gentle, stroking, cheek-to-cheek motion. From then on we nicknamed them 'the kind twins'. His sister, Alice, seemed much more sluggish. Most of the time she seemed asleep, or moved her head and hands slowly, almost imperceptibly, but each time she responded to his gentle stimulation. Once he went back to his turning, stretching, and so on, however, she seemed to plunge back into her state of passivity and/or sleep.

In the following observation Mr E is also present. Rather shy and reserved and also apparently from a humble background, he seems gentle and loving towards his more exuberant wife. He is also very interested in the children and makes very intelligent and sensitive remarks, and asks some profound questions such as whether Luca might have a sense of self and might be testing his 'me, not-me' sensations by feeling the difference between his face and the uterine wall.

Alice and Luca: second ultrasonographic observation (twenty-fourth week) – transcript

DR S: Now this is the right one . . . I am not sure whether it is the first or the second one . . . I will write left and right in any case . . .

ME: Write also that this is the second observation, please . . .

DR S: Very well . . . this is the left one . . .

DR F: This is its heart . . . it is sleeping . . .

DR S: And this is the other twin . . . they are very close . . . their heads are in contact . . . they seem to be hugging each other . . . they still have some space at this stage . . . but they seem to like each other's contact . . . they are really very close . . . they are not Siamese though . . . they are almost certainly a boy and a girl . . . and divided by a membrane . . . nor could they become Siamese at this stage . . . they simply like each other's company . . . last time too they were hugging each other . . . look how this one keeps its hand close to the other . . . is this the one that moves more? . . .

MRS E: Yes, I think so . . . during the day the movement is all on one side . . . this side . . . the other one seems to move much less . . . during the night too . . . this one is much more active . . . I am particularly sensitive to their movements during the night as I often wake up . . . during the day or when I move about I pay less attention to it . . .

DR F: They seem to be in close contact . . .

MRS E: Is there a preferential position for twins? . . .

DR F: No, each twin has its position . . .

MRS E: But I mean, in view of the delivery . . .

DR S: So far they are both cephalic . . . therefore they are all right . . . look its heart has accelerated . . . probably it is waking up . . .

MRS E: (sounding thrilled) Yes, I saw that . . .

DR S: Its hand is on the body of the other one . . . it is moving it . . . sort of stroking the other one with it . . . the one who is moving should be the boy . . .

MRS E: Perhaps I can feel something . . . some slight movement . . . always on this side . . .

DR S: These are its feet . . . it is sort of kicking against the wall . . . again . . . again . . . again . . . it seems to want to get out . . . looks at its hands now . . . they are joined . . . as if it were praying . . . (Mrs E laughs.)

DR F: It is moving its hands now . . .

DR S: It is definitely awake now . . . it is moving everything . . . it is clenching its fists . . . how funny . . . sort of protesting with its fist . . . now it is spreading its fingers again . . . bringing its hands near the wall . . . touching it . . . testing it . . . not much to explore there! . . . look, now it is kicking against the wall . . .

MRS E: Well, I can feel it! . . .

DR S: Now its hand is near its head . . . touching its face . . . now back to the wall . . . back to the face . . . back to the wall . . . back to the face . . . back to the wall . . .

MR E: Perhaps it can feel the difference . . . this is me, this is not me . . . me . . . not me . . . me . . . not me . . .

DR S: Now it is exploring the wall . . . with hands and feet . . . touching it all . . . it is bored now! . . . kicking again . . . it got tired of exploring such a narrow space! . . . always the same . . .

MR E: Poor little thing, it must feel cramped in there . . . it seems to want to get out . . .

DR F: It is too soon now . . .

MRS E: Are its movements all right? . . . they seem to be rather fine movements . . .

DR S: Yes, these kind of movements imply a good central control . . . well-developed . . .

MR E: Looking at it moving like this, one forgets how small it must be . . . it seems much more mature . . .

DR F: Now it is flexing its hand . . .

MRS E: I can't feel that . . .

DR F: These movements are too light . . .

MRS E: Yes, when its movements are stronger I can feel them quite clearly . . .

DR S: It is moving all its fingers one by one . . . thumb . . . index . . . middle . . . ring finger . . . little finger . . .

MRS E: (smiling) My husband likes playing the piano . . .

DR F: Now it's raised its legs . . .

MRS E: I felt that . . .

DR F: Its hand is here . . . sort of stroking the other one . . .

(Dr F gives me the probe to hold, then continues to describe.)

DR F: Here is its thumb . . . it's closed its hand now . . . now it's crossed its arms . . . it is a funny fellow this one! . . . now it is kicking against the wall again . . .

MRS E: Look! . . . I can feel it! . . .

DR F: Move the probe . . . let's have a good look at its face . . . it is not touching it . . . the other one is just there . . . both heads are still in contact or at least very close . . . the other one is still sleeping . . . or at least not moving . . . it is keeping its hands crossed on its stomach . . .

DR S: The active one must be the male . . .

MRS E: Yes, the other one looked like a female last time . . .

DR S: That would be ideal to have a boy and a girl . . .

MRS E: Yes, then I don't need to have any more . . . I am doing it all at once . . .

DR S: The second one is making some slight movements with its hand . . . rather sluggish . . . as if it were still asleep . . .

MRS E: Sometimes if I put my hand on my stomach, they stop moving . . . particularly the left one . . . as if it could feel it . . .

DR F: (to me) You can move the probe on the other one . . . we can't really see their sex today . . . this one is sort of leaning its head on its arms . . . this one moves less . . . the other time too . . . and it is much more curled up . . . actually it is all curled up . . .

MRS E: How can one be sure it is not the other one? . . .

DR S: Because right and left always remain the same . . . their dividing membrane is vertical . . . we can't see much of this one . . . it is too curled up . . . just a bit of its face . . . still leaning over its arms . . . this movement is just your breathing . . . the other one is moving . . . this one doesn't react . . . I thought twins would interact much more . . . well, last time it took this one a while before responding to its twin . . . well, look, perhaps it is beginning to respond just now . . . it is moving its hand and its face slightly . . . turning it towards the other one . . .

MRS E: I can't feel any movement . . .

DR F: It is just moving its face . . . sort of stroking each other's face . . . cheek to cheek . . .

DR S: (coming back – he had gone into the adjacent room) How is it going? . . .

DR F: One is sleepy today . . . the other one is moving . . .

MRS E: Can the probe influence their movements? . . .

DR S AND DR F: No . . .

DR F: This one is sleepy . . . later on as with single pregnancies we should find a diminution of the length of each phase . . . I mean sleep and wake become much more differentiated . . . and well-differentiated sleep and wake each become much longer . . . it's more hazy now . . . though the other twin seems pretty much awake . . .

MRS E: Yes, I felt it moving . . .

DR S: Their heads are still very close . . . they seem to be kissing! (Mrs E laughs.)

DR F: They rub their heads together . . . they are really kind, these twins! . . .

MRS E: Is that its eye? . . .

DR S: Yes, you can see the bony margin . . . but it is not possible to see its head very well as it is all curled up . . . now it has folded its hand . . . sort of scratching its nose . . . probably trying to put its thumb in its mouth . . . it is trying . . . but the thumb is turned outside . . . just very slight movements . . . (Silence)

DR F: The time should be almost over now . . . (then talking to Mrs E) I will see you again in a fortnight for their measurements . . . and then again in a month for the observation . . .

DR S: They are both moving now . . . rubbing and stroking their heads . . . cheek to cheek . . . certainly they don't suffer from agoraphobia . . . they are always so close . . .

DR F: Last time too they moved their heads together . . .

The observation is over. Mrs E dresses again and Dr F gives her her file, then she starts talking about something else with Dr S. Mrs E says goodbye to me very warmly, saying, 'I will see you in a month's time . . .' Her husband says goodbye to me too and they go out.

Alice and Luca: fourth and fifth ultrasonographic observations (twenty-eighth and thirty-second week) – summary

As the children grew Mr E became more and more worried that Luca in particular might be feeling claustrophobic: 'Poor thing . . . he looks so cramped in there . . . he seems to want to get out . . .'

A few days after this observation Mrs E felt some contractions. She was given some medication and was told to stay in bed for a while. When she came back for the following observation she seemed rather anxious and was greatly reassured by the fact that all now seemed to be going well. The stroking contacts between the two children were particularly evident on that day, and Mrs E commented, 'They seem to cuddle up together . . . look how he strokes her . . . ' Her husband was also struck by their contact, and while observing them again posed some very profound metaphysical questions in his simple, but intelligent way: 'I am quite convinced that they know there is another person in there . . . that they feel boundaries . . . and have a sense of being themselves . . . but other people perhaps could argue that she is not aware that his movement comes from outside herself . . . or perhaps that they are too self-centred and absorbed to realize the existence of something and someone outside themselves . . . though these images are pretty convincing . . . ' Later he added, 'Of course I cannot prove it . . . but they seem to me to be already two very separate beings . . . each with its own clear identity . . . '

In the following observation Luca is found to have grown very little since last time and Mrs E's blood pressure is up slightly. She seems rather anxious today and her husband seems very concerned about her.

Alice and Luca: sixth ultrasonographic observation (thirty-sixth week) – transcript

DR S: Let us start with their measurements . . . the boy is smaller . . . considerably smaller . . . 1.9 kg. . . . the girl should be weighing about 2.4 kg. . . . OK, you can start with the observation now . . .

DR F: I will start with the first twin . . . the boy . . . he is cephalic . . . he is moving his mouth slightly . . . sticking his tongue out . . . moving his mouth again slightly . . . sort of mimic movements . . . he hasn't the space for much movement now . . . he is moving his hand . . . it is near his face . . . sort of opening it . . . spreading all his fingers and moving them one by one . . .

MRS E: I can feel him moving . . .

DR F: He is making some very fine movements . . . now it looks as if he's sucking, but very slowly . . . his mouth is almost in contact with the other one . . . as if he were kissing her . . . light kissing movements . . . his mouth is not open now . . .

Prof. C (the head of the obstetric ward) comes in, followed by another obstetrician, his assistant.

OBSTET: What are you looking at? . . .

DR F: The head of a twin . . .

OBSTET: Oh . . .

PROF. C: How are they doing? . . .

DR F: The second one, a girl, is considerably bigger . . . and now she has turned round . . . she is podalic . . . the other one is smaller . . . weighing about 1.9 kg. . . . Mrs E is a primipara . . .

(Mrs E seems considerably disturbed by the news that the girl is now podalic. She breathes audibly and rather anxiously.)

PROF. C: What week? . . .

DR F: The thirty-sixth . . . what shall we do . . . shall we try to have a natural delivery? . . .

PROF. C: Yes, I would think so . . . you should try at least . . .

DR F: I was thinking that too . . . let labour evolve naturally . . .

PROF. C: Then one can see during labour . . . according to how it proceeds . . .

DR S: She is coming back for a check-up next week . . .

PROF. C: The smaller one is cephalic . . . he is winning the race . . .

DR F: The other one is less clever . . . she has turned round in the podalic version, whilst she had always been cephalic before . . .

PROF. C: She can still follow her brother's example . . . and turn round again . . . and with a pelvis as large as their mother's there should be no problem anyway . . .

MRS E: (looking anxious and hurt by this last remark) But she hasn't got much time to turn round . . . we are near term . . . (Prof. C goes out.)

DR F: Look what the boy is doing! . . . he keeps banging his head against the cervix . . . he wants to get out! . . . he is rather independent this one! . . . his sister is much more quiet . . . he is also doing something with his legs . . . sort of touching his sister with them . . . rubbing his feet against hers . . . he is not kicking her though . . . they always seem to like stroking each other . . .

MRS E: What would happen if the delivery were to start soon? . . .

DR F: Nothing . . . it would be no problem now . . . actually it would almost be better . . . as they grow better outside than inside the womb at this stage . . . twins on average are always delivered three to four weeks earlier . . .

MRS E: And are you sure about their sex? . . . I mean, are they really a boy and a girl? . . .

DR F: Last time it seemed rather clear . . . the bigger one looked really like a girl . . . this time she is all curled up . . . and it is difficult to observe twins well at this stage . . . they are all in a tangle . . .

Dr F now gives me the probe to hold. She goes out a moment.

MRS E: Dr F is much stronger than you are . . . you are slim . . . why

135

on earth did she turn round just now? . . . she was in the right position during the entire pregnancy . . . and why do it now? . . . of course she can always turn round again . . . but they look so crowded now! . . . but they don't seem to be annoyed by each other's presence . . .

MR E: I always have the impression that they realize that they are not alone . . . and that on the whole they like being together . . . he seems to be leading the way . . . well, in any case we shall soon see whether this is true or not . . .

DR S: (coming back from the room next door) Aren't you bored? . . . are they doing anything today? . . . the smaller one is banging his head against the cervix . . . (then yawning) . . . you know that probably I will be going to London for a month over Christmas? . . . to Queen Charlotte's Maternity Hospital . . . but I don't know a word of English . . . I shall have to take some lessons now . . .

MRS E: Why don't you take my sister as an interpreter with you? . . . she knows English quite well . . . and she has lived in London for a year . . .

DR S: Soon you will need your sister as a baby-sitter . . . you will be terribly busy . . . look at the boy now . . . he seems impatient to get out . . . moving his arms and legs . . . sort of swinging them . . . what chaos! . . . just think what it will be like in a short while! . . .

MRS E: I can feel him . . . he seems to be banging against my stomach . . .

DR S: He is really bored, this one . . .

Dr F comes back.

MRS E: I hope the other one will turn round . . .

DR F: They still have plenty of amniotic fluid . . . which is good . . . so she might . . .

DR S: And they are not too big . . . but then twins never are . . . they never weigh more than 2.5 kg at birth . . .

DR F: She is not doing anything today . . . her brother has turned his head slightly towards her . . . usually he takes the initiative . . . it takes her a while, but then she follows him . . . look, she is doing it now! . . . she is responding to his stroking . . .

DR S: (talking to Mrs E) You took the news well when we told you they were twins . . .

MRS E: Well, by now I have got used to it . . .

DR S: I have been told by a priest I know that they do terrible things to twins in Dahomey . . . they have a missionary hospital there . . . and apparently they have some unbelievably cruel tradition there . . . they think twins are evil or something . . . can we stop now? . . .

DR F: In fact they are not doing much today . . . most of the time they

136

seem to be keeping to themselves . . . probably they are preparing for birth . . .

The observation is now over. Mrs E gets ready to go. Dr F tells her that she will visit her the following week and we arrange to keep in touch.

A few days after this observation Mrs E was taken into hospital as her blood pressure was found to be still high. Soon after, she began to have labour pains and the children were born rather quickly. Luca led 'the race' and came out first, but his sister too turned round almost at the last minute and followed him.

Alice and Luca: post-natal observations up to the age of four – summary

When I went to visit her in hospital the following day, Mrs E seemed very pleased to see me and told me about the delivery, saying, 'He came out first . . . then she came out too . . . the difference of weight is very noticeable . . . he is all skinny and bony and looks like a small bird . . . and their character, you know . . . just like we had seen inside . . . he is very lively and alert . . . you remember how he used to move and play all the time . . . she is completely different . . . she is very calm . . . '

Later on her husband and her father also came in. She introduced her father to me. He looked like a farm-worker, with big rustic hands and thick leathery skin wrinkled by the wind and the sun. He spoke with a marked southern accent and soon made a rustic comment, saying, 'We will need a cow and a goat and plenty of grass to feed them . . . ' I was later to get to know him as a very gentle man who came in every day to do his daughter's shopping, fetch the newspapers, and give her a lot of help. Mr E also seemed pleased to see me and confirmed that they were 'just like in the womb . . . he is much more active and alert . . . ' We could only glance at them through the screen of the nursery. Mrs E told me that she was hoping to go home soon. 'They told me that I could have already gone home with one, with Alice, leaving Luca here . . . but I couldn't bear the thought of leaving him here all alone . . . ' Then she told me that she was very relieved that they were both well, 'They breathe . . . eat . . . and digest well . . . I was so scared . . . I was really anxious when I was pregnant . . . I worried about them all the time . . . '

The following week Mrs E was still in hospital. She told me again that they had suggested she go home with Alice, 'but I refused . . . I couldn't bear the thought of leaving him behind all alone . . . '. While

I was there she was trying to feed Luca (she was using a bottle, filled with her milk). He looked really tiny and had enormous green eyes. He looked very alert and, except for size, much older than his age. His stare and expression had a peculiar intensity and somehow also dignity. Mrs E told me that she took turns with the nurses when feeding them. 'I don't want to be unfair . . . so once it's him . . . and once it's her . . . ' She also told me how she had always tried to be near them. 'When he was in the incubator . . . I went near them . . . I touched them and I spoke to them . . . '

In the following few months when I visited Mrs E at home I rarely saw the children as they were mostly asleep when I came and I had the impression that Mrs E also had a particular need to have me there for herself. She had decided to give up work until they were old enough to go to nursery-school and she told me that she found isolation (not from her family: they were all there to help) and the constant demands from the children rather heavy to bear, though she was also very pleased to be with them. Each time I visited her she told me about her family and her life, while she offered me coffee and quite a few bottles of delicious olive oil from her small village. She also wanted to know about me, my children, my family and my work, and so on. But far from feeling intruded upon, I found her warmth and spontaneity as well as her generosity quite touching. Her life had been hard, but Mrs E spoke about it with dignity and seemed to have always faced her difficulties with great courage and faith. Born in a small, poor village in the Aeolian islands and being the eldest of six children, she had helped her mother in rearing them, while her father was away in Belgium trying to earn a living. 'We all lived together in the same room . . . even my small flat now looks like a palace to me . . . ' When she was thirteen her father lost his job through tuberculosis and they decided to try their fortune in the North, in the big car factories in Turin. She had to start working at fourteen and still remembered the harsh impact of Turin and its sophisticated people teasing her for her accent and her clothes. 'But now it is different . . . I am older now . . . when I was sixteen I met my husband and it made all the difference . . . he is loving and kind . . . and the rest didn't matter any more . . . '

Traces of her husband could be seen everywhere in the house as, apparently, as soon as he came home he built some new toys for the children and spent hours playing and talking to them. The children were far from being absent from Mrs E's conversation; actually they were the centre of it, and each time Mrs E told me how they were getting on. As with many young mothers she received advice from practically everybody, but she seemed to know intuitively what was good for them. 'The doctor told me to keep their room dark as light might upset them ... but this seems nonsense to me: they are not still inside! They have to gradually get used to this world ... they need to learn to distinguish between day and night ... he also told me: not too many sounds .... but of course they hear our voices ... they have to get used to people ... they actually like sounds and respond to them ... my husband is very fond of classical music ... so we put an amplifier in their room and they seem to love it!'

From the little I saw of the children at the time, they seemed in fact really to love life, though each in their own particular way. Luca was remarkably alert, he looked around with great interest, he smiled, and even moved his lips as if wanting to utter some words while making some sounds. Alice seemed more babyish and cuddly and on the whole less interested and aware of her surroundings. As Mrs E said, 'He is much more intelligent ... he realizes immediately when I pick him up ... he is delighted ... he likes to interact ... I noticed that he even makes some sounds ... I couldn't believe it ... at such a young age ... Alice is different ... she is more of a baby ... she likes to eat a lot ... she just seems very concentrated on her mouth ... she is less bright than him ... ' This was also my impression: with Alice it was probably not so much a problem of not accepting living in the outside (as it had been, for instance, with Marco), but more a problem of intelligence. She was certainly happy and content, but basically less bright than her brother.

Then Mrs E went on holiday for two months; the heat was rather unbearable that year and her mother-in-law had offered them her small house in the mountains. When I saw them again Alice and Luca were about six months old. Alice now appeared to be a contented and rather placid child who smiled a lot, but did little. As Mrs E said, 'Physically she is still much bigger than him ... but he is certainly much more alert ... but we knew that already from the womb, didn't we? He was much more alive, he moved and changed position a lot ... he has always been smaller, but more lively ... ' But certainly Mrs E did not use Alice's less bright disposition against her. 'She is much more gentle than him ... sometimes I wonder if I prefer one or the other ... sometimes I think one ... sometimes I think the other ... she seems more gentle ... more unprotected ... probably I have a soft spot for her ... Luca knows what he wants ... and he makes everybody like him ... my husband probably has a soft spot for him ... '

It was around this time that I also began to watch some social interaction between the two. 'Now they really look at each other ...

they really interact . . . sometimes he is jealous of her . . . but mostly he is not . . . usually he starts the contact, and touches and strokes her . . . and she smiles . . . '

During the following months, Luca began to expand his activities widely. He was interested in everything and particularly in rather 'adult' activities such as 'playing' the piano and looking at pictures in books. He also continued to be very sociable and very soon began to utter a few words. As his mother said, 'He's always wanted to grow . . . sometimes you forget how small he is . . . I am reminded of it each time I give him a bath and he still looks so small and frail . . . but he always looks at you in an adult way . . . ' Alice was mostly engaged in rather monotonous and repetitive activities and though she smiled a lot, she began speaking much later than her brother. She also walked later. As her mother said, 'She is always a couple of months behind . . . it takes her a while, but in the end she always follows him . . . '

At one year of age Alice and Luca could walk and were beginning to talk and still took a great delight in playing with each other. On the day of their birthday Mrs E told me, 'I hope I have not made many mistakes with them . . . I am sure I have made some . . . perhaps I spoilt them a bit . . . though I don't think so . . . how can I with two? It is incredible how time passes . . . you remember . . . we used to call them the kind twins . . . I think that it is still true today . . . they are kind with each other . . . sometimes perhaps he may scratch her . . . but it is usually by mistake . . . they touch each other to express their fondness . . . ' By that time their favourite game had become hiding on either side of the curtain and using it a bit like a dividing membrane. Then Luca would put his hand through the curtain and Alice would reach out with her head and their mutual stroking began, accompanied by gurgles and smiles.

In the following observation Alice and Luca are now four years old and they both attend nursery-school.

Luca's wish to grow fast, his hatred for having 'any boundaries' and his love for his 'freedom' and his 'individuality', all seem very evident. Alice always seems to follow him at a 'slower pace'.

Alice and Luca: post-natal observation at four years old – detailed report

I arrive punctually and ring the intercom, but nobody answers it. Mrs E had told me on the phone that she was going to pick up the children from nursery-school and to wait for her in case she was a few minutes late. I wait a couple of minutes, then I see Mrs E waving at me from her car. She parks it near me and rushes out apologizing for being late. I say that I have just arrived. She kisses me warmly on both cheeks, and asks, 'How are you? . . . ', and I return her greeting. She is wearing glasses and seems to have lost a bit of weight. She says again, 'I am sorry I am late . . . but they didn't want to leave . . . they are preparing for their play . . . so they were having a lot of fun . . . '

We move towards the car. I give her a small cake for the children. Alice and Luca are sitting next to each other in two separate small seats. Luca is touching Alice's face and they are both giggling. Mrs E says, 'Luca said that of course he remembered you . . . he said: "the lady-doctor with auburn hair" . . . perhaps it's true . . . he really does remember you . . . ', then she unfastens their straps and takes them out of the car.

Alice is considerably taller than her brother and she looks at me with a rather dull expression on her face. Luca smiles at me. He starts singing and mimicking a rock-dance moving his hips and raising his arms, then stops and says hello to me mimicking a deep and masculine tone of voice. Mrs E says, 'He has to behave like a clown . . . '

Luca runs towards the door. Alice remains close to her mother and gives me her hand while her mother looks for the keys inside her bag. Luca runs and calls the lift. Alice is still holding my hand. From time to time she smiles at me. Mrs E says, 'Their play is on Thursday . . . we'll have to do something too . . . only three parents accepted . . . three out of fifty . . . we have been daring . . . the others were all being shy! . . . ' Luca exclaims, 'What a swindle . . . someone else has called the lift . . . ' His mother says, 'He has picked up all sorts of swear words from nursery-school . . . '

The lift arrives and we go in. As we reach their floor Luca says impatiently, 'Come on, Mummy, open up . . . ', and Mrs E says, 'He always feels hemmed in . . . he hates to have any boundaries . . . ', then she opens the door of her flat. Alice is still holding my hand. Mrs E says, 'He never had any problems at nursery-school . . . she is improving now . . . but to begin with it was terrible . . . she cried all the time . . . '

Luca comes near her and says in a deep tone of voice, 'I am hungry!' (I notice that often during the observation he tries to speak in a deep and masculine tone of voice, as if he were trying to be forty and not four.) Mrs E replies, 'First you have to wash your hands . . . both of you . . . ' Luca protests, mumbling something, and Alice smiles, looking at me.

Mrs E shows me her kitchen, saying, 'I have a new kitchen . . . I had to change it completely . . . everything broke in the other one . . . the sink . . . the tiles . . . the washing-machine . . . we had bought it second-hand when we married . . . it was quite expensive having to buy everything new . . . but it couldn't be helped . . . ' I compliment her on it.

She takes Alice's coat off. Luca runs towards the bathroom and Alice follows him, but at a slower pace. Mrs E invites me to put my coat and my bag down, and then we follow them.

Alice and Luca are now standing on two small chairs next to each other at the sink. They look at each other and they smile while playing with the water. Mrs E goes near them, and says, 'Come on, stop playing . . . ', and washes their hands. Luca and Alice giggle, but soon Luca protests, gets down from his chair and runs towards the kitchen. Alice follows him, but without running, and keeps close to us. We go into the kitchen too. Luca says, 'I want some chocolate! . . . ', and Mrs E, 'I didn't buy any today . . . you can't eat chocolate every day . . . '

Luca protests vehemently. She says, 'Dr Piontelli brought you a nice cake . . . ' He says, 'I don't want it! . . . ' She says, 'He is so stubborn . . . I am sure he will eat it later . . . he has to assert himself all the time . . . you can have some yoghurt if you like . . . ' She takes some plates and cuts the cake. Then she pours some yoghurt into a glass. He says, 'I want the other type of glass . . . '

She says, 'No, you drink it in this . . . his individuality must always be respected! . . . even more so now that he goes to nursery-school . . . All his teachers are enthusiastic about him . . . they say that he is always self-confident . . . they never have any problems with him . . . Whilst they had some problems with her . . . but they are very different . . . they always have been . . . Now they have this theory that twins should be separated at school . . . this can be right in many cases . . . I can understand that . . . but now they follow the theory blindly and apply it to everyone . . . but twins are not all the same . . . For Alice in particular it would have been important to be with her brother at least to begin with . . . till she got used to it . . . she relies on him a lot . . . Sometimes he gets irritated with her, and says, "But I am not your mother, you know!" . . . but generally speaking, though, he likes his freedom, he is nice to her . . . It would have been important particularly for her . . . in fact she cried so much that in the end they had to put them back together again . . . Now she is improving . . . But people stick to theories . . . luckily I am not easily influenced by other people's theories and try to think with my head . . . but many parents are . . . Yet I am not saying that the teachers are no good . . . with the children they are very kind . . . and they show a lot of devotion to their work . . . The fact is that Alice is very different from Luca . . . perhaps they thought that because they were twins they must be the same . . .

but she has always been shyer and he has always been very independent
. . . My husband is a bit like Alice . . . he is shy . . . while I am an
extrovert . . . Everyone is different . . . there is nothing wrong with
that . . . but differences should be respected . . . '

Mrs E now starts eating some cake. She says, 'This is delicious . . . I
have been able to lose a bit of weight . . . but who cares now! . . . '
Alice too says that she likes the cake and wants some more. Luca says
that he would like to eat an apple and Mrs E peels it for him. He
quickly eats half of it, then runs out of the kitchen. Mrs E says,
'Everything feels too tight for him . . . he hates any constriction . . . '
Alice finishes eating her cake and follows her brother into their room.

Mrs E takes a broom and starts sweeping the floor, saying, 'I have to
pick up the crumbs . . . otherwise by the evening it is a real mess . . . '
Then we go into the children's bedroom. The children are playing on
the floor, Alice with some dolls and Luca with some cars. She says, 'In
two minutes all the toys are out . . . and the room is in a mess . . . but
never mind . . . ' Then she shows me some drawings that are on the
wall. She says, 'Luca has done most of them . . . he can draw very well
. . . it must be something genetic . . . on my husband's side . . . people
in his family all draw well too . . . this is us in the summer . . . in the
caravan . . . with the boat and its oars . . . here is my husband
driving . . . then in the second window you can see me . . . and in the
last one their two heads next to each other and them waving from the
window . . . and these are the fishing-rods . . . ' (The drawing is in fact
very nice.) Then she shows me another one and says, 'Look at this one
. . . I couldn't believe it . . . you see all these faces . . . he told us they
were males . . . but then we hadn't noticed that they all had
genitals . . . penises and testicles . . . he showed us that . . . in fact you
can see them here . . . and here . . . (the drawing is very accurate) . . . '
Luca is standing near us now and he smiles. She says, 'He always
wanted to grow fast . . . but Alice can draw too . . . she started
later . . . she followed him . . . ', and she shows me some (less nice)
drawings on the wall.

Luca looks at me and says in a deep tone of voice, 'Pay attention to
me now! . . . I want some attention too . . . ', and he shows me a
cardboard motor-racing track. Mrs E says, 'My husband has made
it . . . he still makes most of their toys . . . he is away now for a few
days . . . his office sent him to Florence to train some people . . . we
went away too for a few days . . . we went to the seaside . . . whenever
we can we take them away . . . on Sunday we went to see a village fair
in a small village near the Alps . . . this town is just impossible and
whenever we can we take them out to breathe some fresh air . . . '

Luca says again, 'Pay attention to me now! . . . ' and he shows me his two cars are running side by side on the race-track. He says, 'They run together . . . next to each other . . . but the small car will get there first in the end . . . it is lighter, but faster . . . '

Alice is now playing with two small teddy-bears and she makes them hug each other. She shows them to me, and says, 'I was scared on Sunday . . . when we went to that fair . . . there were many monsters with big masks and wooden legs . . . ' Mrs E says, 'Yes in fact she got scared . . . ' Luca shows me an old radio from under his bed. Alice goes over to him and they both smile at me. Mrs E says, 'That's my husband's too . . . he likes making all sorts of toys for them . . . do you remember their small house? . . . and the long tunnel? . . . and all the plastic bottles filled with coloured fishes and sea-weed? . . . he has a lot of imagination . . . and they love his toys . . . ' Then, after a pause (it is almost time for me to go), 'But why don't we sit down for a moment? . . . come with me into the sitting room . . . ' We go and sit down. She says, 'Children are a source of continuous anxiety . . . though I realize that I am lucky . . . I get worried over the smallest problems . . . his tonsils . . . or her crying at nursery-school . . . I wonder how people with serious problems cope . . . it must be dreadful . . . I would never have imagined that having children made you feel all this . . . but that is enough now . . . I am on the pill . . . and I would like to go back to work . . . I am looking for a part-time job . . . I have been used to working since I was fourteen . . . I like being with people . . . I can't just stay here and look after the house . . . I am not mad about cleaning . . . in fact each morning after taking them to nursery-school, I go for a long walk . . . then I come back for lunch . . . and I have to clean . . . at least I don't think about them all the time . . . but I am looking for a part-time job . . . I want to be with them when they are back from school . . . I miss them a lot now . . . we have been together all the time for three years . . . night and day . . . I found it difficult to begin with getting used to them being away . . . probably if I found a job . . . nothing particularly exciting . . . just clerical work . . . but you can't expect more now . . . and I'd be very pleased to get one . . . '

It is time for me to go. She says, 'I am always sorry when you have to go . . . but the traffic is very bad now . . . and you have to go back home too . . . I always keep your phone number here, as I know I can count on you if I need something . . . ' Then she shows me some pictures she has taken of the children. She says, 'Why don't you take one? . . . ', and I thank her very much. We go back to the children's bedroom to say goodbye to them. They are sitting very close to each other on the floor, each playing with their own toys. Alice smiles at me and Luca says goodbye to me in a very deep and funny tone of voice. We both laugh, and Mrs E says, 'He is a man now! . . . always wanting to grow fast! . . . ', then she accompanies me to get my coat.

She says, 'My father sends his regards . . . he has given me something for you . . . ' and she goes into the kitchen and gives me a bottle of olive oil. She says, 'This is made with his own olives . . . I hope you and your family will like it . . . ' I thank her very much and ask her about her parents. She says, 'My father is very depressed . . . his favourite brother died . . . ' I say that I am very sorry about that. Then she kisses me on both cheeks, and says, 'I hope to see you soon . . . you know that you are always welcome . . . ', and she waves to me as I get into the lift.

Alice and Luca – summary

Alice and Luca, as their observant mother said, clearly always had 'different selves'.

Luca's hatred of having any 'boundaries' and his love for 'freedom' and individuality seem to date back a long time. As Dr S and his mother remarked while watching him kicking, and turning and stretching his legs against the uterine wall, 'Look at him . . . he is so small and he already seems fed up with being in there . . . ' and 'he seems to be wanting to get out . . . not much to explore there . . . he got tired of exploring such a narrow space . . . '. Luca in fact gave signs of wanting to be born long before the actual time of his birth, as when banging his head against the cervix of his mother's womb. Luca's 'maturity' probably also expressed itself in his search for 'me . . . not me . . . ' sensations already during his intra-uterine life, as his father so intuitively pointed out. He certainly seemed aware of the presence of his sister inside the womb and frequently reached out for her with gentle touching and stroking motions.

Alice, his physically much more favoured sister who still now is almost double him in height and weight, as her mother says, was 'much more of a baby' right from the start. She appeared to be sluggish and sleepy inside the womb and was and still is much more passive than Luca, her tiny yet very bright twin who always 'wanted to grow fast'. Alice moved very little inside the womb. As her mother commented, 'Movement is all on one side', her brother's side. Yet Alice always responded and followed her brother whenever he initiated a gentle head-to-head contact with her from the other side of their thin dividing membrane.

As birth approached, Alice turned round into the podalic position and therefore her brother 'won the race' and came out first. But then, almost at the last minute Alice too turned round and followed him. As her mother commented, 'She always follows him at a slower pace.'

145

When one year old Alice and Luca could often be seen engaged in their favourite game of using the curtain of their living room as a kind of dividing membrane, gently stroking their heads through it as they had in their pre-natal past; a gesture that had won them the nickname of 'the kind twins'.

Three years later, with the advent of nursery school, the more adventurous Luca is still 'winning the race' as he had when they were born. He sings with a deep masculine tone of voice and mimics the fast motions of a wild rock-dance. Having learnt some swear words too, he seems to be now fully 'on the road'. Yet everything he does is not just clever mimicry or fast projection into an adult world. In his drawings Luca shows a remarkable power of observation and considerable skill, well beyond that which one could expect for his age. His teachers are all enthusiastic about him and I too find him a very appealing, free, and far-from-shallow little boy. Luca is also quite capable of reminding us of his need for attention when his mother and I become too engrossed in our conversation. Though still gentle and kind with his sister, he overtakes her in his enjoyment of social contacts and more 'grown-up' life. He is also determined to assert his individuality and not to smother her, as he says 'I am not your mother, you know!' His past as a twin, however, is still very much with him. His two cars are made to run in parallel on the racing-track. 'They run together', he says, 'next to each other, but the small one will get there first in the end. It is lighter, but faster.' Compared with his shy little sister, Luca seems to have 'won the race'.

Alice always seems to follow him at a slower pace. She has certainly remained slightly behind compared to his very fast pace. Separation from her brother in nursery school hit Alice quite hard. She cried so much when parted from him that in the end their teachers reunited them. Now Alice, standing next to Luca, makes her two teddy-bears hug each other in a way that is nostalgically reminiscent of the close hugging and gentle stroking contact with her brother inside the womb. Being just one and not a pair seems a disquieting possibility for her.

Alice and Luca have been fortunate from the start in having parents who not only took the news of their birth so well, but were also gentle and kind to them and always tried to respect their 'different selves'. Mrs E, though clearly quite adventurous herself, as in her love for touring the world on a small motorbike, never showed any preference for Luca and has always tried to be 'fair' to both of them. Their gentle father and grandfather, though not much present during the post-natal observations, have clearly always been there in the background to help.

OBSERVATION NO. 3 – MARISA and BEATRICE

Background

Mrs F, a woman in her early thirties, came alone for the first ultrasonographic observation. She was then in her eighteenth week of pregnancy. Her careful but visible make-up, her well-groomed, tinted hair, her tight and rather low-cut dress as well as her high-heeled shoes all seemed to advertise her profession: beautician in a not very fashionable hairdresser's shop. Only her undisguisable pallor and the dark rings under her eyes seemed to reveal an otherwise well-concealed pregnancy. Mrs F seemed rather reserved and spoke little during the observation. She only laughed when Dr S reminded her how shocked she had been at the news of expecting twins.

Mrs F, with an air of guilt, was later to tell me several times whilst looking fondly and almost tearfully at Marisa and Beatrice (the names subsequently chosen for the girls), that for quite a while she had seriously considered aborting. She had gone as far as making an appointment with another hospital in order to arrange for an abortion, but had then backed down, encouraged by her husband, who kept saying, 'We shall make it . . . you will see . . .' Economic considerations were just one of the motives that had made her contemplate having an abortion. The birth of her son (Allo, who was four years old at the time) had been very traumatic for her and Mrs F was terrified that double birth might mean double hardship and pain. She was also afraid of the double work that caring for twins would inevitably entail with its consequent tiredness and fatigue. But most of all she was probably frightened about her son's jealousy once the twins were born, as she described Allo as a very possessive and very intense little boy.

Though Mr F was soon able to find several other more or less legal odd jobs in addition to his main activity as a rag and bone man and Allo didn't seem to be overwhelmingly affected by the news, Mrs F continued to maintain a rather ambivalent attitude towards her pregnancy throughout. She didn't want to know their sex beforehand. She hoped she'd have boys and was afraid of her reaction if she found out that they were not. Yet as soon as she saw the girls (I visited her in hospital twenty-four hours after the delivery), she immediately took to them and soon became a very loving and tender mother. In a way, I had never had any doubts about that.

The observation that follows is the first ultrasonographic one. Mrs F is eighteen weeks pregnant and she is rather silent and thoughtful throughout, though she follows the activities of the twins on the screen carefully. Her resignation appears to be almost in sharp contrast with the volcanic activity of the girls, who keep fighting, kicking, and pushing each other all the time.

Marisa and Beatrice: first ultrasonographic observation (eighteenth week) – transcript

DR F: We can start now . . . the right one is podalic . . . let's write it down . . . we shall call it right . . . the left one is cephalic . . . the left one is moving . . . the right one is not . . .

DR S: The right one is sleeping . . .

ME: Can you tell me the week?

DR S: It is the eighteenth week . . . I will write it on the tape for you . . . I saw Mrs F three weeks ago for a first check-up . . . and we suspected a twin pregnancy as her womb was so big . . . therefore we decided to have a scan . . . when I told her she was going to have twins, she almost fainted and screamed . . . didn't you? . . .

MRS F: (laughs) Yes, I was really shocked . . .

DR F: We will keep her file here . . . together with all the files of the twin pregnancies we are observing . . .

DR S: Now the left one is moving a lot . . . sort of kicking against the dividing membrane . . . at this stage it is still easy to observe both twins . . . can you see them? . . .

MRS F: Not much really . . .

DR S: All right . . . let me move the screen . . . is that better now? . . .

MRS F: Yes . . . that's better . . .

DR F: The left one is still kicking against the membrane and its twin . . . look, now the right one seems to have been woken up by the blows . . . it is retreating . . . sort of curling up . . . then extending its legs and pushing the other one back . . . again . . . again . . . again . . . it continues to curl and retreat while at the same time pushing the other one back . . . the other one insists with its blows . . .

MRS F: They are both awake now . . .

DR S: Yes, both awake and fighting . . .

DR F: The left one is pushing its legs like mad against the membrane . . . it looks like a battering-ram . . .

DR S: It is sort of pedalling . . . one blow after the other . . . it is not moving its arms . . . I have the impression that its fists are clenched . . . what a bellicose type! . . . we mustn't forget that Mrs F doesn't want to know their sex . . . I mean not now, but later on, we must keep this in mind . . .

DR F: The other one is beginning to move more . . . look, the left one has stopped . . .

DR S: Yes, from what we have seen so far with other twin pregnancies, usually only one twin moves at a time . . .

DR F: These seem different . . . look, the left one has just kicked the right one on its head! . . .

MRS F: (laughs) Yes, I saw that very clearly . . . I can't feel them moving though . . .

DR F: The right one is protecting itself from the blows . . . it's brought one hand over its head . . .

(Dr F gives me the probe to hold.)

DR S: Luckily they have the dividing membrane between them at least . . .

DR F: It is the left one that is particularly bellicose . . . the other one tries to retreat . . . then in the end it fights back . . .

MRS F: I am getting used to the images . . . I can see them very well now . . .

DR F: Now they are moving together . . . both kicking against the dividing membrane . . . they are moving simultaneously . . . the left one is moving more though . . .

DR S: Now the right one is not moving . . . it has curled up again . . . the left one is still moving . . . sort of stretching its legs . . . pointing its feet against the membrane . . . like a ballet-dancer . . .

DR F: Contrary to what we have seen in other twin pregnancies, these two seem to move simultaneously . . .

MRS F: Perhaps they have more space . . .

DR S: They have quite a bit of space till the twenty-fourth week . . .

DR F: I don't think it's a matter of space . . . otherwise they would disturb each other all the time . . . yet we have seen that some twins seem quite impervious to the blows of the other . . . these two on the contrary both seem to be reactive . . .

DR S: I have just read a paper about single pregnancies . . . they say that external shaking . . . like when we try to make a fetus move because we have seen it to be immobile and non-reactive . . . is quite useless . . .

DR F: The data on that is contradictory . . . it is true that single fetuses do not always respond to shaking . . .

DR S: When the observation is over we could try with the right one . . . it seems to be sleeping now . . .

DR F: I don't think it is sleeping . . . at least judging by its heart-beats . . . in fact it is moving its arms slightly . . . its hands are in front of its face . . . it looks as if it might have its thumb in its mouth! . . . Certainly before we started observing twins I had a different idea about

149

them . . . I thought they would all react much more to the other one . . . most of them seem quite indifferent though . . .

ME: I had the same idea too . . .

DR S: The right one is not moving now . . . it looks as if it is lulled by its mother's aorta . . . this one seems more cuddly . . . all curled up and lulled by the sound of the heart-beat . . . the other one too is not moving much at the moment . . . but it seems a nervy type . . . it continues to make slight jerky movements . . . now it is rubbing its face with both hands . . . and again a slight jerky movement . . . in fact its heart has accelerated . . .

MRS F: I can't see it very well now . . .

DR S: Look . . . you can see the head here . . . the right one is not moving . . . the left one is kicking . . . Jesus! . . . it is kicking and punching the other one! . . . look! . . . now the right one has reacted too . . . pushing it back with its knees . . . it doesn't want its space to be occupied . . .

DR F: I wonder if some twins are already intolerant of their co-twin *in utero* . . .

The observation time is now over. Dr F and Dr S start talking about other topics. Mrs F gets ready to go and we arrange to meet again in one month's time.

The following observation takes place about a month later. Mrs F is alone today too. She observes intensely the belligerent activities of her twins who constantly fight and box, 'blow upon blow all the time'. The left one, Marisa, seems to be particularly active in bombarding her sister with blows. Marisa is now smaller than her sister.

Marisa and Beatrice: second ultrasonographic observation (twenty-third week) – transcript

DR S: (writes down the measurements, then) This is the right twin . . . it is moving . . . stimulated by the other one . . . they are moving simultaneously . . . but I would say that the right one reacted to the other one . . . this is the hand . . . actually the fist of the left one . . . they are fighting . . . boxing! . . . literally! . . . look! . . . the hand of the left one . . . then the hand of the right one . . . boxing . . . punching . . . their hands are very close . . . and it is one punch after the other . . . marvellous . . . just as it has been described since biblical times! . . . as if they were skirmishing . . . what blows! . . . the fist of the left one and then the fist of the right one . . . and look . . . these are the feet of the left one . . . it is sort of pointing them against the membrane . . . like a ballet-dancer . . . Look! . . . they are over the head of the other one . . . it is putting its feet on the head of the other one! . . . the left one seems more reactive . . . can you feel them? . . .

MRS F: Yes, I can . . . I can see them too . . .

DR S: All this area is the placenta . . . the left one is keeping its feet over the head of the right one . . . the right one is not moving much now . . . just sort of swinging its head slightly . . . as if to say: no . . .

Dr S gives me the probe to hold and asks me if I have visited the other twins at home. Then:

DR S: The right one is still not moving much . . . let's see what it's doing with its hands . . . both its hands are almost joined now . . . near the navel . . . I mean under the heart . . . as if it were praying . . . the heart is here . . . and one knee is now between its hands . . . here we go again . . . the other one struck again . . . with its fist . . . and this one moved its hand and leg away . . . with a jerky movement . . . now their hands are in contact through the dividing membrane . . . still in contact . . . now they have started fighting again as before . . . one blow after the other . . . again . . . again . . . again . . . (Silence. Dr S yawns.) . . . they keep fighting . . . (Silence. Yawns.) . . . This boxing is becoming monotonous . . . (Silence) . . . we can also see the face of the right one quite well . . . with its bony orbits and its nose . . . look . . . what a blow . . . the other one just struck it here! . . . near the back of the neck . . . They both seem to be awake . . . These two seem to be rather agitated . . . sort of blow after blow all the time . . . can you feel them?

MRS F: Yes, I can . . . last month I was complaining about not feeling them . . . but now it's even too much! . . . they seem to be moving all the time . . .

DR S: Let's go back to the right one . . . look what a funny position . . . it is pointing its hands as if it wanted to get up . . . like an athlete ready to spring . . . just like an athlete ready for a long-jump . . . (Silence. Dr S yawns several times.)

DR S: Let's look at the left one now . . . (I am still holding the probe.) . . . Yes, it's here . . . this is its cord . . . it is pointing both legs against the head and the chest of the other one . . . it is moving . . . actually it is kicking . . . it is moving its mouth too . . . probably it is sucking its thumb . . .

ME: It is opening and closing its mouth . . .

DR S: Yes . . . the thumb is in its mouth . . . its feet are crossed now . . . at this stage they still have plenty of amniotic fluid . . . they

can still play . . . Later the observations become more boring . . . now
you can observe lots of playful activities . . . well . . . not really with
these two . . . they seem to be fighting and not playing at all . . .
MRS F: And what about the delivery? . . .
DR S: I have no idea at this stage . . . we shall have to see later on . . .
according to their position . . . the right one is still in its athlete's
position . . . ready to jump . . . the left one is a nervy type . . . (Silence)
. . . Now the right one has turned round . . . the left one struck it with
a blow on its head . . . it is turning again . . . the other one is
bombarding it with blows . . . just like a boxing match . . . the nervy
one is smaller . . . the right one is not moving now . . . just swallowing
. . . both its hands under its chin . . . she seems calmer . . . the cord is
there too . . .
MRS F: Is it possible to see if they have the cord around their neck? . . .
DR S: Not really . . . at least it is almost impossible . . . I only know of
one paper describing it . . . but normally they are not so silly . . . and
do not twist it round their necks . . . very few do that and get strangled
by it . . .
MRS F: Is it more frequent with twins? . . .
DR S: Not with this kind of twins . . . it is more frequent with
monoamniotic twins . . . those who share the same amniotic sac and do
not have a dividing membrane . . .

After a long silence and many yawns, Dr S tells me that the observation
time is over and we arrange to meet with Mrs F next month.

Marisa and Beatrice: post-natal observations up to the age of four – summary

Marisa and Beatrice went on fighting all the time during the following
ultrasonographic observations and continued fighting right till the end.
Then just as in 'biblical times' during the delivery they fought over
their birthright. Marisa, who by now weighed almost a kilogram less
than her sister, forged ahead like 'a ram' and was going to come out
first. Beatrice, however, it was found, had been cornered into a difficult
position, and to save her life it was quickly decided to do a Caesarean.
Mr F, whom I had met briefly during the last ultrasonographic
observation, phoned me a few minutes later proudly announcing their
birth.

When I went to visit Mrs F in hospital the following day, she looked
very pale and exhausted, but seemed very pleased to see me. She had
spent the last twenty days of pregnancy in hospital as Marisa's weight

was being monitored very carefully. Mrs F had found her stay in hospital very difficult to bear. She was now in great pain, but was very relieved that all had gone well. She hoped to go home soon and was longing to be reunited with Allo, who seemed to have taken the news quite well, except for one or two soiling episodes. She then commented laughingly, 'He was very pleased to know that they were both girls . . . so now he is the only boy . . . my brothers have only got girls too . . . ' Since the girls' weight was well above the normal range for twins (Marisa weighed 2.6 kg and Beatrice 3.6 kg), she had decided not to breast-feed them: she was too tired and anaemic for that, and in fact she really looked terribly pale and worn out. She was also planning to go back to work soon and therefore wanted to place the girls in a kindergarten as soon as they were two months old. During my brief visit, with the exception of the breast-feeding, she seemed to have forgotten all her plans and in fact she went back to work (part-time only) much later, when the girls were nine months old and they were carefully looked after by her mother-in-law.

During the first few days (until some blood tests had been carried out), Mrs F was told that the girls were identical, but she seemed very sceptical about this. She had already spotted very clear differences both in their aspect and in their character. Marisa seemed in fact a very 'nervy type', with big alert eyes and a serious and almost tense expression on her thin, intense face. Beatrice looked quite different, with her small eyes and curiously square face and protruding chin. She also seemed quieter, and her mother told me that she loved being cuddled, while her sister was all tense in her arms. Mrs F told me that the doctors too had noticed that. I was later told by Dr S that Marisa seemed to have reacted with tension and apparent fear to the sudden transition of Caesarean birth, whilst her sister seemed to have 'taken it more easily' and soon quietened down in the nurse's arms. Mrs F was later to attribute Marisa's fear of unexpected changes of position and sudden noises to her Caesarean birth. 'She was probably unprepared for it . . . it must be frightening to be pulled out like that . . . '

Once back home Mrs F decided to divide her time with as much equanimity as possible between the two girls, taking turns with her mother-in-law who came in every morning carrying a huge bag of clean and freshly ironed linen and clothes. She devoted all her attention to just one girl at a time and while looking after one she seemed quite oblivious to the other and quite impervious to her frequent cries. Then as the feed or the changing was over, she devoted an equally undivided attention to the other one. Only on the rare occasions when Allo too was present could she be slightly distracted from her task. But caring for the girls did not seem to be simply a task for her. Mrs F seemed to derive a great deal of pleasure from looking after them. She cuddled and fondled and kissed them and loved talking to them, and both girls responded to her attention with obvious delight. Mrs F showed great passion in caring for the girls and all her nail-varnishes, lacquers, and make-ups soon vanished. As she said, 'No more time for that now . . . I look terrible, but it is difficult to be well-groomed and a mother of young twins . . . '

As for the twins, Marisa continued to be much more 'nervy' and to look much more tense. She seemed very alert and carefully scanned the room with her big serious eyes, and her intense expression made her look much older than her age. Besides being visibly disturbed by sudden noises or unexpected changes of position, she seemed easily upset by any extraneous presence (including mine). As her mother often commented, 'She is always tense and on the alert . . . she can never relax . . . as if some potential enemy were always around . . . ' Even when picked up she often pointed her feet tensely against her mother's chest and frequently her mother said, 'Even my body feels dangerous . . . but why can't you relax? . . . this one is trying to grow fast . . . so that she can master the world . . . ' But what seemed to disturb Marisa most, right from the very beginning, was the presence of her sister. She reacted with desperate screams and yells whenever her mother devoted her attention to Beatrice. When she was only five months old, whenever she looked at her sister she started making loud farting sounds. Occasionally she found some consolation in sucking her thumb or her dummy, though her baleful stare continued to reveal her unmitigated rage.

Beatrice seemed more 'cuddly', she looked much more relaxed, and ate avidly and with obvious pleasure. She seemed less alert and more 'babyish' than Marisa and in fact began to gurgle, sit, stand, and so on, slightly later than her very precocious sister. Beatrice at first seemed to react to Marisa's presence by cutting her out completely, seemingly ignoring her even when Marisa's face was right in front of her eyes. However, when her mother's attention was devoted to her sister for too long, she reacted to Marisa's triumphant gurgles and smiles with loud screams and piercing yells.

From the very beginning, in fact, intense rivalry and jealousy seemed to characterize the relationship between the girls. At first this was mostly expressed in murderous stares and high-pitched yells or an equally aggressive, determined cutting of the other one out of their field of vision. But as soon as they were able to sit up and reach out with their hands a real and unremitting war began. After feeding them Mrs F often sat Marisa and Beatrice next to each other facing the washing-machine. Each time Marisa saw Beatrice reflected in the front of it she hit her over her head with her plastic spoon without even turning round to look at her. Marisa soon became very clever at scratching her sister's face and Beatrice reacted by hitting her back. All Mrs F's attempts at restoring some peace and her pleading, 'But look at her, she is your sister and not an enemy, you know ... why do you have to look away the moment I sit her next to you ... ', seemed to fall on totally deaf ears. As their mother said, 'though they have different characters ... they are both very determined types ... ', and both were very determined to continue their fights.

Marisa and Beatrice continued their fights during the following years. Their murderous jealousy if anything seemed to be increased by age, and keeping them apart was often an ordeal. Jealousy, though, seemed to run in the family, as on the rare occasions Allo was at home he referred to his sisters as 'those two pigs' and having innocent pigs devoured by a lion was apparently one of his favourite games. Mrs F often said, 'He says that he will steal all their money when he grows up ... not that we have much money anyway ... '

Marisa continued to be a 'nervy' type. She was very precocious in her walking and talking and seemed to direct most of her verbal abilities against her slightly less alert sister. As her grandmother once said, 'She is a real viper with her ... ' When she started nursery-school (they were never sent to kindergarten in the end as their grandmother continued looking after them), Marisa with her sharp intelligence became very popular amongst her teachers who apparently often commented on her skills and her precociousness as well as on her 'sharp tongue'. With other children, though, she was found to be 'a bit of a loner', who preferred the company of adults to that of her peers.

Beatrice was slightly backward compared to her and had to be forced to go to nursery-school. As her mother said, 'She doesn't mix much with other children ... and she likes to be cuddled ... but her teachers don't have much time to do that ... ' On the whole, though, she was considered to have adapted well to the new requirements imposed by nursery-school.

In the observation that follows Marisa and Beatrice are now four years old. Beatrice is unwell today and she is at home from nursery-school. Therefore her general behaviour may appear uncharacteristically less aggressive compared to her norm.

Marisa and Beatrice: post-natal observation at four years old – detailed report

I arrive punctually and I press the intercom. I take the lift to Mrs F's floor. She is waiting for me at the door. She greets me warmly, and says, 'Please, do come in . . . '. She looks rather tired and pale, but as usual is carefully made up and nicely dressed with a black skirt, a red cardigan, and black shoes and tights. I give her a cake. She thanks me and we go into the kitchen. Her mother-in-law is sitting there on the bench seat. Beatrice is lying on her lap. She is sucking her thumb and holding a handkerchief in the same hand. The mother-in-law kisses me on both cheeks, and says, 'I am very pleased to see you again . . .' then, referring to Beatrice, 'she is glued to me . . . '. Beatrice doesn't look at me and keeps sucking her thumb rather sulkily.

Allo comes in the kitchen too. He is holding a small plastic skeleton and he shows it to his sister. She looks rather frightened and then buries her head inside her grandmother's lap.

Mrs F says, 'You are frightening her! . . . everybody is at home today . . . except Marisa . . . she is at nursery-school . . . Beatrice is suffering from bronchitis . . . the doctor saw her on Monday and prescribed some antibiotics . . . This winter has been dreadful . . . there has always been something the matter with someone . . . I am not well either . . . I have a terrible cough [in fact during the observation she coughs rather frequently] . . . and tomorrow I'll go to the doctor too . . . I think it's this terrible climate . . . living in this dreadful town . . . with so much pollution . . . I was thinking of sending the girls to the sea for a while with my mother-in-law . . . I asked about the prices only this morning . . . I was very busy in the salon . . . but they were just dreadful . . . I don't think we could afford them . . . '

She opens the parcel containing my cake and starts cutting it. Allo in the meantime has gone back to his room. She says, 'Allo is mad about cakes . . . Beatrice doesn't like them . . . she prefers ice-cream, chocolates, or sweets . . . but the doctor forbade me to give them any sweets . . . he says they are very bad for their teeth . . . but then they see other children . . . and they are often given a sweet as a reward at nursery-school . . .'

She offers us a piece of cake and sits down and eats some too, saying, 'This is delicious! . . . '. She then calls Allo and tells him to come and have some cake too. From his room he replies that he is busy right now, but he will come in a minute. Mrs F says, 'He is also at home . . . his school was on strike today . . . ' While her grandmother is eating her cake, Beatrice covers herself more and more with the table-cloth saying almost in a whisper, 'I like being alone . . . and in peace', then she slips from the bench and curls up in the fetal position under the table, still sucking her thumb. She is completely out of our sight now.

Mrs F says, 'She is a bit shy . . . she always says that she doesn't like people . . . more than two people around is already too much for her . . . ' She looks at her watch, and says, 'I have to give her her antibiotic now . . . she doesn't like it . . . Come on Beatrice . . . come out . . . you have to take your medicine now . . . '

Beatrice moans from under the table. Her mother pulls her out. Beatrice sucks her finger and complains. Her mother begs her to be good and take her medicine. Beatrice closes her mouth. Mrs F says, 'I'll give you some ice-cream after that . . . '

Beatrice says, 'I want some water . . . '

Mrs F: 'All right . . . drink some water . . . ' She gives her some water to drink, then almost forces the antibiotic into her mouth. Beatrice grimaces and asks for some more water. She spits some of the antibiotic into the glass. Her mother shrugs her shoulders, and says, 'The doctor told you that he will give you a really bitter one next time . . . ' Beatrice goes and curls under the table again sucking her thumb.

Mrs F calls Allo, saying, 'Your cake . . . ', then puts the coffee on. Beatrice climbs on to her grandmother's lap and covers herself with the table-cloth, saying once more, 'I am fine when I am alone . . . '.

Her grandmother says, 'Beatrice is a cuddly child . . . Marisa is not . . . she is terribly jealous . . . yesterday she hit me on my face . . . she came back from nursery and Beatrice was lying on my lap . . . and she just hit me . . . Then she looked at me with a murderous look . . . and she didn't forgive me until I put Beatrice down and picked her up instead . . . She looked really murderous . . . she is incredibly jealous . . . They all are in this family . . . but Marisa in particular . . . She often hits her sister . . . poor Beatrice, they all hit her . . . Sometimes she responds too . . . but generally she gets hit . . . particularly by Marisa . . . '

Mrs F puts some ice-cream in a cup for her, but Beatrice again retreats under the table. Allo comes in with his plastic skeleton. He sits down and eats some cake, then asks for a Coke. Beatrice comes out from under the table and sits next to her grandmother, saying, 'I want some Coke too . . . ' Her grandmother shows her the ice-cream, but she gives it back to her, saying, 'It is still too hard . . . ', and her grandmother starts moving the spoon until the ice-cream is almost completely melted.

Allo asks his mother to help him finish assembling the skeleton. She says, 'You should ask her . . . she is a doctor, you know . . . ', then she tries to fix its feet, but soon gives up saying, 'I can't do it . . . they feel too slippery . . . ' I try too, but with no success. Mrs F says, 'Allo is very good at school . . . he likes everything and has a fantastic memory . . .

157

compositions are the only things that he doesn't like . . . but his teacher gives them such silly compositions . . . I can understand him getting bored with them . . . '

She looks at her watch, and says, 'Well, I should get started now . . . I have to go and pick up Marisa from the nursery-school . . . I shall only be a few minutes . . . ' She looks at Beatrice. She is eating her ice-cream, but at the same time is almost continuously rubbing her left eye. She says, 'It is all swollen . . . something must have got in . . . stop touching it . . . ', and she gets her coat and goes out. (I had almost lost any hope of seeing Marisa today.)

Beatrice starts rubbing her eye with the handle of her spoon. Her grandmother tells her not to do it. She leaves her ice-cream and disappears again under the table. Allo goes and gets several books from his room. He shows them to me. They are all about human anatomy. His grandmother says, 'Everything has changed nowadays . . . when I was at school I had only one big book . . . I still have it at home . . . we had to learn everything by heart . . . now it has all changed . . . they have dozens of books . . . they have to do all sorts of projects . . . '

Beatrice sticks her head out from under the table. Allo immediately puts the small skull in front of her. She tries to touch it and he screams, 'Leave it! . . . you are a pig! . . . ', and grabs it.

His grandmother scolds him saying, 'Be nice to her . . . '. Beatrice sits next to her. She sucks her thumb (and still has her handkerchief in her hand), then suddenly she slaps her grandmother's face. Her grandmother pretends to hit her back. She says, 'She gets hit all the time . . . (then to Allo) . . . you should show her your toy . . . ' He shows her the skull and she holds it.

The grandmother says, 'My mother-in-law used to keep her husband's skull in her room, next to her bed . . . I couldn't bear it . . . I had known him . . . it was like a shrine for her . . . but it upset me terribly . . . yet each time I went inside her room, I couldn't help it, I kept staring at it . . . once I was dusting the room and I covered it with a duster . . . it was too much looking at it . . . but then my mother-in-law came back into the bedroom from the bathroom and got cross with me . . . I pretended not to have done it on purpose . . . but she got very cross . . . she didn't believe it had just been absent-mindedness . . . '

Beatrice is listening to every word she is saying. Then she takes half of the plastic body that should cover the skeleton and holds it, saying, 'How nice . . . it is only half . . . ', then she touches its navel and says, 'What is this? . . . ' Her grandmother says, 'It's its navel . . . you have one too . . . ' Beatrice: 'And my sister? . . . ' Her grandmother: 'You both have one . . . you were in the tummy together . . . but each of you had a cord . . . ' She holds the half body for a while, looking rather lost in thought and then starts whispering something inaudible to it, looking very absorbed. Then she takes some of the pieces of the skeleton and starts looking at them. She bends them slightly and her grandmother says to Allo, 'Put it away . . . otherwise she will break it . . . or else you will lose some piece . . . '

Allo picks up all his pieces and goes back to his room. Beatrice starts sucking her thumb again. Her grandmother says, 'Why don't you hide under the table-cloth . . . your sister will be here any minute now . . . then we can pretend that you are not here . . . we will play a joke on her . . . ' Beatrice hides under the cloth and her grandmother covers her completely with it. She says, 'The other day Marisa hit her because she was jealous of her . . . and I said: "Don't you ever do that again!" . . . otherwise I shall go and get two more girls . . . she stared at me murderously and said: "You try! . . . I will tear everything to bits and destroy everything in this house!" . . . she was livid with rage . . . ' She laughs.

Mrs F comes in with Marisa. Beatrice sticks her head out. Marisa ignores her, pretending not to see her and looks at her grandmother very seriously, then suddenly looks at her sister and says, pointing her index-finger towards her, 'You are a witch! . . . '. Beatrice stares at her rather murderously too. Mrs F explains, 'They are preparing an end-of-year play at school . . . Beatrice will be the witch and Marisa a ghost . . . (then to her mother-in-law) . . . I am afraid you will have to prepare their costumes . . . the instructions are here . . . your fame has spread and all their teachers know that you are a good dressmaker . . . ' Her mother-in-law looks up as if in despair, then they discuss the details of the costumes.

Marisa and Beatrice still look murderously at each other. They look very different: their features are different. Marisa is quite pretty, with big intense eyes, while Beatrice looks much less attractive with her rather square face and curiously protruding chin. Marisa is still considerably smaller and thinner than Beatrice and her expression is much more determined and adult-like. They are also dressed completely differently and their hair-styles are different too.

Allo comes in and takes some of his books away. Marisa takes some too, saying, 'I will help you . . . ' Beatrice tries to help him too, but Marisa hits her on the face. Beatrice hits her grandmother's face. Her grandmother says, 'I had nothing to do with it . . . ' Mrs F continues to talk to her. She explains about the costumes and then gives her detailed instructions for the following day. The children in the meantime all go out. Mrs F says that she will go to do some shopping first and then to the doctor and they discuss all the arrangements for the children. The mother-in-law says, 'What a day! . . . I will be exhausted by the evening . . . no need to go to gymnastics with these three! . . . ' Mrs F goes and makes a phone call. She talks to someone about work.

Marisa comes in holding two plastic dinosaurs, one big and one small. She puts them on the table, and says, 'The small one is smaller . . . but it is much cleverer . . . ' and she hits the big dinosaur with it and makes it fall on the floor. She says, 'This happened all the time in those days . . . ' Her grandmother looks at her, and says, 'Time flies . . . they are already four . . . in two years' time they will be at school . . . ' Mrs F finishes phoning and comes back. Marisa goes out.

Mrs F says, 'They have their own room now . . . and they decided to have separate drawers . . . they did it all by themselves . . . I found that out the other day . . . Marisa's drawer is very tidy and filled with things . . . she knows exactly what is in it . . . Beatrice is much more untidy . . . she throws everything in it . . . everything has to be separate with them . . . woe betide me if I exchange their clothes! . . . '

Beatrice and Marisa are now fighting over a small chair, each pulling it in a different direction. It is very late and I should go, but I have the impression that Mrs F still wants to talk or tell me something and therefore I decide to stay a little while longer. Eventually Marisa manages to grab Beatrice's hair and she hits her. Beatrice hits her back, but Marisa is very fast at getting out of the way.

Allo switches the television on and Beatrice lies on the sofa next to him to watch it. Mrs F says, 'Marisa doesn't like looking at telly . . . she organizes all her games . . . she always has something to do . . . she is always busy with something and moves all the time . . . ' In fact we see her hopping and running and going in and out of the sitting room. Then we hear Beatrice screaming. We all run towards her and see that she has fallen on the floor. We also notice that the small chair is on the sofa and Allo says that she has fallen from it. Mrs F picks her up saying, 'You mustn't do that . . . it is dangerous . . . who put the chair there? . . . ', and Allo replies, 'Marisa'. Beatrice stops crying and Mrs F says, 'Luckily it was just a fright . . . ' Then she cuddles Beatrice a little saying, 'She is a cuddly child . . . Marisa is not . . . when I pick her up, she tenses all up . . . she can't relax . . . This one is cuddly . . . she moulds herself to the shape of my body when I pick her up . . . ' Then she puts Beatrice down and we go back to the kitchen.

Mrs F says, 'Marisa has been ill for two weeks . . . with nervous colic . . . in the evening she was all curled up and crying with pain . . . saying that her stomach was hurting . . . then she vomited . . . the doctor examined her carefully and said that there was nothing the matter with her . . . just nervous colic . . . He prescribed some medicine . . . but she kept vomiting all the time . . . The doctor was worried . . . she was losing weight . . . He asked me if something was happening in the family . . . like, say, fights . . . but no, I couldn't think of anything . . . of course sometimes I quarrel with my husband, but nothing dramatic and in five minutes it is over . . . I just couldn't think . . . Then I asked the teachers at nursery-school and they told me: Marisa is really dominated by her sister these days . . . I couldn't believe it! . . . Usually it is the other way round . . . Then I thought: perhaps that is why . . . perhaps they have changed roles for a while and Marisa resents it . . . perhaps that caused the tension . . . I hope it won't happen again, otherwise I shall ask your help . . . '

I say that she knows she can phone me should she be worried about something. She says, 'A friend of mine told me that her daughter had to see a psychologist for that . . . she was suffering from the same thing . . . the chemist too, he told me that these things are serious and might need treatment . . . So, if I am worried I will phone you . . . Now I'd rather wait a while and see if she is better . . . She has always been older than her age . . . The other evening her father said something to her . . . and she replied: "You mind your business and I will mind mine" . . . '

Her mother-in-law adds, 'She wants to be grown-up . . . she cleans everything . . . she helps . . . it is impossible to talk to her like a child . . . '

Mrs F says, 'The other day we went to the circus and my husband then picked us up . . . He laughed . . . He said that Marisa was the only one sitting up straight . . . with her spine completely straight . . . she would like to become a ballerina in fact . . . Next year perhaps I shall take them to ballet lessons . . . They both seem to like the idea . . . The problem is that I practically live in the car . . . always driving around . . . work in the morning . . . then picking them all up from school or nursery . . . then Allo goes swimming or plays football twice a week . . . '

Her mother-in-law says that she has to go and I say that I have to go too. I say goodbye to the children. Allo and Beatrice are still watching television and Marisa is playing with her two dinosaurs: the small one is winning. The mother-in-law tells Mrs F that she has cooked some lasagne and a roast and left them in the fridge. Mrs F smiles. I say goodbye to her and she promises to get in touch with me if she is worried about Marisa. Then I also say goodbye to her mother-in-law and I go.

Marisa and Beatrice: summary

Marisa, the smaller twin, seemed to be a 'nervy type' right from her pre-natal days. Beatrice looked more 'cuddly' in the womb, lulled as she was by her mother's heart-beat. But each time her peace was short-lived, as she had to protect herself from her sister's incessant blows. As Dr S pointed out, Marisa looked like a 'bellicose type' and a 'battering ram', kicking as she did against her sister and the dividing membrane. Nor was Beatrice simply passive towards her bellicose co-twin, but often actively tried to punch her back too. As Dr S said, 'Luckily they have a dividing membrane between them at least . . . ', fighting as they both were. 'Boxing! . . . literally! . . . one punch after the other . . . just as it has been described since biblical times . . . '

Then during the delivery, just as in 'biblical times', Marisa and Beatrice fought over their birthright. Though it is rather doubtful whether one could ascribe so much intentionality to their moves inside the womb, in more distant 'biblical' times Beatrice would have certainly died as in the end only a prompt Caesarean birth saved her life. Their battles for a life-space, though, had certainly begun much earlier than that and can be seen to continue pretty much unchanged up to the present day.

At four years old Marisa and Beatrice seem to go around always nursing the same grudge of not having been able to be alone from the start.

Beatrice apparently does not mix much with other children. She covers herself with the table-cloth and declares, 'I like being alone'. As Mrs F comments, 'More than two people around is too much for her.' Later Beatrice says again, ' I am okay when I am alone . . . ', and by curling up like a fetus she seems to long for that solitary peace she has never been able to enjoy right from the start. As she says, looking at her brother's plastic skeleton, 'How nice . . . it is only a half . . . ' A few minutes later she seems far from reassured when her grandmother explains to her, 'You were in the tummy together . . . but each of you had a cord.' Having had an individual cord probably feels like a wretched compensation for someone who had never wanted to divide her uterine space with another half in the first place. Both children now have decided to have separate drawers. As their mother comments, 'Everything has to be separate with them.'

Marisa, too is described as a bit of a 'loner' and her grandmother says that she is a 'viper' and a 'witch' with her sister, always trying to hit and hurt her because she is so 'jealous of her'. As soon as Marisa comes in she and Beatrice look murderously at each other. Soon the hitting starts and their poor grandmother is caught up in it too. Their fight becomes very vicious and they start pulling each other's hair as well. Later Marisa tries to make her sister fall down, by deliberately giving her a chair in a dangerous position. Mrs F then tells me how Marisa had some 'nervous colic' which she thinks may be due to the fact that apparently Beatrice is beginning to rebel against her sister at nursery-school. Her explanation is probably not far from the truth. Marisa, too, seems to have never worked out her 'pre-historic past'. Towards the end of the observation she hits the bigger dinosaur, saying that the small one is 'much cleverer' and is 'winning over the big one'. Marisa is still considerably smaller than Beatrice just as during their pre-natal past.

Jealousy, though, seems to 'run in the family'. Mrs F at the beginning almost considered aborting her twins as she was so afraid that jealousy would have been unbearable for Allo, her son. Allo clearly shows a strong jealousy now towards the twins. He greets Beatrice with a skull and immediately tries to frighten her by showing her a plastic skeleton. As soon as his sisters were born he nicknamed them 'those two pigs', and having innocent pigs devoured by a lion was apparently one of his favourite games.

Though Mrs F and her mother-in-law (and presumably also Mr F) always tried to be fair and as impartial as possible, dividing their time equally between both twins, both Marisa and Beatrice received just a 'half' of what they feel they could have had otherwise.

OBSERVATION NO. 4 – GIORGIO and FABRIZIO

Background

This observation had not been planned, but then Dr S told me that one of his patients was almost certainly expecting MZ twins as so far he had not been able to detect any dividing membrane. Given the extreme rarity of this type of pregnancy, we decided to ask the parents' permission to observe the twins. Mrs G was then about twenty weeks pregnant. The observations, though, were reduced to only three, for the reasons I explained at the beginning of this chapter.

Mrs G, a woman in her late twenties, though by far the most well-off of all the mothers I observed, was very interested in the possibility of receiving some money from us and seemed rather disappointed when Dr S told her about our almost non-existent budget. She nevertheless agreed to be observed, though she refused to have the tape-recorder on during the first two scans. Therefore this observation is certainly in many ways quite incomplete, but I hope that it may nevertheless be of interest to the reader.

During each ultrasonographic observation Mrs G came accompanied by her husband, who was about her age. His rather peculiar Byronic aspect made him look like an absent-minded poet from another age, and his ethereal and studied pose contrasted greatly with his wife's aspect. Mrs G looked shabby and fat, her clothes were tatty, her legs hairy, and her hair unwashed, but she none the less constantly wore a superior look on her face, as if she were too busy and too preoccupied with other much more important matters to indulge in such feminine trifles. I was told by Dr S that she worked as a social worker in a child guidance centre and was involved in a rather ambitious programme of child-rearing research. I was only too soon to find out what her rearing methods were like.

Mr G was a researcher too: socio-economic theory was his field, and his area of interest focused on the dubious economic activities of Panama and off-shore tax-havens such as the Dutch Caribbean. He had never visited those islands, but he wrote constantly about them from his small desk overlooking a congested street.

Both Mr and Mrs G seemed clearly very ambitious. They soon voiced the fact that their as yet unborn twins were not supposed to interfere in any way with their careers and the routines and pleasures of their lives. Yet something quite sadly pathetic showed under all their superior arrogance. Already one could feel that they were not going to fulfil their ambitious dreams, locked as they seemed in rather mad idealization of themselves. But once one observed how they treated their twins it was much more difficult to feel sorry or sympathetic towards them.

Mr and Mrs G kept very silent during the observations and looked rather absent-mindedly towards the screen, as if what was being displayed was not a matter of their concern. This, though, may not have been surprising, as the activities shown by their twin boys seemed either nonexistent or else very monotonous indeed.

Most of the time Giorgio and Fabrizio (the names subsequently chosen for them) were totally immobile and always so tightly intertwined as to render it impossible to tell who was who and which was which. The little initiative one could detect in them seemed to stem from Fabrizio, the smaller of the two, and then a few minutes later, as if by reflex, the same activity always spread to Giorgio, his considerably bigger twin. But the activities on the whole were few (a slight movement of the hand, an almost imperceptible stretch, a tentative opening of the mouth, and so on) and very far between. As Dr F pointed out, 'These two just seem to be leading a parasitic life . . .

they seem to be just vegetating or sleeping all the time . . . ', and while saying this he yawned. After each observation the twins were in fact subjected to some stimulation to see if they responded. Only once did their immobility seem to elicit some anxiety in their mother, who exclaimed, 'Come on . . . do move, my little ones! . . . '

The observation that follows is the verbatim transcription of the tapes of the third ultrasonographic session, the only one where I was permitted the use of the tape-recorder. Mrs G on that day had arrived a few minutes early, while we were still recording Mrs E, and seemed rather struck by the friendly, relaxed atmosphere in the room. When her turn came, she then gave me permission to record the comments about the observation this time.

Giorgio and Fabrizio: third ultrasonographic observation (thirty-third week) – transcript

DR F: I am writing thirty-third week . . .

DR S: Look how close they are . . . their hearts too are very close . . . they fit into each other perfectly . . . like the two halves of a puzzle . . . only one is turned upside down . . . I mean one is cephalic and one is podalic . . . apparently the big one is podalic . . . their chests are totally in contact . . . almost like Siamese twins . . . the ideal would be to have two probes . . . it's so easy to confuse them otherwise . . .

MRS G: Can you show them to me? . . . I can't understand a thing . . .

DR S: They are one over the other . . . here is the small one . . . and here is the bigger one . . . the small one is cephalic and is over the big one . . . but it is very difficult to distinguish which is which as they are so intertwined . . .

DR F: The small one seems to be growing smaller . . .

DR S: It's a growth retard . . . we shall have to consider that . . . can you feel them moving? . . .

MRS G: They never move much . . . but when they move they seem to move together . . . I feel the movement everywhere . . . and I can't distinguish which is which . . .

DR S: I shall start with the small one . . . it's important to see if he is all right . . . though it's not possible to be absolutely accurate with ultrasounds . . . I mean we can't be absolutely sure of their weight . . . we can't tell if this one is as small as it looks here . . . this is why we check their growth several times . . . twins are particularly difficult to measure . . . yet this is the only safe way to measure their growth . . . this one seems to be sleeping now . . . the other one too . . . they always do the same thing at the same time these two . . .

165

Long silence. Dr S yawns several times, then he asks Dr F if it is not possible to try and wake them by shaking Mrs G's abdomen, but Dr F says that she wants to observe their spontaneous motions first. Dr S gives me the probe to hold. He goes out, saying, 'They could go on sleeping for an hour . . . ', and we hear him talking to someone next door.

MRS G: Could you please show me the different parts of its body . . . I never understood anything during all these observations . . .

I point out head, arms, legs, and so on. Dr S comes back.

DR S: Are they still sleeping? . . .

DR F: Yes, they both seem deeply asleep . . .

DR S: They can go on sleeping for 20 minutes to half an hour . . . they haven't moved yet? . . .

DR F: No, not yet . . . I was looking at their heart-beat . . . no, they are really asleep . . .

DR S: Later we shall send Mrs G upstairs so that she can have tocodinamometry . . .

DR F: They never moved much during the other observations either . . . and they have been like this all the time . . . all in a tangle . . . even when they had more space . . .

DR S: They are monoamniotic aren't they? . . . we have never seen a dividing membrane . . . their placenta is also the same . . .

DR F: Yes, I think that it is very likely that they are monochorionic and monoamniotic . . .

DR S: It's still not moving . . . its hand is near its mouth . . .

DR F: Are you tired, Mrs G? . . .

MRS G: No . . .

DR S: I shall soon fall asleep . . . look now! . . . it has moved its head and its hand slightly . . . the other one is still immobile . . .

DR F: There are about two centimetres of difference between the two . . .

DR S: It is moving again . . .

DR F: (talking to Mrs G) It is quite common for twins to have a very different weight . . . particularly with monoamniotic twins . . .

DR S: We shall see her again in a fortnight . . .

DR F: No, she is coming back tomorrow . . . we have decided to hospitalize her . . .

DR S: (to me) Move the probe on the other one now . . . here it comes . . . the right one . . . it is turned in the podalic version . . . (to Mrs G) . . . Why don't you turn on your left side? . . . you will be much more comfortable . . .

ME: They are moving their chests now . . .

DR S: Yes, almost in time . . . these are respiratory movements . . .

DR F: It's a mess though . . . you can't understand which is which . . . they are so tangled . . .

DR S: The left one moved its legs . . . and now the right one is moving them too, I think . . .

DR F: The movements of the right one usually follow a few minutes after the movements of the left one . . . but today there is altogether very little movement . . .

(Very long silence)

DR S: I think we can stop now . . .

Giorgio and Fabrizio: post-natal observations up to the age of four – summary

Mrs G was in fact hospitalized the following day. She was monitored carefully and regularly for about two weeks and the twins seemed to be doing all right. But then her amniotic fluid was found to be stained with meconium and since initial signs of fetal distress could be detected a Caesarean was decided upon. She was by then thirty-five weeks pregnant. Fabrizio and Giorgio were born quickly and weighed respectively 1.5 kg and 2.1 kg. I was allowed to visit them in the intensive care unit once a week for about half an hour.

On the first day Fabrizio appeared to be suffering a lot. Both he and Giorgio, given their weight and gestational age, still looked very much like 'fetal-infants' (Gesell 1945), subjected to the hardships of life too soon, with all sorts of life-saving devices being forced on them. Fabrizio looked pathetically thin and small with his head shaved and his body full of needles and probes. He shivered almost constantly and from time to time was shaken by strong jerky movements. His brother, being heavier, looked quite different from him and seemed much more peaceful in his sleep.

The following week Fabrizio was still in the incubator and looked as if he couldn't find any peace. He shivered a lot and still shook with strong jerky movements, but from time to time he also reached out with tentative movements, as if searching for something, though as soon as he met with the hard and presumably colder surface of the incubator, he withdrew his leg with an expression of intense pain on his face. From time to time he let out some very feeble, bird-like cries.

Giorgio seemed immersed in a deep sleep. He didn't react to the varied and loud sounds in the nursery; the noise of the nurses' clogs, their voice or the other babies yelling from next door, and so on, yet as soon as his brother let out his feeble, bird-like cries, incredibly, he opened his eyes and each time kept them open as long as Fabrizio continued his whimpering sounds.

In spite of his unfavourable start, however, Fabrizio seemed to be much more 'tenacious' than his more favoured brother and by the following week their roles seemed to have changed, as Fabrizio now looked much more peaceful, was out of the incubator, and was steadily gaining weight. The nurses commented on the fact that Fabrizio seemed to be more 'vital' than his bigger brother, 'probably because he is smaller and had to struggle more . . . '. They also commented on his 'determined' character and on their mother's apparent lack of interest in them. On that day I was again struck by the fact that Giorgio and Fabrizio seemed to recognize and respond to each other's feeble cries.

This was almost the last time I was going to see Giorgio and Fabrizio properly, at least for some time. When they were about a month old they returned home and from then on a nightmarish infant observation began.

Once home Mrs G and her husband seemed determined to forge ahead with their careers and to be disturbed by their sons as little as possible. Mrs G, in particular, also seemed determined to be disturbed as little as possible by me and in fact cancelled most of her appointments, often forgot about my visits, and even when I was finally admitted into the house, left me alone with the children who were sleeping in their almost permanently dark room. As Mrs G said, 'They have to get used to being alone . . . I am not going to waste my time with them . . . ', and apart from what was strictly necessary she and her husband in fact never 'wasted' any time with them.

Though Giorgio and Fabrizio, to begin with given their difference in weight, looked quite different from each other and for at least the first months continued to look more like fraternal twins, their parents never wasted any time in finding out obvious differences between them. They decided from the start that the twins were absolutely identical and indistinguishable and that was that. From then on Fabrizio and Giorgio were always dressed the same and were provided with bracelets with their names on them 'otherwise we would never be able to tell who was who . . . '. Mr and Mrs G, if anything, seemed to take pride in the rarity of their twins. Not only were they afraid that the twins would represent a waste of time, but also that they might weigh too heavily on the family budget. Giorgio and Fabrizio were never given a cot or a cradle, nor later a child-sized bed. At first they slept in their prams and later, until they were finally big enough for an adult-sized bed, they were made to sleep on the foam and plastic covered mattress of their play-pens, as 'a play-pen is much more useful than a small bed . . . they play in it and don't wander round the house . . . ', and in fact their play-pens for a long time became a kind of cage for them. The children were never allowed out of it, and then once they began to crawl were never allowed out of their room.

These were just a few of the hardships they had to endure. Their mother (particularly when it came to baby food) never prepared their food, as she had 'no time for that . . . I buy ready-made food for them . . . they say that it is not so good . . . but I don't care . . . '. Their nappies were changed only once in a while, as there was 'no time and no money for that'. But most of all nobody was prepared to spend any time cuddling them or talking to them. 'They can keep each other company . . . I am not going to waste any time teaching them . . . '

Their feeble cries were silenced either with dummies or with shouts and later Mrs G went as far as using cold showers to 'quieten them . . . '. To begin with if they cried during the night they were simply 'shut away' in the kitchen, as 'we need to sleep during the night'. Each day (so I was told), no matter whether it was raining or snowing, boiling hot or freezing cold, they were taken out for two hours, so as to 'calm them down . . . '. They were also taken out on the bleak days after the Chernobyl disaster, when all Italian streets became suddenly deserted of any child. If Mrs G for any reason was too busy for that, she put them out in their pram on their small terrace overlooking a very congested and very polluted street.

Since their jobs allowed them some freedom, Mr and Mrs G took turns with the children, and they were also often helped by their parents, who lived nearby. Therefore they lacked neither time, nor money, nor help.

As described below, I tried several times to intervene but without success, and I did not think that the physical damage to the children – the only sort that government authorities would respond to – was sufficient to warrant a formal report to the social services, especially in view of Mrs G's involvement in her research programme.

As to Giorgio and Fabrizio, they soon seemed to learn things the hard way. On the rare occasions I was allowed to visit, they were mostly silent or asleep. The few movements I could make out in the dark room mainly came from Fabrizio. Giorgio often followed with the same movements a few minutes later, and soon their movements became very repetitive and their stare very blank. On the few occasions the children were awake, I was often shown only one child at a time, for, as Mr G put it, 'You just need to see one . . . the other one is exactly the same . . . ' Most of my visits were spent sitting on a chair in a silent, dark room. I was never offered a coffee or even a glass of water

169

and, each time, as if to add to my discomfort, after saying that they were too busy to spend any time with the children or with me, Mr and Mrs G, whoever happened to be there at the time, never failed to shut him or herself into the toilet across the hall and to expose the children and me to the noise of their ablutions.

When the children were six months old, Mrs G left for a long holiday with them. She came back looking very fat and fed up. I was able to see a bit more of the children now (perhaps ten minutes on each visit). Fabrizio always seemed to lead the way and Giorgio usually followed within a few minutes. Not that their activities were very varied, as they could only go from monotonous head-banging to equally monotonous swinging back and forth for hours on end within the narrow boundaries of their play-pens. Not surprisingly, both children were rather backward in their motor and intellectual development; but this did not seem to worry their parents in the least.

Giorgio and Fabrizio's development continued to be very slow. They uttered their first words when they were three and a half and were beginning to go to nursery-school. By that time they were also beginning to look strikingly similar as their weight was now the same. But Fabrizio always 'led the way' both in his motor and verbal development. Giorgio usually followed within a fortnight. Fabrizio's leadership also applied to their daily activities. Whenever I visited the Gs and was allowed a glance at the boys, each time that Fabrizio initiated an activity, within a few seconds Giorgio usually followed, shadowing as if by reflex all his brother's actions. Not that they were doing or were allowed to do much.

When the twins were almost three years old, Mrs G decided to get pregnant again, as according to her studies the ideal family had to be made up of three children. And in due time a little girl, Victoria, was born.

Yet at around that same time Mr and Mrs G's plans began to crumble. Mr G was never offered his teaching post at the polytechnic and he had to take up several not very important jobs. Mrs G's dreams broke down too as funds were withdrawn from her research and eventually even her child-guidance centre was closed down.

In the observation that follows Giorgio and Fabrizio are now four years old.

Giorgio and Fabrizio: post-natal observation at four years old – detailed report

I arrive punctually and ring the bell. Mrs G asks several times from behind the door, 'Who is it?', then eventually she hears my name and opens the door, saying, 'Oh, my God, it's you! . . . I completely forgot! . . . ' She lets me in. She is holding Victoria in her arms. Mrs G looks enormous and shapeless. She seems to have aged a lot and put on an enormous amount of weight. Her hair is cut very short and she is wearing a tatty overall. I am quite struck by her aspect. She looks almost like a tramp and her expression too seems to have changed from the impenetrable hardness and unerring conviction of before to an air of defeat. I can hear the television on full volume.

She says, 'I completely forgot . . . Fabrizio has been unwell . . . and I have been very busy . . . I had to take him to the doctor . . . my mind was so full with all sorts of things . . . and I completely forgot about you . . . ' Victoria looks at me. She is also wearing tatty clothes and her face is quite dirty. She is sucking a filthy dummy and stares at me rather blankly and with a fixed smile on her face.

I give Mrs G a small cake for the children. She goes and puts it down in the kitchen, saying, 'You are always so kind . . . you shouldn't really . . . ', then looking at Victoria: 'You just saw her briefly . . . that was after the Caesarean . . . before you went on holidays . . . I could hardly speak then . . . but a Caesarean was inevitable . . . she was still very high . . . and anyway it was too dangerous to wait . . . '

She kisses her, and says, 'She is very different from them . . . she is very affectionate . . . a cuddly child . . . and she is very good . . . she never cries or complains . . . ' In fact during the entire observation Victoria will never cry or wriggle and will always keep her rather fixed smile on her face.

I am still standing in the doorway and I still have my coat on. Mrs G says, 'Please, do come in . . . take your coat off . . . ' I take it off and put it down on the table (the sitting room and dining room are just one big room now). Fabrizio and Giorgio are sitting in front of the television. They are sitting on the floor and are both drawing something. They look very skinny and seem to have lost a lot of weight. Their similarity now is very striking. Their faces are rather dirty and they are wearing shabby clothes. But what strikes me most is their almost defiant and cruel expression, quite different from the sad and forlorn look of just a few months ago.

As we go near them they start fighting ferociously over a red pencil. Fabrizio screams with rage. Mrs E says, 'They fight a lot . . . almost all the time . . . ', then, talking to Giorgio, 'Leave it to him, you can have it later . . . ' Giorgio leaves the pencil, but still looks enraged. She shows me Fabrizio's arms and face, saying, 'You see, he has a rash . . . I thought it could be German measles . . . but the doctor said no . . . he has no temperature and has no lymphadenitis . . . she said it is not an

171

infectious disease . . . but probably an allergic reaction . . . she thought it might be due to penicillin or Bactrim . . . but that was a fortnight ago . . . it seems strange to me . . . perhaps he just ate something . . . '

While she is talking Fabrizio stops drawing and sits on the sofa. He takes a bottle of talcum-powder and starts spreading his legs with it. Mrs G says, 'Don't put too much of it on . . . he feels rather itchy . . . the doctor prescribed me some antihistamine drug in case it got too itchy, but I didn't buy it . . . I also forgot to buy the special mentholated talcum she mentioned . . . then it was too late to go out and I couldn't leave them on their own . . . this winter has been terrible . . . they have been ill with something or other all the time . . . and in fact they have lost quite a bit of weight . . . but the worst was when they had bronchitis almost a fortnight ago . . . they both had a very high temperature . . . and they became delirious . . . they could no longer distinguish dream from reality . . . and couldn't tell night from day . . . it was quite frightening and they had to be put on penicillin . . . we were all mad . . . all the winter has been like that . . . since they started nursery-school . . . one of them was always ill with something . . . Victoria too . . . all three took turns . . . '

She lies on the floor and I sit down too. Victoria is all over her body, but Mrs G seems to pay very little attention to her. Only when Victoria occasionally drops her dummy on the floor, Mrs G sticks it back inside her mouth. She says, 'I give her her dummy all the time, so there is no danger that she might pick up and swallow something her brothers have left on the floor . . . '

Fabrizio is now back on the floor. When he was sitting on the sofa, Giorgio had stopped drawing and was watching television. Now Fabrizio starts drawing again and a second later Giorgio does too. Giorgio is sitting in front of Fabrizio and cannot see what Fabrizio does, yet always a fraction of a second later he will do almost exactly what his brother does. Fabrizio draws a circle and then a small protuberance on the top of it. I ask him what it is, and he says, 'It is our house in Monticello . . . ' He scribbles. 'And here is the street leading to it . . . ' The street becomes more and more tortuous till it ends up in a tangled mess covering the entire sheet. Giorgio too is drawing a circle with a small protuberance on it. I ask him what it is, and he says, 'It is our house in Monticello . . . and this is the street . . . ' His street is less tangled though, and he seems to be drawing more carefully. Fabrizio crumples up his drawing and throws it away on the floor, then says to his mother, 'I want some more paper . . . ' She laboriously stands up and says, 'OK, I will bring you some . . . they love drawing . . . they didn't before . . . but now that they have started nursery-school they spend a lot of time drawing . . . '

She picks Victoria up and goes into another room. I catch a glimpse of her husband in it. I had somehow been aware of someone else's presence in the house from the beginning of the observation, but had not yet seen him. He is sitting at a desk. Mrs E takes some sheets of paper and closes the door, but a minute later her husband comes out and says hello to me. He is wearing a strange knee-length damask house-coat which gives him a rather outdated and bizarre look. He looks rather depressed. He says hello to me in his usual manneristic way and I ask him how he is. Even before I've finished asking him, he starts pouring out all his problems and failures. He says, 'I didn't get the polytechnic job in the end . . . though they say that another one might come up soon . . . and I'd be the first one on the list . . . but this is what they said last time . . . it was quite a blow . . . I spent ten years of my life waiting for that job . . . the best years of my life . . . and I am back to square one . . . I can only wait now . . . but it is more and more difficult waiting without having any certainty . . . so I had to consider all sorts of other jobs . . . like teaching evening classes . . . and the odd consultancy job . . . and I still work free at the university . . . I am terribly busy in fact, but I feel like I am wasting a lot of time . . . running around from one job to the other . . . yet I have to earn some money . . . my family is quite big now . . . '

Mrs G is standing next to him with Victoria in her arms. Victoria stretches her arms towards her father. He picks her up. Mrs G says, 'She dotes on her father . . . when he goes out in the morning she cries . . . otherwise she never cries . . . '

Mr G adds, 'But I have published a book . . . it is about off-shore tax-havens . . . I will give you all the details . . . perhaps you can buy a copy, if you are interested . . . ' and he goes and gets some paper and writes down the title and other details of the book. The publisher is completely unknown to me and I have the impression that he is desperate to sell some copies.

Victoria is back in her mother's arms now. Mr G says, 'Leave us your phone number . . . perhaps we can meet one evening . . . when they are asleep and talk in peace . . . ' I give him my phone number (I gave it to his wife many times before). He says, 'Excuse me now, but I have to get back to work . . . ' and he goes back to his desk while his wife closes the door.

Mrs G lies on the floor again. I sit down too.

Fabrizio is drawing a kind of square with two eyes and a mouth. His mother asks him what it is. He says, 'It is my pillow . . . ' Then she looks at Giorgio, who is also drawing a rather similar square with mouth and eyes and asks him too what he is drawing. He says, 'My pillow . . . ' She says, 'How come that your pillows have a mouth and two eyes? . . . ' Fabrizio adds short arms and legs to his pillow. He says, 'Because pillows move . . . I was never alone, even at night . . . ' Mrs G says, 'Yes, your pillow keeps you company . . . ' Giorgio adds, 'When I lean my head on my pillow, it moves . . . '

Fabrizio throws his drawing away. He draws something else: a kind of circle with many cord-like figures attached to it. He says, 'This is a dragon . . . just one body, but two heads . . . all linked together . . . it is a terrible monster . . . ', and he shows it to his mother. Giorgio scribbles a circle too, and says, 'This is also a dragon . . . no, well, perhaps it is a stork . . . ', and he adds to his scribble a sort of head and a beak.

Mrs G says, 'They are always wrangling with each other . . . yet they can't do without the other one . . . typical of twins . . . ', and she looks lost in thought. The television is still on, and she says, 'Fabrizio, please switch it off . . . ', but he shouts back at her. She says, 'Luckily there is television . . . when they come back from nursery-school they switch it on and I can have some peace again . . . usually I pick them up at 4 o'clock, but the nursery-school is actually open till 6 o'clock if needed . . . then they watch television . . . and at 7.30 they all go to bed . . . we have some peace . . . and they have to rest . . . rest is necessary because they have to get up early to go to nursery-school . . . '

Fabrizio tries to grab a pink felt-pen from Giorgio. He shouts, 'It's mine . . . ' Mrs G says, 'Stop fighting! . . . you can have it later when he has finished using it . . . ' Fabrizio and Giorgio look murderously at each other, then Giorgio retreats with his pen and a sheet of paper into the corridor. Mrs G says, 'They always want the same things at the same time . . . '

Fabrizio draws a kind of circle with two eyes and an appendix. His mother asks him what it is. He says, 'It's a pig . . . and this is its tail . . . ' Giorgio has come back silently and is now sitting in front of him again. He also draws something. His mother asks him what it is too. He says, 'It is a pig . . . well, no, perhaps it is a horse . . . its legs are too long . . . ' Fabrizio throws his 'pig' away on the floor and his mother asks him 'Why?' (the floor is by now covered with sheets of paper) and he says, 'I didn't like it . . . its tail was not right . . . it was not curly . . . ', and he draws two more pigs, saying, 'Pigs all look the same . . . '

In the meantime Mrs G gives Victoria a biscuit to eat. She drops all the crumbs on the floor and then picks them up and puts them in her mouth. After a while Mrs G notices that and she sticks her dummy in her mouth. Victoria brings up some milk and it falls on the floor and on her mother's overall. Mrs G goes and gets some toilet paper and wipes Victoria's face and the floor with it.

She says, 'Everything is dirty . . . I am always dirty . . . but she is a nice child . . . one doesn't realize that she is there . . . they are fond of her . . . when I came back from the hospital, their grandfather was here . . . they picked her up and said: she is ours . . . and it was all all right . . . she is very good with them . . . they can do anything to her . . . she never cries . . . but she is different from them . . . she moves a lot . . . they were always immobile . . . they remained for hours on end in their room . . . she seems to want to talk . . . they didn't utter a word till a few months ago . . . now they are quite articulate . . . but till they were three, not a word . . . they were isolated . . . she is a very sociable child . . . now with nursery-school things have improved . . . but before whenever we went out, they ignored other children . . . they have become more sociable now . . . particularly with girls . . . not so much with boys . . . they don't play any of their games . . . they don't like football or cars . . . so they don't have many friends . . . but the girls dote on them . . . they attract them because they're different . . . because they look the same . . . and they go along with it . . . '

Fabrizio is now drawing some more 'pillows' with mouth and eyes. She says, 'But your pillow is not like that . . . you don't sleep on top of your brother at night! . . . ' Fabrizio draws an empty circle without any mouth or eyes. He says, 'This is your face . . . ' Giorgio has stopped drawing now and he is watching television rather blankly. Mrs G says, 'I am sorry I never offer you something . . . but with them . . . ' Giorgio stops watching television and gives a sheet of paper and a pencil to his mother, saying, 'Draw something for me . . . a stork . . . ' She draws it for him saying, 'It looks more like a goose . . . it is not a very nice stork . . . ' Fabrizio comes near her too. He asks her to draw another stork for him. She draws one and says, 'This one is not very nice either . . . it is enormous . . . with a big tummy . . . it is the mother stork . . . '

Giorgio and Fabrizio now start fighting over a yellow felt-pen. Mrs G says, 'Stop fighting! . . . you can take turns with it . . . ' and they stop. Both start colouring their stork. They are rather careful and skilled. After a while Giorgio says, 'I can't find the top of my felt-pen any more . . . ' Mrs G, says 'Let's look for it . . . otherwise Victoria might swallow it . . . she picks up anything off the floor . . . ' We all look for it except Fabrizio, who is still colouring his stork. After a while I realize that Fabrizio is actually holding two caps very tightly in his left hand. I point this out to him and he seems surprised. He says, 'I hadn't realized that . . . ' He continues colouring his big stork. Mrs G says, 'We are all careful with her . . . she gets everywhere (in fact Victoria has only been moving over her mother's body) . . . she explores . . . the other day I found her with her hands inside the plant-pots! . . . that never happened with them . . . they just stayed inside their cots . . . they could be left alone for hours . . . they never moved . . . ' Now Fabrizio starts colouring the space around his stork with a brown felt-pen. Giorgio asks his mother for a pair of scissors (his second bit of initiative in this observation). She says, 'Go and look for them . . . but don't give them to Victoria . . . ' He comes back with his scissors and starts cutting his drawings, saying, 'They cannot be left like that . . . joined together . . . they have to be separated at some point . . . '

It is time for me to go, but Mrs G picks up Victoria and starts talking to me. She seems to find it unusually difficult to let me go today. She says, 'Victoria just plays with their toys . . . she is not interested in hers.' She follows me as I pick my coat up, and asks, 'Is your son at school full time? . . . I don't know what to do with them . . . twins are kept separate at school . . . and I prefer them to be separated . . . but there might not be enough classes for two . . . I couldn't possibly take them to two different schools . . . of course they are right in saying that they must be kept separate otherwise they become too similar . . . but we shall have to see whether this will be possible . . . they are very similar . . . I don't mean just how they look . . . but they also behave very similarly . . . before you just couldn't tell them apart . . . but since nursery-school they have started fighting . . . sometimes they hate each other . . . yet they can't do without each other . . . '

She goes near them and switches the television off. She says, 'They like to have it on, even if they don't watch it . . . for them just the voice is enough . . . any voice . . . ' Fabrizio gives her his stork, saying, 'You have to hang it up in our room . . . ', then Giorgio comes too, gives her his stork, and says, 'You have to hang it up in our room . . . ', then they both go back to drawing.

I say goodbye to them, but they don't seem to pay any attention to me. I walk towards the door. Mrs G follows me. I notice that near the door there is a pile of dirty nappies on the floor (I hadn't noticed them when I came in). Mrs G says, 'They still wear their nappy at night . . . Giorgio has started to call me sometimes during the night . . . but not Fabrizio . . . Fabrizio still does his stool in his nappy . . . he is frightened of the bathroom . . . I mean he calls me each time he has to pass a motion . . . it is not that he does it in his pants . . . he calls me . . . and I have to take his nappy and put it on my lap . . . then after a second, he just shits on my lap . . . I can't scold him . . . he is too terrified of the loo . . . I hope gradually he will get used to it . . . but this has also been a terrible winter . . . they have always been ill with something . . . next September I will probably start another job . . . but just part-time . . . ' Then, after a short pause, 'Do you by any chance know of a good cleaner? . . . I need one . . . I would like someone just for some cleaning . . . I hate doing it . . . just a couple of hours a day . . . perhaps I shall phone you to see if you can find one (I haven't said anything) . . . I have always treated you abominably during all these years . . . I never offered you anything . . . kept you waiting . . . forgot about your visits . . . but I was too busy with them . . . '

Victoria now plays with the cord of the intercom. Mrs G says, 'I really need a good cleaner . . . I hate having to clean . . . it is so monotonous . . . I'd rather iron or cook . . . ' Then she opens the door. Fabrizio comes there too and they all accompany me to the lift.

Giorgio and Fabrizio: summary

In the womb Giorgio and Fabrizio lived in a 'tangle' from the start since their shared genetic endowment coincided with a shared amniotic sac. As Dr F pointed out, 'They fit into each other perfectly . . . like the two halves of a puzzle . . . ' In fact, Giorgio and Fabrizio from their pre-natal days were always so tightly intertwined as to render it impossible to tell who was who and which was which. Most of the time they were completely immobile. As Dr F said, 'These two just seem to be leading a parasitic life . . . they seem to be just vegetating or sleeping all the time . . . ' The little initiative one could detect in them always seemed to stem from Fabrizio, the smaller twin, and then a few minutes later, as if by reflex, the same activity would spread to Giorgio, his considerably bigger twin. As Dr F pointed out, 'The movement of the bigger one usually follows a few minutes after the movement of the small one . . . ' Mrs G could not tell their movements apart, as she said, 'They never move much . . . when they move they seem to be moving together . . . ', nor did she seem to worry much about their remarkable stillness.

Giorgio and Fabrizio clearly had a traumatically premature birth. Yet so many horrific experiences have later been added to this initial fact that it is probably impossible to distinguish now any specific traces of their birth amongst the many traumatic events that have constantly shaped their lives. Most of the time they were left alone in their room and their room was kept so dark as to render it impossible to 'tell night from day'. A list of the cruel and neglectful treatments they were subjected to would sound like a catalogue of horror stories.

The most striking continuity between their pre- and post-natal behaviour is that most activities were and are initiated by Fabrizio and then copied by Giorgio, a fact of which their parents seemed to be unaware. Even though their parents have never made any effort to distinguish between them, always stressing their being identical, for

177

quite a long time after their birth it was quite easy to tell them apart, Fabrizio being clearly smaller and much more 'tenacious' and 'determined', as the nurses of the intensive-care unit remarked.

Now, at four years of age Giorgio and Fabrizio look strikingly similar and each wears a cruel expression on his face. Mrs G looks fat and defeated and her husband too complains about his shattered dreams. Giorgio and Fabrizio shout at them, Mrs G says that Fabrizio 'shits' on her lap, and Mr and Mrs G seem to have become almost their slaves. Such reversal of roles seems in tune with the sinister atmosphere of madness, dirt, and total defeat pervading all the family. Dirty nappies are piled up at the door, Victoria's face is filthy, the boys are thin and neglectfully dressed, and Mrs G almost looks like a tramp. Mrs G says that this has been a terrible winter and then describes how when they were ill Giorgio and Fabrizio even became delirious, as if they could no longer 'distinguish dream from reality . . . and could not tell night from day', and one wonders if this just applies to that one feverish episode. It is rather difficult to distinguish now who is who, though Fabrizio seems to be leading the way and Giorgio usually follows a few minutes later as if by reflex, and he also repeats his brother's words.

Their drawings now seem to reflect their history, starting from their remote past, when they were not allowed solitary peace, but even the 'pillow' they were resting upon had a mouth and eyes and could move. As Fabrizio says, 'Pillows move . . . I was never alone even at night . . . ' In the womb he was never alone, without even a dividing membrane to keep him apart from his twin. While drawing his 'dragon' with 'just one body, but two heads . . . all linked together . . . it is a terrible monster', Fabrizio seems to describe the 'monstrosity' of twinship as experienced by him. Giorgio too seems to be faced with the same problem when later, while cutting his drawings, he says, 'They cannot be left like that . . . joined together . . . they have to be separated at some point . . . ' Giorgio and Fabrizio seem to hate each other now, yet as their mother says, 'They can't do without each other', and they both seem to be almost inextricably 'tangled', just as they were during their pre-natal days.

At the end of the observation Mrs G recognizes that she has treated me 'abominably' during all these years yet even now, in spite of my having offered on other occasions a different kind of help, she treats me more or less like a cleaner and even asks me to help her look for one. What is most worrying though are the visible effects of her 'abominable' treatment on her children. Though they could be said to have been tangled 'like the two halves of a puzzle', immobile, or 'just vegetating or sleeping all the time' since the distant days of their pre-natal past, nothing since then in their external environment seems to have helped them to become more autonomous and differentiated. From the beginning their only comfort seems to have been that of their mutual presence which they now depend upon but hate. Even when in the intensive-care unit, Giorgio was able to recognize and respond to his brother's feeble and bird-like cries. Right from birth, given the constant darkness and almost total silence of their room, it was often only too difficult for them to distinguish night from day. The nightmare seems to have extended well beyond their pre-natal past into their post-natal world.

An observation of such abnormal nature as the one of Giorgio and Fabrizio naturally poses many serious ethical problems about the morality of Infant Observations. One cannot just watch without intervening or commenting on such monstrous behaviour. When human (physical as well as mental) lives are at stake, one cannot refrain from trying to intervene. Yet Giorgio and Fabrizio's situation was a particularly difficult one. Given their mother's involvement in child-rearing programmes, she seemed to have an unfailing belief in her upbringing methods and her theories. Though I offered her on several occasions assistance in many ways – suggestions about the boys' upbringing (very much contrary to my usual behaviour) and psychological assistance for herself through a referral to a colleague – these offers were never accepted and all my comments and remarks were always treated with equal contempt and often with overt hostility as well. On the other hand, had I asked some external agency (social services, court, and so on) to intervene, my appeal would have certainly remained unheeded, both given Mrs G's particular involvement with the social services and the fact that on corporeal inspection the twins' physical growth would have been found to be within the norm and no signs of physical abuse could have been detected on them. Only these would have justified realistically some kind of intervention from 'above'.

Concluding remarks on twins

On the basis of these observations I would like to offer tentative answers to some of the questions I asked about twins in the Introduction.

First, could a relationship, or at least characteristic movements between twins, be observed *in utero*? Here, as must be amply clear by now, the answer must be 'Yes'. By the time of the first ultrasonographic observation, characteristic behaviour patterns between the twins *in utero* appeared to have been clearly established and these patterns were continued after birth. There was a partial exception in the case of Fabrizio and Giorgio, whose abnormal experience after birth may have made them both more dependent on each other and more hateful to each other than they might have been with a more supportive, more 'ordinary' type of upbringing. Even in their case, the tendency observed *in utero* for Fabrizio to act first and for Giorgio to follow him was still very noticeable in the post-natal observation at four years of age. Study of other MZ twins is obviously a research priority, though very difficult to arrange for the reasons described in Chapter 3.

Second, does twinship throw any light on the question whether rudimentary forms of mental and emotional awareness begin before birth, especially in view of the fact that a twin has an opportunity *in utero* to interact with another being similar to himself? This question cannot of course be answered with any sort of certainty from my data; as noted in the previous paragraph, however, characteristic patterns of relationship behaviour between twins are established *in utero*, but one cannot say how much mental and emotional awareness is involved. So far as I could see with my infant/mother observation technique after birth, twins were no more precocious post-natally than singleton babies in giving clear signs of object recognition and responsiveness.

Third, is the uterine environment the same for each twin? Clearly it is not, the most obvious difference being that one twin is usually less favoured by its position inside the womb compared to the other. In all four cases, however, the smaller twin proved to be more alert and advanced after birth, the difference being much more marked in the case of Luca and his 'slower' sister Alice and Delia and her more withdrawn brother Marco.

Fourth, does twinship throw any light on the hypothesis that the mother's emotional state affects the fetus? Only the case of Mrs D and her twins Marco and Delia is relevant here. Mrs D had a temporary but near-psychotic breakdown in pregnancy, but her emotional state appeared to have little effect on the intra-uterine behaviour of Marco, who remained withdrawn, or Delia, who remained active, much as before. However, it may well be that only some types of emotional disturbance in the mother affect the uterus and the fetus, and Mrs D's disturbance was not of this sort.

4

Child analysis

I have chosen the six case histories reported in this chapter specifically because they show links with pre-natal and perinatal experience. They have been chosen from among several small children, twelve in all, whom I have had the opportunity to treat over the last ten years. Not all these children, including some very disturbed ones, showed this sort of link with their past. Reading the present chapter without being aware of this would be misleading; it is not my intention to suggest that all disturbance or all behaviour can be connected with pre-natal experience.

Giulia (case no. 1) needs no presentation, as her history has been described in great detail in Chapter 2. Her treatment, because of my unusual knowledge of her past, will be described in greater detail than that of any other child. I hope the reader will have the opportunity here to compare the impressions derived from her observations with those arising from the account of her treatment, including a detailed report of three sessions from three different stages.

In describing each of the other cases I will try to focus almost exclusively on those aspects of their treatment and of their history which seem to me to be more closely linked with their remote past. Therefore in my accounts I will neglect other important elements of these children's treatment and post-natal life and could, therefore, rightly be criticized for presenting what may seem a too unilateral and superficial view of each case. Their treatments included many other elements that cannot be discussed here for reasons of space, and whilst I do not want to deny or diminish the importance of post-natal emotions and events in the shaping of each unique human being, my emphasis will be, as I said, on those elements which appear to show a repetition or at least a link with what I suspect may have happened previously inside the womb.

181

Whenever feasible, as with the observational material described in the previous two chapters, I have introduced a verbatim report of one session in the description of each child, usually drawn from the very initial stages of the analysis. Giulia again is an exception, as three of her sessions belonging to three different stages of her treatment are reported in detail.

CASE NO. 1 – GIULIA (three years old)

Giulia's early history certainly does not need entering into in any further detail, as my unusually long acquaintance with her and with the main 'components' of her environment (including her intra-uterine environment) have already been described at length in Chapter 2.

What needs justifying here is the rather unorthodox nature of her treatment. A few days after seeing her for the consultation already described in detail, I met Giulia's parents to discuss my impressions with them. Mr and Mrs A came together this time, and their plea that something should be done for their child matched my worries about her. But by then Mr and Mrs A had also known me for a long time and were deeply attached to me. Therefore, when I suggested that Giulia should be referred to another colleague for treatment, they both were adamant in their refusal and no reasoning could succeed in changing their minds. Given Mrs A's particular mental make-up, which I had come to know through my regular visits to her in her mother's home, one could perhaps well understand why she refused to part with me. Mr A too, though, was determined in wanting help only from me. With his usual apparent cynicism he justified this by saying to me, 'No offence . . . but I don't have much faith in most of the gurus that seem to abound in your profession . . . much show and little substance . . . usually I trust my computers more . . . they talk less, but give precise results . . . but I have known you for a long time and I know the kind of person you are . . . Giulia is my daughter and not a machine . . . I would not entrust her to just anyone . . . actually I would only entrust her to you . . . sorry to be so imposing . . . but I am afraid you have no other choice . . . '

Therefore, wanting very much to try to help Giulia as well as her parents, as Mr A said, I was left with practically 'no other choice' and I then took Giulia on at a perhaps less than symbolic price.

Giulia could also be brought to see me only twice a week: the journey to my town was too long and Mrs A was too busy looking after her new child on her own to envisage any other realistic arrangement. Due to the increases to their family, they had had to move recently into a new flat, rather far from Mrs A's mother who, given her age and the various minor ailments afflicting her, could not be counted upon to travel so far every day.

Apparently the change of house had greatly affected Giulia, who seemed 'quite disoriented' in her new, bigger flat and often expressed the wish to go back to her old 'messy, small', but much beloved home.

Giulia, therefore, came to her sessions almost always accompanied by her father, whom I began to get to know as being very tender and affectionate, as well as far from just someone in the background. By that time, though his health was beginning to pose serious problems for him (as well as for Giulia and Mrs A), as his kidneys were beginning to function rather poorly, this had, in fact, been an added consideration to my accepting their plea to help their child, though, as I said, in this rather 'unorthodox' and non-intensive way.

All this certainly rendered it more difficult for me to analyse Giulia compared to any other child patient of mine. Usually I feel much more comfortable with intensive, five-times-a-week treatment, and my previous long knowledge of her and of her family, as well as my clear wish to help her, certainly rendered me less free from 'memory and desire' (Bion 1967) than I would usually try or wish to be.

Giulia's therapy also only lasted under two years, as by then she had apparently improved greatly in many ways, at least superficially, and as accompanying her to the sessions on the other hand was proving to be too much of a strain on her parents.

Giulia's treatment therefore could in many ways be considered of very little 'scientific' value indeed. In spite of all these various limitations, though, I feel that it may still be of interest to the reader for its unusual match between intuitive observation and evidence acquired through psychoanalytic procedures.

Giulia spent practically all her first session busily wrapping and sealing all her toys with the paper, the Sellotape and some Kleenex she had with her, till, as she said, 'nobody is outside' and 'nobody can come out any more . . . '. Then she seemed more relaxed and relieved. Her father had accompanied her that day and before leaving had handed her a packet of rather realistic chocolate cigarettes. Giulia now, after sealing all her toys and making sure that the door of the playroom was securely closed, sat down on the couch with her legs wide open and started licking her cigarettes voluptuously one by one, while saying, 'Now I can really enjoy some peace . . . nobody is going to disturb me in here . . . ' During that first session, after wrapping all her toys, Giulia reacted to my comments and interpretations with big, beaming smiles while staring ecstatically into my eyes, as a kind of 'twin soul' lost in the contemplation of an unreal and much idealized love. My words seemed to be 'sucked in' with the same voluptuous pleasure she showed in licking her chocolate cigarettes. Yet I already had the uncomfortable feeling that my interpretations were treated by her as just a kind of pleasurable source of sound to be enjoyed sensuously, while their meaning was lost. Then the end of the session, even if it had been mentioned beforehand, seemed to be perceived by her as a sudden and unexpected shock. Her eyes, just a second before, lost in the unreal contemplation of my face, now looked terrified, and Giulia dashed out of the room as if I had suddenly turned into a potential persecutor. She immediately asked her father for something to eat and drink, and her father, who seemed rather well supplied, instantly took a tin of Coke out of his coat, and Giulia gulped it all down in one breath.

Giulia came back for the following session looking quite frightened and terribly upset, as if the unexpected separation from me had transformed our idealized 'fusion' from an unreal 'oneness' into an insurmountable abyss. Giulia refused to take her coat off, screaming as if terrified and she covered her face with it, while trying frantically to stick her hair into her nose and noisily sucking her thumb, without ever looking at me. After I interpreted at length her fear of me, she came into the playroom, sat down at the small table, and immediately pointed to a small hole in it, asking, 'What is this? . . . ' in a frightened tone of voice, sucking her thumb as she spoke, all the time avoiding looking at me. When I pointed out to her how she had to be completely wrapped up, closing every possible hole, including her nose, she said, 'I have to be completely wrapped up . . . ', and covered her face even more. When I said to her that even the sight of me or my voice seemed to upset her, she replied, 'Your voice comes from the outside . . . it upsets me . . . I want to be left alone . . . I don't want to hear any noise any more . . . ' Her capacity to deny the reality outside seemed very strong indeed, and Giulia spent the remainder of her session completely wrapped up in her coat and asleep, apparently totally impervious to any comment I made.

During the following sessions, and for quite some time, Giulia seemed more and more terrified. She spent her sessions completely wrapped up in her coat, she stuck her hair into her nose, she sucked her thumb desperately and never even glanced at me. Whenever I spoke, she screamed. Her sessions, my words, and my room seemed to represent not only a terrifying and unbearable outside, but also a setting and a place that deprived her of all the pleasures that otherwise compulsively filled her life. In the bareness of my playroom, she found no food, no smells, no tastes, no sounds, no things to touch and voluptuously enjoy. It is impossible to report any of these sessions in detail, filled as they were just with piercing cries and endless shrieks. Each time I had the impression of witnessing a terrifying withdrawal crisis brought about by abstinence from some powerful drug, while Giulia screamed frantically, 'I want something to eat . . . I want a Coke . . . a Bounty . . . a Mars bar . . . a hot-dog . . . some bread . . . I have to have something to eat . . . give me something please . . . ' Then after more shrieks, 'I want my mother's hair in my nose . . . I want my old house . . . I want to sleep . . . I want some sweets . . . ', and then, sweating and in total panic, 'Give me something . . . anything, please . . . ' Finding nothing else she grabbed some paper and hid it inside her coat, looking like some crazed drunkard stealing the first even remotely alcoholic thing he sees from the crowded shelves of a supermarket. My faith in my capacity to help her reached a low ebb in those days: I had the impression that unless Giulia felt, and indeed was, wrapped up inside some kind of substitute uterine wall within which she could instantly and constantly satisfy her addiction to pleasure and food, she was simply going to fall to pieces and disintegrate.

Yet somehow we survived and gradually my presence and my voice ceased to represent a terrifying outside filled only with persecution and pain.

Gradually, the interior of my room came to represent yet another sheltered and padded inside and for quite a while I was probably perceived as no more than a pleasurable semi-inanimate component of this sheltered world. In the inside Giulia seemed free to enjoy all the sensuous pleasures that formed such an essential component of her life.

Very soon Giulia's sessions took on the quality of elaborate schools of *haute cuisine*. Giulia used any possible container to prepare what she called delicious roasts, tasty stews, varied and elaborate first courses, desserts and cheeses from every possible corner of the earth and of every possible kind, and I must say that this was quite an unusual therapeutic experience for me. My voice, by now considered quite pleasant, seemed to have little more than the function of a glass of port after a six-course meal or that final touch of spice on a carefully prepared titbit.

The session reported below is the first of a rather long series of sessions with this peculiar 'flavour'.

Giulia: first session – summary

Giulia, in collusion with her parents, comes well-equipped with all sorts of sweets and foods. I had never before seen a pair of eight-pocketed dungarees and least of all a pair of eight-pocketed dungarees filled with every imaginable kind of food. Giulia blushes as she sees me, as if I had caught her red-handed. Her father seems rather embarrassed, and justifies his giving in by saying, 'We have to survive somehow . . .' All this session in fact seems to show how food and the constant thought of it play an important role in Giulia's survival. Once plunged 'in', Giulia now feels 'no need', as her needs seem to be instantly satisfied. Giulia's voluptuousness seems evident throughout, she seems really 'crazy' about food, and the session is soon transformed into a real culinary feast.

My function seems purely marginal in it. My interpretations are 'tasted' like food and I have the peculiar counter-transference experience of feeling equated to a good chicken broth or a cream cake. My words are easily and voluptuously sucked in and compared to sweets or the refreshing ice in a cool drink. I feel no more animated in this session than a kind of placental background (Grotstein 1981) to be licked voluptuously and at will. One cannot help being reminded of her licking feasts when floating comfortably inside the womb. In this situation I find it very difficult to keep my interpretations at the right level and depth. Not that this seems to make much difference to Giulia, busy as she is imagining her 'feast'.

When the door-bell rings near the end, Giulia somehow puts 'a lid' on it and tries to deny this unpleasant reminder of the outside by retreating even more into the all-absorbing act of cooking. She starts preparing a 'nice risotto', which normally takes at least twenty minutes to cook. In the end, when she really has to go and face the outside, as a last resort she tries to retreat inside her drawer, though she realizes that she is probably too big for it. Some distant fears seem to emerge now, buried perhaps in her perinatal past, as she is afraid that both she and the container that should keep her 'in' might break, causing the end of them both. Again one can't help being reminded of her past and in particular of her mother's desperate cries during the delivery, 'Please help me . . . she will never come out . . .', and her fears that they were both going to die, though clearly there can be no tangible proof of how these two distant events could be still linked in time. As they are leaving, however, her father tells me that Giulia is beginning to feel better in the outside and has at long last been able to go out of her house.

Giulia: first session – detailed report

Giulia arrives punctually with her father and I hear her chatting merrily with him. When I open the door she smiles at me, though she blushes slightly and lowers her eyes without looking at me. I notice that she is holding a bag full of rice in her hands.

Her father says to her, 'Show Sandra how many pockets you have in your dungarees . . . eight pockets . . . each filled with something different to eat . . . bread . . . sweets . . . biscuits . . . chocolates . . . crisps . . . ' Probably he notices my amazed face, and adds, 'We have to survive somehow . . . she is very pleased to come now . . . she keeps repeating: if only I could fly there . . . '

Giulia says to him, 'You can go now . . . no need for you to stay . . . ' Her father goes out.

Giulia comes into the playroom. She takes a half-opened packet of chewing-gum out of one of her numerous pockets and shows it to me, saying, 'They are called crazy chewing-gum . . . they tickle your tongue when you chew them . . . ', and she shows me how she puts some of the chewing-gum on her hand and licks it with a voluptuous expression on her face. I say that she is showing me how she is really 'crazy' about food. When she wants to lick or eat something she has to have it instantly at hand. Like when she wants to see me and would like to fly so as to be here at once.

She smiles, and says, 'You have known me for a very long time . . .' I say that I seem to know her tastes.

She goes on licking her chewing-gum, and says, 'I will have a drink now . . . and then do the dishes . . . no need for you to come in the kitchen too . . . ', and she goes to the sink and drinks some water. I say that she seems to be using every possible excuse, even doing the dishes, to fly to the kitchen as soon as she can. She laughs, and says, 'I like what you said . . . it's true . . . my mother believes me when I say that I have to clean something . . . and instead I eat . . . '

I say that she liked what I said, she found it funny and tasty. She says, 'Your words are sweets to me . . . ' I say that I am not allowed to do much cleaning with her though. She says, 'No need . . . '. She takes a sweet and eats it. I say that she feels 'no need' for me, my words are sweets, and she can have plenty of those without having to wait for me.

She rolls up her sleeves, and starts looking for her hens inside the drawer, then she puts them in her cup and fills it with water. She says, 'Now I will prepare a nice chicken soup . . . these chickens first . . . then some butter . . . and a pinch of salt . . . some herbs . . . celery . . . carrots . . . an onion . . . a couple of potatoes . . . that should do . . . let's put it on the stove . . . ' She seems almost able to taste the things she describes, and she licks her lips frequently.

I say that all she can think of is food and I am just a silly chicken to be boiled. She says, 'A good one, though . . . ', but then somehow she doesn't seem to listen to any of my words any more and seems very absorbed in what she is doing. Soon the session seems transformed into a kind of cordon-bleu cookery course and the room into a kitchen filled with all sorts of food, like a kind of Babette's feast. She says, 'I just love cooking . . . now let's prepare a good roast . . . actually one of the chickens could be roasted . . . here is another pan . . . some salt . . . butter again . . . rosemary . . . and why not a pinch of mustard too . . . that should add a good flavour to it . . . ' Then she pulls out her drawer, and says, 'This is my fridge . . . ' She puts every possible container in it, and says, 'Lovely, now it's really full . . . ' and looks at it with a delighted expression on her face. I say that she feels no need, emptiness or void, when her head and her pockets, as well as her stomach are full of food, but she also becomes very cold with me, she sends me away, as she did with her father before.

She says, 'I love ice . . . particularly if it is in a soft drink . . . now this is milk . . . let's keep it in the fridge for tomorrow . . . the fridge must always be open . . . so I can have access to it when I want . . . just plunge in . . . ' I say that she plunges 'in' and forgets about tomorrow and keeping things cold. She says, 'I have all I want in my fridge . . . ' She takes a cup and puts it on the table, saying, 'This is a cream cake . . . never forget the dessert . . . here is some chocolate too . . . delicious after coffee . . . here is some cream . . . to go with the coffee . . . and on the cake . . . as a decoration perhaps . . . and here is some liqueur . . . and oh, we mustn't forget about bread . . . I must have some bread in here too . . . I don't want to have to go out and buy it . . . ' I say that she seems to have completely forgotten about me and all the things that exist in the outside.

The door-bell rings. Her father has arrived some ten minutes early. Giulia looks annoyed. She makes sure that the door of the playroom is well closed. She says, 'I am too comfortable in my kitchen . . . ' I say that she is too comfortable when she plunges 'in' and feels inside, she just wants to remain inside and any reminder of the outside annoys her.

She looks back at her chicken, and says, 'Now we put a lid on it . . . raise the gas a bit . . . very good . . . ' I say that she doesn't get burnt when she is inside. She just puts a lid on everything that is hurting her and feels excited and hot at the thought of food.

She takes the Plasticine and starts cutting it to bits. She says, 'This is what I need now . . . some delicious vegetables . . . I will just brown them a bit . . . and then a good blow out . . . let's put a lid on them too . . . ' I say that she is trying to cover the hurt that she feels when she has to go out. She knows that the door-bell just rang. She takes her bag with the rice, and says, 'Now a good risotto . . . ' I say that we have to finish. She seems very reluctant to go. She looks at her drawer looking almost frightened, and says, 'I could try fitting in there . . . ', then, 'But what if it breaks? . . . we could both break . . . the drawer and I . . . that could be the end for me and for it . . . ' I say that she knows she is too big now to be inside, her time has come to go out.

I open the door. She goes towards her father and hugs him. He says to me, 'She is much better now . . . she went out with some friends on Sunday . . . she doesn't find it so difficult leaving the house at long last . . . ' Then he notices that her face is all flushed, and says, 'Gosh, you must have had an exciting time! . . . ' He says goodbye to me and they go out.

Soon Giulia's sessions became even too 'exciting', as they resembled real orgies more than just simple 'feasts'. Her highly sensuous nature seemed to explode, and other pleasures, in particular of a sexual-masturbatory kind, became prominent during them. Giulia seemed to drown herself in wild parties of sex, food, and drink. Giulia also began to appear for her sessions dressed a bit like a whore, with dark sun-glasses, black transparent tights, a revealing mini and a long chocolate cigarette constantly hanging from her protruding lips. Her obesity added a sad note of obscenity to all this, and Giulia, like her mother when I first saw her, looked like an old-fashioned whore, as often portrayed in Fellini's films.

Giulia: second session – summary

The session that follows is one of the first belonging to this orgiastic spell. Giulia appears dressed and behaving like a loose woman, smoking, pacing the room, and swinging her hips as if she were waiting for her next client. Contrary to the session reported above, Giulia now seems much less 'innocent' and much more determined in her behaving like a 'pig'. As she says, 'I am beyond caring now . . . ', but she seems not to be beyond being aware of what she does. At some point, when blushing after my comment on her growing too fast and on her readiness to perform all sorts of 'illicit' acts, she seems to realize that I have caught her at fault. But that doesn't stop her from going ahead and filling herself with drunken excitement all the time, as she says, 'Never empty, but full . . . '

There are no limits, 'no doors', to her getting drunk with excitement now. Her obscenity is quite evident. Sex and food, though, seem to be confused together and are 'both nice'. Not surprisingly 'oral sex' seems to be particularly attractive for Giulia, as when she licks her 'grissino' and her pencil as if she were performing an expert act of fellatio, till the imaginary penis grows 'big' and 'hard'. Then Giulia is really 'beyond caring now', and like a drunkard on a binge she is determined to drink more and more, without any restraint, beyond all caring about the following day. As she says after belching, 'I am a real pig now', and she goes as far as symbolically emptying her bladder on my floor. When gone so 'far', Giulia is not only full of drunken pleasure and excitement: her sensuous nature seems to be completely satisfied, but also once more and once again Giulia seems to succeed in blurring the outside. As she says, 'You don't exist when I have gone too far . . . I am alone in here . . . you are too blurred . . . '

Yet towards the end of the session Giulia seems rather frightened and asks, 'How can I come down? . . . how can I come out? . . . ', and somehow I seem to succeed in sobering her up. When she sees her mother she seems quite frightened about the blindness that so much excitement might entail, as she says, 'The cows have lost their eyes . . . '

Looking back at this session I cannot help being reminded once more of Giulia's behaviour at various stages during her past. Though these links may well seem, and in fact may be, too far-fetched, her voluptuousness seems to date back a long time and was probably already heralded by her sensuous licking inside the womb as well as by her inclination in those distant days to keep her hands almost constantly between her legs, something that both I and the obstetricians probably felt too incredulous and inhibited to comment upon. Her voluptuous licking of an imaginary penis also reminds me of the days when Giulia incessantly licked the cord.

Then, when Giulia starts getting 'drunk', I am also reminded not only of the glimpse I had of her mother's house, full of empty bottles and unemptied ash-trays but also of Giulia's later 'sensuous feasts'. Her mother's comments also come to my mind, when she used to call Giulia a 'little whore' and say that Giulia was not only mad about food, but was also 'crazy about men'. These associations, though, must remain in the realm of suggestive, but hypothetical, links.

Giulia: second session – detailed report

Giulia and her father arrive a few minutes late. She is wearing a red leather jacket, a white mini-skirt and a pair of big, dark sun-glasses. She is holding a small white leather bag which she keeps moving back and forth as she walks towards the playroom swinging her hips, with a chocolate cigarette dangling from her slightly made-up lips.

Her father says, 'I am sorry we are late . . . the train was late . . . but she has been very good . . . no complaints . . . she has been running fast

... you can stop running now! ... only she chooses to dress as she likes ... she hates prohibitions of any kind ... and something always dangling from her mouth ... ' He waves her goodbye and goes out.

Giulia doesn't turn round and swings straight into the playroom, then starts pacing back and forth as if she were a miniature harlot walking the streets. She says, 'I keep smoking now ... I like it very much ... ' I say that she seems to be running too fast today and behaving as if she were grown up and ready to disobey all rules. She blushes slightly and looks away from me, as if she had been found out.

She takes her cups, and says, 'I will fill them now ... they must never be empty, but full ... ', then she puts her cups on the edge of the table, saying, 'They are better here than in the fridge ... there is a door on the fridge ... ' I say that she likes to have no doors and no prohibitions. She never wants to feel empty, but always full.

She sits on the table with her legs wide open looking rather obscene. She inserts a finger inside her cup and licks it. Then she puts her hands between her legs while moving her tongue over her lips. She looks very excited and her face is all red now. I say that she's filling herself with prohibited excitement now. She puts her finger in her mouth and then almost inside her vagina, saying, 'This or this, they are both nice ... ', and she laughs. I say that eating or rubbing her vagina are the same for her, in both ways she gets very excited and hot.

She lies on the table with her legs wide open, then takes a 'grissino' from her bag and starts licking it as if she were performing an expert act of fellatio. She laughs. I say that she really seems addicted to speed now. She says, 'This is nothing ... ' I say that there are no limits, no doors to her getting excited. She empties all the contents of her drawer on to the floor, and says, 'Who cares ... I am beyond caring now ... ' I say that she seems too drunk to stop now, she throws away all that she cares about.

She drinks from all her containers saying, 'This is wine ... this is beer ... this is liqueur ... ' and laughs, looking as if she were more and more drunk. I say that she is drunk with excitement now and she seems determined to have a binge of drink, excitement, and food. She says, 'Now I will give myself a nice present you know ... ', and she takes a pencil and pretends to be putting it inside her mouth again, but then says, 'Too small ... ' and wraps the pencil all up in a scarf she has in her bag and then laughs, saying, 'It's big enough now ... it's all right ... ' I say that she gets all excited at the thought of making the penis grow all big in her mouth. She replies, 'Big and hard ... ' I say that I am made to feel totally impotent and unable to stop her now.

She pours the cup of water on the floor and laughs. I say that she is provoking me now by peeing on the floor. She belches, and says, 'I am a real pig now! . . . ' She drinks some more water from another cup, saying, 'I just go on drinking! . . . ' I say that she is really determined to get drunk with excitement. She laughs, 'It's wine . . . it's wine! . . . ' I say that she's behaving like a real pig and she knows it.

She pours another cup of water on the floor. I say that perhaps it is time to sober up before she finds herself throwing up on the floor. She says, 'I can do what I like when I am in here . . . ' I say that she seems to ignore that I am there to stop her from going too far. She says, 'You don't exist when I am too far gone . . . I am alone in here . . . you get all blurred . . . everyone else does too . . . ' But then she suddenly looks worried, and says, 'How can I come down? . . . how can I come out? . . . ' I say that she is now asking me to help her to sober up.

I help her to come down from the table. She goes and looks at her animals. She looks worried, and says, 'The cows have no eyes . . . I thought they did before . . . but they seem to have lost them now . . . yet they had them . . . ' I say that she is afraid of going blind when she gets so drunk with excitement and behaves like a pig or a cow. I must keep my eyes open for her. She says, 'You have got big eyes . . . ' The door-bell rings. Her mother has come to fetch her and Giulia runs towards her saying, 'The cows have lost their eyes . . . '

Yet during the following months Giulia began to open her eyes, and some guilt began to appear as well as a growing concern for the objects and people populating her life and she no longer seemed 'past caring' about herself and other people.

Though Giulia often seemed to move and float almost as if in tune with my interpretations, as if she were still at one with me, gradually she began to perceive me more as a separate entity belonging to the world outside.

Her drives too became more symbolized and Giulia now spent many of her sessions drawing big whales, hot-air balloons and huge planes which she dreamed would transport her through the doors of perception into distant and fantastic realms. Soon the whales were filled with small dots and circles, the other children, or 'eggs', living inside, all bearing the name of Gerardo, the hated usurper of her space. Giulia now began to express her jealousy towards him more graphically and less impulsively. It must be remembered that she had actually tried to strangle him during the consultation with me. Her attacks were now simply expressed on paper, as if she were a lawyer writing petition upon petition for some unforgivable wrong.

Parallel to all this the inside began to represent not only her 'paradise lost', her 'messy and small' but much beloved old home, but also and mainly a potentially deadly trap. Her agoraphobic fears were now replaced by claustrophobic anxieties, and often Giulia asked me to keep the window slightly open for her, otherwise she felt 'trapped in the inside', just as about three years before her mother had felt trapped while giving birth to her.

A few months later on Giulia, who by now seemed to find it natural to go out for walks and to go to nursery-school, began to emerge in her sessions as a less regressed child compared to the blind, animalesque figures of her 'cows' represented in the session above. Using an Aristotelian analogy she seemed to have taken on a more 'human' and less 'animal soul'.

The session reported below, one of the last sessions with her, takes place soon after a holiday. I was not aware at the time that Giulia was going to stop her treatment within a short time.

Giulia: third session – summary

Though Giulia still comes well-equipped with chewing-gum, some progress seems evident throughout. While looking back at her blind and deaf horse, Giulia seems to reflect on her 'old' previous state, which she calls a 'nonsense' now. Giulia seems to be able to 'repress' her old state and her distant past by pushing it 'back' into the unconscious of her mind and by moving on, as she says, to 'something else'. Giulia now seems to have a past and to be less at one with her old state. She also has a past and a history with me, and she wants to look back at it and be reminded of her start. Her whales and hot-air balloons can now be looked at without her being carried away by them. Giulia seems more able to look at her feelings with a certain detachment and insight, without being swamped by them. She can also sit next to me without 'gulping' me and my words down and without instantly having to get 'in'. Though she says that 'enough is enough', she can contemplate the idea of other children taking up her much-beloved old space, something that was vehemently denied during her consultation with me and during many of the sessions that were to follow it.

Yet Giulia's past is still very recent, and, while I was not aware of it at this stage, she probably already knew that she was not going to have much future with me. As so often happens towards the end of an analysis, she thinks back to the time when her brother was born and how this caused her to break down like an 'egg'. Her shell still seems quite fragile and can 'easily break'. Giulia says quite clearly that she would need more time with me: the time we have had has not been 'enough'. Her breakdown and her falling to pieces were very real for her and she still wears a 'real scar' which has not 'faded away'.

Though Giulia (and her family) are miles away from any of the sophistications of psychoanalytical language and I have never mentioned the word 'transference' to her, her saying, amazingly, 'I am making a transference on to you . . . ', seems pretty real too, as her transference seems much more intense and much more human now. I do not feel like some insignificant object in the background any more and my 'outline', the perception Giulia has of me as a separate entity, also seems much more real to me. One could say that Giulia is beginning to show signs of having really seen the 'light' now. But our separation still hurts her too much, and at the end Giulia goes back to her licking and to tasting her beloved chewing-gum. Yet, now, she also seems able to accept her mother telling her that she will have to wait till she gets home for something to eat. Her mother too seems to have acquired some strength, when she says, to her, 'I am not your personal bar . . . ', something that I was made to feel she indeed was for quite a while when Giulia simply got 'in' and helped herself to her drinks and her food.

Giulia: third session – detailed report

Giulia arrives punctually with her mother, and when I open the door she comes straight into the playroom after waving goodbye to her. She is holding a comic in her hands and I notice some chewing-gum sticking out of her pockets. Her mother comments, 'She is so pleased to come here now . . . she is delighted when she leaves the house . . . ' Then she goes out.

Giulia smiles at me and goes straight to her drawer. She looks carefully at her animals, then picks up the horse, and says, 'He is without eyes . . . he cannot see . . . probably he is deaf too . . . but why? . . . it's nonsense to be blind . . . this must be an old horse . . . '

I say that she looked at me before, and she smiled. Her mother told me that she likes going out now. She no longer feels blind and deaf to the outside like the old horse, having to live all the time locked inside. She says, 'I went out to the park yesterday . . . ', then she drops her 'old' horse, and says, 'Let's leave this old horse now . . . so we can move on to something else . . . '

She takes her folder with all her old drawings inside. She says, 'I want to look at them again . . . come and sit near me . . . can you remind me what they were? . . . ' I say that she wants me to remind her of how she felt before, when she first came to see me. She looks at her first drawing. She says, 'These are a lot of dots . . . all inside a big circle . . . like Gerardo inside mummy's tummy . . . ' and she giggles, then

194

adds, 'I can remember that now . . . I was in a state . . . ' I say that once she feels better she can also remember her past and what happened when Gerardo was born and she went blind with rage.

She looks at her other drawings, saying, 'This is a hot–air balloon . . . this is a whale . . . this is a dolphin . . . these are some small penguins . . . and these are some eggs . . . this is just a mess . . . ' I say that it is a mess if there are more eggs and more dots; if her mother becomes as big as a whale again and other children are born. She is beginning to accept Gerardo now, but other children could be too much.

She says, 'I like Gerardo now . . . but enough is enough . . . my mummy said that too the other day . . . ', and she starts pretending to hit my head. I say that she is hammering me because I too should get it well into my head, 'No more babies, enough is enough'. She smiles.

She says, 'I will draw something else now . . . here are some small eggs . . . and here is a hen . . . she is quite big and fat . . . I will colour it well . . . oh, my! . . . it's just a big mess . . . '

I say that it is really a mess for her when I become big and other eggs are inside. She says, 'Eggs can easily break . . . I was an egg too . . . that was a while ago . . . but not too long ago . . . ' I say that she broke like an egg when Gerardo was born and she still feels fragile now.

She goes and gets some paper which, at the beginning of her treatment, perhaps during the first session even, she had used to wrap some Plasticine in. She takes her scissors and opens it smiling. She seems surprised and perhaps also slightly frightened not to find anything inside. She says, 'It's empty! . . . who has done this? . . . it was here . . . how could it possibly have fallen out? . . . it's all in pieces now . . . it should have remained inside for longer . . . '

I say that she feels she should remain protected by me for a longer time, otherwise she is afraid that she may fall to pieces again.

She shows me a scar on her arm, and says, 'This is real . . . a real scar . . . it will never fade away . . . ' I say that she was really scarred when Gerardo was born and he took her place. Her going to pieces felt very real to her. She says, 'Never mind . . . let's not think about that . . . I will get my comic now . . . there are some stickers inside . . . then I also have some chewing-gum . . . '

I say that she transfers on to her chewing-gum and on her presents all her scars and forgets about them. She starts chewing her gum and using her tracing paper. She says, 'I am transferring it to you . . . ', and she gives me her paper. I say that she easily transfers her worries and pains, provided she has something in her mouth, but she also wants me to know how real her pain was in the past. She says, 'I am making a transference on to you . . . the background paper is not so important now . . . what is important is the real outline . . . you can begin to see it well . . . particularly if you look at it in the light . . . ' She asks me, 'Do you by any chance have a chocolate or a sweet today? . . . '

The door-bell rings. She seems reluctant to go. Then she goes out, and I hear her asking her mother if she has a chocolate or a sweet. Her mother says, 'I am not your personal bar . . . you can wait till we get back home . . . ', and they go out waving to me.

A few days after this session Mrs A phoned saying that her husband was unwell and it had become too much of a strain for them to bring Giulia to see me. Giulia, in any case, according to them, was much better now. Then Mr A had to be admitted to hospital, and less than two months later we were in fact obliged to stop Giulia's treatment.

Her mother has continued to keep in touch with me. Apparently Giulia has really improved in the world outside. Many of her fears seem in fact to have 'faded away' and, according to Mrs A, 'the world is her oyster now . . . ', her metaphor being always in keeping with the realm of food and with an added hint of champagne.

It may well be that Giulia's shell has simply enlarged a bit, transforming the entire world surrounding her into yet another protective and comfortable niche, but at least now she seems to be able to enjoy the company of other children at nursery-school and seems happy to go out as well as moving with her old joy within the walls of her house. I am also told that her father's health seems to have improved slightly.

During her last session, putting aside for a moment pans and casseroles, Giulia said to me, 'You understand me . . . you have known me since birth . . . you know what I am like . . . I will always like eating . . . I love food . . . we all have our tastes . . . ', only food now seems to be less of an obsession for her and Giulia has even lost quite a bit of weight. On the other hand, I am sure that Giulia was right in saying what she said and in maintaining that she is what she is and will always love food and will always be a rather heavy eater as well as what one would call a *bonne vivante*. We all have our tastes. Her propensity for sensuous enjoyment and for food may well take on a defensive quality at times, but it is also very much part of her 'nature'. Her strong tastes seem to date well back to before her birth.

CASE NO. 2 – TINA-VERA (two years and three months old)

A longer version of this case report was first read at a meeting of the British Psycho-Analytical Society on 7 May 1985 and was subsequently published in the *International Review of Psycho-Analysis* (1988) (15: 73–81).

Tina-Vera (often called by her parents just Vera) started analysis with me when she was two years and three months old. She still could not walk and indeed she could hardly stand. She looked flabby and disjointed, and in order to move around she used to crawl on the ground like a lizard or a snake. Numerous and thorough neurological investigations had repeatedly excluded any neurological cause. Together with her motor retardation she also showed many other psychical symptoms. I will come back to this a bit later, just mentioning a few for the moment: she sought isolation, she avoided any physical contact, she seemed to ignore people around her and so on. She was therefore diagnosed as psychotic, and referred to me for analysis by a neuropsychiatrist who knew of my interest in treating young children.

When I saw her parents for an initial interview, they immediately started linking her first problems to the time of her stay inside the womb – something apparently ignored or at least not reported by my colleague. Tina-Vera was a wanted child. I do not know whether her pregnancy had been planned or not, but certainly both parents seemed very pleased to have another child, as they already had a son of four. The first months of pregnancy were apparently 'easy' and Mrs H reported no sickness or any other trouble: 'I was feeling well and my life went on as before . . . ' She was also visited monthly by her gynaecologist who thought that the baby was growing well. Mrs H's first worries began around the fifth month of pregnancy when she knew, from her previous experience, that she should have begun feeling the baby's first movements. 'I began to worry . . . I felt nothing at all . . . I still remembered very clearly how Leo [her son] used to move and kick a lot . . . in fact he still does now . . . he is always bouncing around and says, that he wants to become an athlete . . . but with her nothing at all . . . '

As time went by her worries increased, but in spite of numerous check-ups, including ultrasounds, nothing could be found and, apart from stillness, there was no other indication of danger for the child's life and development.

When the ninth month of pregnancy elapsed, since Tina-Vera was already quite big and slightly overdue, the gynaecologist decided to induce birth. Then something, indeed, went wrong during the delivery and only an almost miraculous intuition and intervention by the midwife saved Tina-Vera from certain death as she was found to have the umbilical cord doubly and tightly knotted around her neck. This is something that it is almost impossible to detect, at present, with ultrasounds. (The cord can often be seen as a characteristic image if it is at an angle. If knotted around the neck of the fetus it would be almost indistinguishable from other soft tissues of that region, particularly during a routine examination lasting only a few minutes.) It is also impossible to know whether her stillness inside the womb was due to the danger of strangulation should she have moved, or to some kind of preference for lying still while being wrapped by the cord. (In the course of ultrasonographic observations the fetus can frequently be seen playing with the cord. Strangulation therefore is caused actively, though probably accidentally, by the fetus.)

What remains undeniable is the fact that Tina-Vera's birth must have been an extremely traumatic, excruciatingly painful event. Whatever the intra-uterine experience, certainly her birth did not make the transition to this world an easy or pleasant matter for her. As her mother said, 'She must have been terrified . . . she was born with her hair standing on end as if with reason . . . '

Nor was life easy for her during the first month outside. Tina-Vera's neck remained swollen for months and her face and her eyes infused with blood. For a fortnight she was kept under an oxygen tent, as apparently her autonomous breathing was extremely difficult and probably also extremely painful. Tina-Vera was discharged from hospital when she was about one month old.

Once outside Tina-Vera met with what I am inclined to regard as two basically good parents. The economic background of the family though was a rather modest one, and both parents had to work full-time from the start in order to support their growing family and their respective parents, who lived nearby. Because her mother had to work, Tina-Vera was never breast-fed, and initially she was left mostly in the care of her two grandmothers, who took turns looking after her. Though her mother soon gave up working full-time in order to be with her, it is likely that her conspicuous initial absence also had a strong impact on Tina-Vera at the time.

According to her mother, Tina-Vera spent the first five months of her life practically completely inert and apparently asleep. She seemed to react to nothing and nothing could wake her up. Even when being fed, she kept her mouth open and motionless with milk dribbling profusely out of it. Yet Tina-Vera mysteriously continued to grow and put on weight. Then when she was about five months old she seemed to wake up and spent the following five months screaming non-stop, night and day, as if terrified. But it was particularly the slowness of her motor development that worried her parents and pushed them repeatedly to seek medical opinions about her, but even the most organically minded doctors found no apparent or obvious organic cause.

When Tina-Vera was eventually referred to me she could only move round like a snake, and like a drunken one at that. She also looked, and probably still does to a certain extent, like a strange creature from another primitive world. Her head was big, her nose flat and dilated, her teeth pointed and small and horribly blackened and eroded by decay. Her eyes looked either frightened or completely dull. She seemed to ignore people and always tried to keep away from them. She showed no affection towards her parents or her grandparents. By then Tina-Vera was beginning to talk, but her speech too had a strange, non-communicative quality. She went on and on with what sounded like totally incomprehensible and endless monologues made of bits of disjointed or oddly fused words. All she seemed to want was to be left alone in her strange and solitary world.

Unfortunately, in Tina-Vera's case I was left with little opportunity to test my understanding as she always was very unresponsive to my interpretative work. This is also one of the reasons why it is almost impossible to reproduce any of her sessions in detail.

What immediately struck me in analysis was how Tina-Vera seemed constantly to re-live her past imprisonment and entanglement inside the womb. Particularly at the beginning of her analysis Tina-Vera always came to her sessions with a long heavy chain tightly doubled around her neck, a chain given to her by her parents. Often her dummy was hanging from it. Her parents told me that Tina-Vera 'lived with it' and 'couldn't part from it', though they made no connections with her previous life. She would then pass from her mother's hand to mine without any interruption, as if still tied to a long rope that she could not or would not let go. She also always came to her sessions holding some object or toy which she pressed horizontally against her navel. As her mother said, 'She can't do without it . . . she always has to hold something in her hand . . . '

Once inside the playroom she would often continue to hold on to some rope-like object such as the belt of my overall or particularly the cord of my curtain, which she used for all sorts of complicated windings around her face and her neck. For a long time Tina-Vera never used any toy except the string and the Sellotape which she had immediately grasped during one of her first sessions and had then proceeded cleverly to unwind and entangle again around her face and her neck. Then, again, at the end of each session, Tina-Vera left either holding my hand as before or the curtain cord till she reached her mother's hands without any break.

Apart from using my hand as an appendix of her body, not differentiated from the numerous cord-like objects which she almost constantly held, Tina-Vera seemed to ignore me completely, as if I didn't exist for her. Once inside the room she would immediately retreat into one of her interminable monologues made of incomprehensible, broken, and oddly fused words, while lying or, later on, standing immobile in a distant corner of the room staring at her hands or at the wall. Or else, all the time monologuing, she would retire under the table, curl up in the fetal position, and soon fall asleep. Her favourite hiding-place was always my curtain, which she used as a divide and a screen from the outside world. Once inside it, apart from talking to herself non-stop or using the cord for all sorts of complicated wrappings, she would also spend hours in a trance-like, nirvanic state seeming totally oblivious of my presence outside.

Tina-Vera's withdrawn state often seemed not only charged with nirvanic oblivion or with an active search for isolation and deaf-blindedness towards the world, but also appeared at times strongly erotized and hypersensual. Tina-Vera spent hours playing with her hair, her tongue, and her hands, endlessly caressing, touching, and stroking them, and while doing this she often seemed enraptured as if in a kind of voluptuous dream. Her voice then took on a sexy tone and her movements became like the motions of a hard-core film. From behind the curtain I could hear all sorts of extremely realistic 'boudoir' laughters and sighs which made me feel like an unwilling spectator at an improvised peep-show. The main actor of all her sex scenes was always the cord of my curtain, which she treated as a cord and a penis at the same time. She wrapped it sensuously around her neck, she licked it frenziedly with her tongue, she inserted it deeply inside her throat and between her legs. But it was particularly the wrapping of it around her neck (something that she did frequently and seemed almost addicted to) that seemed to rouse the most intense orgiastic frenzy in her. Other cord-like objects such as the string and the Sellotape or a long roll of Plasticine, which she made by joining different strips, were, at different times, all used for the same purpose.

All this, as well as providing a source of endless and intense pleasure, and isolating her from the world, seemed to serve the purpose of sheltering her from something akin to, yet I think much more primitive than, ordinary jealousy. What seemed intolerable to Tina-Vera was the fact or the thought of something else occupying her physical uterine space, be it a penis or another object such as the body of another child. During her orgiastic scenes Tina-Vera seemed right 'in', watching, participating, and orchestrating every detail of a kind of primeval scene. Her sensuality was therefore also used defensively so as not to feel outside and to combat the thought of some other concrete object occupying her physical space.

Being outside while something else was inside was absolutely intolerable for her, and this fact had to be annihilated or denied. Tina-Vera found it particularly intolerable waiting in the waiting room. She banged and screamed at my door, and often as soon as I opened it I found her already rushing right inside. Once she was inside she usually ignored me, and I often felt that my playroom was concretely equated with my inside. At other times, as soon as she entered the waiting room (which is not illuminated from the outside) Tina-Vera immediately switched off the light making it as dark as the darkest cave, and then, having annihilated her perception of being outside, sat there silent and immobile usually in some sheltered corner of the room. I could often hear her mother saying things like 'But why on earth with all the space you have here, do you always have to end up in some kind of hole?' Sometimes, if the wait had been particularly long (coming from out of town they often arrived early), or else when approaching some longer break, once inside she would often push her head violently between my legs, screaming, this time clearly, 'Open!' or 'I want to get inside'.

Whenever the phantasy of living inside occupying all my space proved to be just a phantasy and even for a second Tina-Vera felt outside or could not deny my separate existence, her usual reactions were fury or terror and often a mixture of the two. Her fury was accompanied by sudden kicking, biting, and scratching fits during which Tina-Vera looked like a wild and savage beast. Often her attacks ended suddenly in a superior laughter and then Tina-Vera quickly withdrew into one of her favourite hiding places and again ignored me.

Her terror of coming out and of being outside was particularly evident at the beginning of her analysis. At times my door, every tiny hole or any crack on the wall seemed suddenly to terrify her like the sight of an abyss. Passing through my door at the end of a session could be accompanied by strangulated screams. The sight of a hole on my table could make her suddenly choke and withdraw in terror, while searching frantically for the safe and familiar wrapping of the curtain. Even defecating and urinating gave the impression of being equated with birth, and Tina-Vera usually tried to resist these physiological needs by straining and squeezing her legs, while screaming and sweating profusely, looking like a woman in labour left alone in the coldness of a delivery room.

Sometimes her usual perspective seemed reversed, and my dark waiting room became a safe and peaceful inside, while I had the impression that my room came to be equated with a terrifying outside filled with unbearable persecution, to which Tina-Vera often reacted with a sudden deep sleep reminiscent of the deep sleep of her first five months of life.

Nor did all the dangers come from living outside or the only safety and pleasure from living inside. Tina-Vera in fact seemed to be caught in a sort of impossible trap: if she came outside she risked dying, but if she remained inside she died just the same. At times the inside of my room seemed to become a deadly trap, the inside of my body a mortal device, the womb her prison and her grave. Vera would then try desperately to disentangle herself from the suffocating wrapping of the curtain or the strangling turns of the cord, and when her fears became particularly intense, she would try to stagger out of the room while calling desperately for her otherwise unmentioned parents. Usually, soon after, she was back inside and was back to her complicated and sensuous wrappings with the cord.

There were other ways in which Tina-Vera tried to reproduce both her past entanglement and isolation inside the womb. Her monotonous monologues and solitary activities often made one feel sleepy and bored, or, to quote her mother's words, 'In the end one tends to forget that she is there and everybody leaves her alone . . . ' Often I felt almost resigned to leave her forever inside her private space. On the other hand sometimes one got the strong feeling of such a lucid determination to pursue her aims, that, again to quote her mother's words, 'One feels like strangling her . . . '

Yet Tina-Vera probably made some progress, as by the time she left she could move and walk almost like any other child and was reported to be more affectionate at home. She also looked less alien and strange.

Most of the time though, working with Tina-Vera felt like a lost cause and a hopeless enterprise, as no matter how hard one might try to pull her towards another world, one felt that her attachment to the cord and to the uterine universe was always bound to win in the end.

I do not think it would have been just a matter of time: when Tina-Vera stopped her treatment at the age of seven, her parents having decided to try and send her to school, her attachment to her past was still tenaciously defended by every possible means at her disposal.

CASE NO. 3 – TILDA (two years old)

Tilda, by far one of the most severe cases I have come across in my career, had just turned two a few days before starting 'emergency' analysis with me, her very life seeming to be at stake. Though extremely uncertain about the outcome of any treatment with her, I was nevertheless moved by her parents' despair and by their equally desperate requests that we try psychoanalysis as a last, tenuous hope. Not that her parents seemed to expect any miracle from me; they were just desperate not to leave any stone unturned for their child. Had she lived in another century Tilda would probably have been brought to an exorcist in a last-ditch attempt to free her of the forces that seemed to possess her, and that would have certainly rendered her an ideal candidate to be condemned to the stake.

When her parents came to see me, Tilda looked like a little mummified corpse, with her dried skin sticking to her tiny bones, her sparse hair, her sunken eyes, and thin crooked nose. By then she had completely stopped growing and was rapidly losing any remaining weight. Every possible sort of test and medical treatment had been tried on her, till even her very organic-minded doctors had concluded that 'it must be all in her mind' and had therefore referred her to me. By that time Tilda had not only stopped growing and seemed dreadfully undernourished, but also could barely sit and did not utter any even distantly human sound. Yet Tilda was far from being immobile like a corpse. All the time she seemed animated by crazed, restless, incessant motions, such as twisting her neck, stretching her legs and her arms, rolling her eyes and noisily sucking and smacking her tongue. She could also barely be parted from her mother's body without causing almost inhuman shrieks, massive foaming, and frightening convulsive motions. Because of this she was almost constantly carried around by her mother, looking like some crazed appendage to an otherwise pleasant, though by now distraught and exhausted, person.

Mr and Mrs I, both in their early thirties, though clearly quite worn out, looked like warm-hearted and caring people who were prepared to do anything for their only child.

Tilda's pregnancy had been carefully planned and eagerly wanted by both, yet it had been difficult right from the start. As Mrs I recalled, 'During the whole nine months I simply vomited all the time . . . in fact I even lost weight at some point . . . ' Mrs I, a rather short and plump woman certainly not lacking in appetite, remembered how she vomited in particular all the foods she had always liked: 'It was strange, but I had the impression even then that Tilda didn't want to have anything to do with me, my life and my tastes . . . '

Mrs I also became increasingly worried, as she never felt any movement from her child, 'only after the seventh month, just some slight scratching . . . but otherwise the most total stillness . . . '. Her gynaecologist repeatedly reassured her, saying that the child was growing well and its heart-beat presented no irregularities of any kind. Two rather early scans had shown no apparent anomalies in the placenta or in the child. After nine months, though, Tilda was not born and gave no signs of wanting to be. She remained turned 'upside down', in the podalic version, and since she seemed now rather small, the doctor interpreted this as a sign that probably Mrs H had miscalculated the time when conception had taken place. But when even the tenth month elapsed and Mrs I's amniotic fluid was found to be slightly stained, he decided to intervene by inducing birth. The delivery was then quite precipitate as Tilda apparently was born almost suddenly, in less than an hour, and no complications were derived from her being podalic, 'but this was because she was well-formed, but rather underweight . . . she looked old and like a small mummy . . . all wrinkled and bony as she was . . . almost just as she looks now . . . '. No apparent causes were detected for her being so small for her gestational age (Tilda weighed slightly less than 2.5 kg). 'The placenta seemed normal . . . but of course one never knows . . . who knows what had happened in there . . . we shall never know . . . '

Certainly once born and outside Tilda continued with her total immobility and, as her mother said, 'To begin with she didn't know how to suck . . . I thought that this was something quite natural for a baby . . . but not for her . . . she had no idea that she had to open her mouth . . . and even when it was caught open, the milk would just dribble out . . . ' Tilda would spend her days mostly asleep in what her mother called 'a heavy, impenetrable sleep'. After a fortnight or so Tilda began to open her mouth when given the breast, but then clung to it for hours on end. Since Tilda was so small and was putting on very little weight, Mrs I literally spent her days with her child clinging tenaciously to her breast. Mrs I had to sit there immobile, as any movement of her body seemed to arouse endless screams from her child. Except for her tenacious attachment to the breast, any other living object in the world outside seemed to be completely ignored by Tilda. As her mother said, 'It took her months before opening her eyes slightly . . . not that she seemed to like what she saw much . . . ' Tilda mostly seemed to keep her eyes closed and generally avoided other people's gaze. Apart from sight, any tiny awakening of her other senses seemed equally unbearable: 'Whenever she heard a sound, she would scream as if she had been lacerated by it . . . ' Mrs I's diet also had to be kept monotonously the same, as she had noticed that Tilda just clung to the breast without sucking from it if she ate anything different, thereby presumably causing a change in the flavour of her milk.

When Tilda was six months old her first teeth began to appear, and soon after her mother had to wean her. With weaning, if possible, things became even worse and Mrs I noted an even more dramatic change in her child. 'She was beginning to open her eyes by then . . . and I am sure that she recognized me in some ways . . . ' but as soon as weaning started and some distancing from her mother's body had to take place, 'She didn't look at me any more . . . not even the oblique gazes I had noticed a few weeks before . . . '.

Soon her parents noticed that even from a motor point of view Tilda was making no advance at all (she would never grasp any object and by eight months could not yet sit if unsupported), and from then on a sad pilgrimage to many specialists began (not that they had not often consulted their paediatrician before), but no plausible organic cause was ever found for her frightful state. In the end when Tilda came to me, when she was approximately two, not only could she not walk or talk, would not play, and never looked into people's eyes or even looked at people's faces, but also she was losing her already insubstantial weight and her doctors feared that given her state even a mild infection could prove fatal.

By then her previous immobile state had been substituted almost completely by vortical, wild motion and frequent, continuous screaming. Not even when carried around in her mother's arms practically all day long did she seem to find any peace in the warm embrace of her body or in the soothing comfort of her voice.

In analysis I soon realized that it was practically impossible to separate Tilda from her mother's body as even the tiniest distance from it seemed to induce terrifyingly violent convulsive fits that made one fear that any separation at that stage could have quite literally meant her death. Therefore for several months, in fact for exactly nine months, I found myself having to treat her together with her mother. It is impossible to describe any of Tilda's sessions in detail, filled as they were with just chaotic vorticose movements and totally meaningless sounds. To begin with any tiny sign of life, including my very simple and very tentative interpretations, seemed to represent for Tilda an unbearable persecution to which she reacted with screams, shrieks, scratches, and kicks.

Almost to my surprise, though, my voice, from seeming actively persecuting, as it did for quite a long while, began gradually to be mostly tolerated and apparently ignored. During her sessions Tilda would now simply cling to her mother's body, but not just to any part of it: she would only cling to her mother's abdomen, apparently ignoring all the rest. She would never look up at her face, but sometimes very slyly and suddenly managed to scratch it viciously. She would never touch her breast, save occasionally to push it away. But, as I already described, not even in the restricted area of her mother's abdominal wall did Tilda seem to find any peace. She continued to move restlessly, changing her position continuously, and each time her mother had to adapt to her new position, or suffer unbearably piercing inhuman screams.

Yet from the initial chaos gradually I realized that Tilda seemed to begin to differentiate among three distinct areas inside my room, and towards each of them she would now show a quite distinct behaviour. One was the extreme end of the playroom, the farthest from the door, where I keep a globe-like, rather pot-bellied lamp. The other was the central part of the room, where she lay on her mother's tummy. Then there was the area towards the door where I would usually sit. Tilda, all the time clinging to her mother's body, would now often stretch her arms towards my lamp with the kind of desperate nostalgic look of someone forever torn away from an eternal love. My lamp in its bellied stillness and total, constant immobility seemed in fact to represent a kind of lost nirvana, a realm of the inanimate from which her senses had been awakened totally against her will. Tilda showed quite clearly that it was in fact towards that state and that realm that she longed to return. Sometimes, after stretching frantically towards the inanimate peace of the lamp, Tilda, exhausted and covered in sweat, would fall in a deep, equally inanimate sleep.

Even the central part of the room, represented by her mother's body, or better by the restricted area corresponding to her once distended womb (the only area where she lay), seemed to be something too animated and frighteningly alive for her. The comparatively little movement and animation to be found in life inside the womb seemed to be too frightfully hectic compared to the static, inanimate, dead peace to be found before the beginning of life itself.

Yet the zone represented by her mother's womb was still preferable to the third area, the one where I was and that now seemed to represent to her the gate and the passage towards the outside world. While sitting on her mother's lap Tilda would just move restlessly, as if she could find no peace, but whenever she turned towards my chair and me Tilda would immediately scream in a mixture of terror and rage. Besides my presence, I think this was also caused by the door, a kind of opening towards the world, beyond which, Tilda knew, her father was waiting for her, ready to take her out and back home. Certainly for a long time I was associated with her father, the one who had decided to pull her out of the 'impenetrable sleep' of the inanimate and started in her the unarrestable flow and animation of life. The long stretch and invisible line connecting the stillness of my lamp, to the unpleasant animation of the womb and the unbearable persecution represented by all the stimuli in the outside seemed to reflect her brief history from non-existence and inanimation to the unbearable persecution of life.

In the sessions, strangely, it took me exactly nine months to the day to try and pull Tilda out into the world a bit and separate her at least from her mother's body. Towards the end of those nine months Tilda seemed somehow to have reconciled herself to some extent with her mother's body, or at least the central, abdominal part of it. Gradually she seemed capable of relaxing for a few moments in it and she sometimes allowed her mother to rock her a bit. Soon after she was also able to sit in between her legs, though always tied to her as if by a kind of invisible umbilical cord. Then one day she quickly came out of her legs, feet first, she screamed, then managed to throw herself inside her drawer and remained there immobile and curled up in the fetal position, looking like a small mummified corpse inside its grave, and soon plunged in an impenetrable sleep. As her mother commented: 'Exactly as she did after birth . . . '

Not that Tilda could be even remotely considered to be psychologically aware or born, and in analysis very little was solved by her not so symbolic birth, as in fact many insurmountable problems only began with that.

One of the most frightening and unexpected facts I was faced with after her parting with her mother's body during the sessions (her mother now waited for her outside the playroom), was that Tilda, who had till now almost miraculously been spared from any disease, was suddenly assailed by all sorts of illnesses and frightening allergic reactions which once again brought her very close to death. The parting from her mother's body seemed to have left her in some mysterious and totally inexplicable way completely open and unprotected towards the insults of the outside, as if so far an intangible immunological tie had still united her with her mother's flesh. Once such protection was removed, Tilda seemed left with no defences against disease, while at the same time her otherwise immature immunological system seemed to reject vehemently all sorts of potentially beneficial agents from the outside (Tilda's allergic reactions were directed against foods favoured thus far and a wide range of drugs).

Yet somehow Tilda survived and almost against her will recovered and even put on weight.

Her only meaningful actions now seemed to be her nostalgic stares and stretches towards my rounded lamp. Only occasionally did Tilda manage to find some peace by throwing herself back inside her drawer, as she had done on the day of her symbolic birth, soon plunging into an impenetrable sleep, curled up in the fetal position and completely immobile.

Whether it was due to my tentative interpretative work or to her longing to touch the representative of her paradise lost, one day Tilda, just as suddenly as she had been 'born', stood up and began to move tentative and peculiarly rigid steps towards my lamp. Her parents were overjoyed – 'Lazarus has been resurrected!' commented her father – but I was only too aware that her first tentative steps were directed back towards the representative of the inanimate peace to be found only in her grave.

From then on her sessions, if possible, became even more of an ordeal, as I could not take my eyes off her even for a second and had to follow her wherever and whenever she moved, as in her constant and crazed motions she risked hurting herself all the time.

Yet a slow and incomplete 'resurrection' in analysis continued, though with only too many backward steps.

At the age of four Tilda suddenly began to utter a few words. Not surprisingly her vocabulary was limited to a very few, very sharp and very clear commands, such as 'No!', 'Keep away!', and 'Leave me alone!' By that time Tilda would walk about in the playroom with a rigid, marching gait while holding a pencil in her hand, moving it incessantly like a mad conductor wanting to orchestrate every least detail of a too animated and uncontrollable world. Only too often was I dealt a clever blow on my head with her baton whenever I tried to utter a word, and very frequently some sly scratches were directed with unerring accuracy towards my eyes.

Yet Tilda by now seemed at least slightly more aware of the existence of the world outside, but such awareness only elicited from her violent fury and murderous, destructive attacks. Tilda tried to break and tear everything to bits, often using her sharp teeth to produce deep lacerations in almost all her toys as well as in my overall (I had in fact to keep a special overall for her). Tilda would now walk about the room with her scissors in her hands, scissoring the air madly while sucking her tongue vortically.

Most of the time Tilda seemed to be caught up in an orgy of movement, destruction, and rage. The vortical sucking of her tongue too now took on a more libidinous tone. Tilda seemed to find it a sublime and irresistible pleasure to destroy all perception from the outside and seemed intoxicated by her activities aimed towards this. Often, while scissoring wildly and moving about in the room, she would stop for a moment and try to use her blunt scissors to behead herself. I was told by her mother that while Tilda seemed to ignore any other child, she now seemed fascinated by a very severely brain-damaged child in the neighbourhood whom she watched for hours on end and tried to imitate. Only occasionally would Tilda stop her frenetic destructive activities to plunge into an inanimate, catatonic immobility before falling into her impenetrable sleep.

Often Tilda spent a good deal of her sessions pacing the room, shouting at invisible enemies, 'Go away . . . go away . . . go away . . .', then suddenly she would attack me, trying to bite me and scratch me while tearing my hair and my clothes, looking like a deranged maenad in the middle of a wild, crazed rite. But it was mainly my abdominal wall with its possible contents that was attacked with scratches and spits and sly kicks. Tilda would now also shout at my stomach and sometimes would even go as far as interrupting her usual constipation by 'letting go' and, though protected by her nappy, literally covering my lap. No rival was to enter the territory of her mother's womb. Tilda in fact now often seemed to pace the room as an animal intent on marking its territory with various secretions and smells: while doing this she farted and belched and peed, raising her leg like a dog. Her territory by now seemed to embrace all the space of my playroom, which seemed equated with a jealously guarded inside.

It became very difficult now to make Tilda leave the playroom. Near the end of each session, Tilda would point her feet against the door and refuse to leave. Her father would often have to pull her out 'feet first' towards the waiting room.

Some tenuous signs of letting go then began to be there: sometimes Tilda sat on my lap looking at me, or she smiled or even, occasionally, cried with a sad, forlorn tone in her voice. She became clean and dry, and the words 'daddy' and 'mummy' began to be part of her limited vocabulary.

But by now Tilda was already nearly seven years old, and so much developmental time seemed to be irretrievably lost. Her parents then decided to try and have another child. As Mrs H said, 'I am getting on . . . I will always continue to do my best for her . . . but I feel that I would really like to have another child . . . ' Nine months later a little brother, Romano, was born, and Tilda had to leave her treatment, as it was no longer possible for her parents to bring her to see me.

After the end of Tilda's treatment Mrs H kept in touch with me and occasionally I have seen Tilda again. Though Tilda has certainly improved in her life, her development is still greatly thwarted in only too many ways. Even now her pull towards life seems so tenuous and her drive towards death so strong, that I doubt greatly whether she will ever be like any other child.

CASE NO. 4 – ALEXANDER (three years and four months old)

Alexander, a sturdy and attractive though peculiarly absorbed and vacant-looking fair-haired little boy, was referred to me at the age of three years and four months for a rather generic 'accident-proneness' and because by that age he could not yet speak. His parents, both strikingly attractive and intelligent young people, were very worried about him. Though Mr and Mrs L were only in their early thirties, Alexander was already their third child. After him another little boy, Peppe, had been born and was six months old at the time. Apparently Peppe's birth had worsened Alexander's condition and his parents were now rather desperate for help.

Mrs L, who could certainly be considered an expert in children and pregnancies, told me that she had felt that something was wrong or at least strange with Alexander well before his birth. Alexander from the early stages seemed to move a lot 'just like an athlete . . . I never felt any of my other children swinging from one side to the other of the womb and kicking the wall and turning round and round in such an acrobatic way . . . he seemed to enjoy an endless freedom of movement . . . ' Things, though, became more complicated as pregnancy proceeded, as not only Alexander was on the whole less free to move, but also apparently became acutely aware of sounds and seemed intolerant of many of them. Mrs L, a talented writer, loved music, and she used to listen to it all the time while typing her latest manuscript, mostly at night.

At first Mrs L had noted how Alexander seemed to 'love' the regular and monotonously unchanging ticking of her typewriter: 'He seemed to dance in tune with it, as if at one with it . . . ' Madrigals and any rather predictable and regular form of music from the sixteenth century seemed to have the same effect on him. Apparently Alexander went 'mad' whenever his mother listened to anything more modern and discordant, such as Stravinsky or Mahler, not to mention Stockhausen or Nono, both of whom she was very fond of. As Mrs L said, 'He simply went mad whenever he heard any of that . . . his movements became wild . . . and it felt as if he were crazed with rage . . . '

Soon Mrs L had to stick with her regular ticking and her largely predictable madrigals and pavanes. Then one evening, when Mrs L was eight months pregnant and was peacefully typing after having put the other children to bed, she suddenly felt a great commotion in her womb: 'Alexander began to move frantically . . . he seemed crazed with something . . . later I realized that he had probably felt that the delivery was approaching . . . a few hours later in fact the first contractions started . . . I was taken into hospital and the contractions continued during the entire night . . . I was monitored rather carefully . . . but the dilation was little and slow . . . then in the morning I was administered some oxytocine and the contractions increased in strength . . . dilation too was beginning to increase . . . but then suddenly Alexander, who had so far been cephalic, managed somehow to turn round almost at the last minute and to sit on my cervix in the yoga position . . . with his bottom acting as a kind of plug . . . we were all amazed and a Caesarean was instantly decided upon . . . I was really stupefied as my other children had all been born naturally . . . '

According to his parents Alexander did not constitute an active part of family life till he was about one year old, as he seemed to sleep almost all the time. His general non-reactiveness had been noted from his hospital days. The doctors called him the 'mollusc child', and administered him some mild cardiotonic to try to keep him awake. Apparently the only time when he was awake and almost alert was when he was being bathed. 'As soon as he was put in the water, he seemed to wake up and began to move . . . he is still mad about water now . . . ' I was later to find out that Alexander, as soon as he was able to crawl, had risked drowning several times, as the moment he saw a river, a lake, a puddle, or, above all, a full bath-tub, he simply plunged in and just slipped underwater without even taking a breath. Apart from literally 'losing his head', as his mother said, whenever he saw even a few drops of water, he seemed otherwise not to be the least bit interested in the world surrounding him.

When at one year of age Alexander began to wake, noises still upset him greatly, and he seemed generally intolerant of any even minor change. As his mother said, 'Alexander according to me, has always tried to reduce the world to a small microcosm to keep under constant control . . . ', and 'He seems to live all the time on some kind of cloud . . . noises bring him down to earth . . . '

His motor development, though, seemed to proceed at a fast pace. When he was one year old he could walk about securely. His vocabulary nevertheless was limited to a few incomprehensible sounds.

A major drawback in his development was represented by the birth of his younger brother when Alexander was two and a half years old. As soon as his rather observant eyes realized the visible change in his mother's body, he seemed to become 'uncontainable'. He banged his head against her stomach and 'tried to get in . . . pushing his head against my legs . . . '. When his brother was born Alexander tried to substitute him in all sorts of possible ways 'till in the end we had to give in somehow . . . he resented most of all his brother's pram . . .

therefore he was allowed to sleep in it sometimes . . . ' Soon his growing body, though, pushed him out of the comfortable but too limited space of the pram.

It was mainly his verbal retardation as well as his accident-proneness that worried his parents and prompted them to seek my advice. When Alexander was brought to see me for a consultation at the age of three, the only word he could utter clearly was 'water'. Four months later, when I had a vacancy and we started analysis, few more words had been added to his limited vocabulary.

As to his 'accident-proneness', I had no idea of its extent at the time, nor was it described in much detail by his parents until much later, when I had already learnt its tragic extent during my sessions with him.

During his first session Alexander seemed to be trying by every possible means not to experience any separation. As soon as he entered into the playroom he pointed at his head, as if he wanted to take it off, and then, by pointing at my tummy, indicated that he was 'in here'. Then he turned the tap on and soon the room was flooded by water and transformed into a watery inside. Soon after he said 'Peppe no' and then asked 'wee'. After weeing 'out' rather concretely his hated rival, whilst saying again 'Peppe no' and 'Peppe out', Alexander seemed to become 'insane' when, on coming back from the toilet he noticed in my waiting room a painting representing a swimming-pool. He just wanted to plunge into it, and banged his head against it while saying, 'water . . . water . . . inside . . . inside . . . '. By plunging 'inside' he seemed to lose any distinction between outside and inside and seemed unable to function at a symbolic level. The swimming-pool became concretely equated with a watery inside very much as described by H. Segal (Segal 1957). His uncontainable fury at separation then became quite evident. Not being able to plunge 'in', Alexander tried to get rid of his head and all the perceptions connected with it, by hitting it. Then in his fury he tried to destroy the world all around. In the end he looked deflated and limp, and his limp state seemed reminiscent of the description of him as a 'mollusc child'. A few minutes later he seemed to be again 'wrapped inside' and to comfort himself with a monotonous medieval tune. His peace was soon interrupted by the arrival of his parents and Alexander again seemed 'crazed with fury' at having to separate. The end seemed to be experienced by him as a violent birth, and he tried to resist it by sitting down in the yoga position, just as he had done in his distant past.

The session that follows is Alexander's second one. Many other important elements seem already to be hinted at in it.

Alexander: second session – detailed report

Alexander arrives punctually, accompanied by both parents. He is in his father's arms today, looking like a sort of koala-bear hanging on to him. His father brings him into the playroom and lays him down on the couch. Then both his parents disappear rather quickly.

Alexander bursts into tears of despair, sounding both terrified and at the same time enraged. Gradually he drops his head backwards looking floppy and apathetic, as if he has lost the ability to lift it up. I say that he seems to feel too small to be left on his own, like a newborn infant who cannot yet lift his head. I remind him of his parents leaving him just now and of my leaving him yesterday, when he seemed unready to go. He stops crying immediately and raises his head saying, 'I small'. He puts both hands over my head for a second, but then pushes them against my stomach as if wanting to break in and tries to insert them between my legs saying again 'I small'. I say that he feels too small to be left outside. If he is left on the outside he becomes all floppy and unable to stand and this throws him in despair. He smiles at me while pretending again to drop his head backwards and to look limp and unsustained. Then he stands with his feet on my feet and smiles while looking at me. I say that I shouldn't walk away and go out, but should just carry him wherever I go, like a child inside following my steps. He smiles and gives a firm 'Yes'.

Then he goes to his drawer. He takes the fence and several little animals out. He puts the animals inside the fence, but then suddenly he notices that somehow he has picked up the baby together with the animals. He throws it away furiously and with great rage tries to break everything within his reach. He seems to have completely lost his head and looks totally crazed.

I say that he can't stand feeling like a baby, it drives him crazy. He calms down. He looks at the sink. He turns the tap on. He hints that I should give him some toys, but then stops my hand, saying, 'One'. I say that he has to be the only one. He says, 'Peppe no'.

He picks up a small duck from amongst the little animals. He smiles. He immerses his arms inside the water, then tries to plunge his head in too. I stop him and I say that he has now become the little duck completely immersed in the water. He takes the sponge and the mop and soaks them with water and then floods the entire room, transforming it in a kind of lake or swimming-pool. I say that all the room is full of water now like a swimming-pool and he is the duck inside. I remind him of his wanting to enter the picture of the swimming-pool in my waiting room yesterday. He smiles. He goes towards the lamp. He touches its hot metallic top. He smiles. I have to

213

stop him as I am afraid that he might scorch his hands. He smiles again, then starts moving dangerously near the window-sill, sort of jumping all over the place. I say that once he is inside, that he has plunged in, he thinks he can do anything and will not hurt himself or feel any pain. He jumps from the sill almost hovering in the air like a Peter Pan and lands miraculously uninjured on the floor.

He wets the floor some more and from time to time he makes some tentative swimming movements. I say that he feels he has no restrictions or limits once he is inside. He feels free and he thinks he cannot be injured or harmed by anything. I have to carry all the worry for him. While I am saying this he slips on the wet floor and nearly hurts himself. He just seems surprised and shows no reaction otherwise. He goes and opens the door and puts his head out for a moment looking into the waiting room, but almost immediately he withdraws it, saying, 'Hurt'. I say that he gets hurt once outside. He thinks he is invulnerable, 'no hurt', once inside. He pours some more water on the floor, and says smilingly 'fish'. I say that he is happy and can swim like a fish in the inside, but he is also mute as a fish.

We hear some noises coming from the flat next door. He suddenly looks frightened. He curls up on the couch covering his ears with his hands. He says, 'Not like it', and starts moving frantically and kicking in all directions, as if he had gone mad. The noise ceases.

The door-bell rings. Alexander refuses to go. He holds on tightly to the sink, then he sits down in the yoga position in front of the door. His father has to intervene. He picks him up. When Alexander is in the waiting room, he somehow manages to free himself and darts back into the playroom and in a second curls up in the fetal position in his drawer, till his father, amongst many yells, kicks, and screams, manages to drag him away.

Alexander's ravaging and uncontrollable fury continued to be present for a very long time. Whenever his illusion of being wrapped in a restricted microcosm controlled down to the last detail was shattered by any alien perception or dim awareness of separation, Alexander simply 'lost his head' and started attacking furiously and blindly whoever and whatever was at hand. His 'mad' and frantic frenzy often reminded me of the amazement his mother had felt whenever Alexander seemed to go suddenly and uncontrollably wild inside her at the first discordant notes of a Stockhausen piece or his somehow mysteriously sensing that the changes brought about by the delivery were about to take place.

His attacks often had a precise spatial distribution. My waiting room was mostly equated with separation and an entry into an unpredictable outside where he would, as he said, be 'hurt', whereas the playroom mostly stood for a comfortable and well-controlled idealized inside where Alexander felt free to bounce and to move. Once he plunged 'in', his sessions were on the whole orderly and ritualized, following a rather detailed and unimaginative orchestration which was repeated day after day. First Alexander used to wet all the floor. Then, each time, he tried to take off all his clothes and to wet his hair and his face, often while trying at the same time to fill even his nostrils and his ears with water. As soon as the room was more or less transformed into some kind of lake or swimming-pool, Alexander seemed to revert dangerously to a kind of ill-fit marine life and seemed really to lose any perception of potential dangers of terrestrial life and of the various laws governing the outside.

When trying to hover freely in the air as light and as carefree as Peter Pan, Alexander seemed to have completely lost any sense, let alone notion, of gravity. (Though the fetus cannot be regarded as living in a state of complete weightless buoyancy, the influence of gravity, as compared to life after birth, is only minimal.) And when, as frequently happened, he ended up hitting against the hard ground, his only reaction, as in his unexpected fall of the first session, seemed to be that of genuine and complete surprise. This surprise, though, was repeated almost every day. It was very difficult during the sessions to try to prevent all his falls, and Alexander seemed totally incapable of learning from the hard experience of hitting the ground each time. His parents later told me that Alexander had in fact risked his life several times by actually trying to fly out of the window of their flat, totally oblivious of the fact that any flight would have ended on the concrete below. By then they had put up a thick, unbreakable mesh at all the windows.

What might have otherwise seemed like suicide attempts were in fact performed by Alexander in all innocence and apparently in all good faith. Whenever he tried to float in the air with the lack of consciousness and the recklessness of a Peter Pan, no suicidal volition seemed even remotely to guide his acts: he simply seemed to believe he could fly, thus defying the gravitational laws governing life in the outside.

Unfortunately when plunged 'in' and transformed into a marine creature long past its time, Alexander's thinking became concrete in many other ways and again in all innocence he risked his very life.

As in the second session, when he heedlessly touched the hot metallic top of my lamp, Alexander seemed to be amazingly insensitive to heat and pain, two of the least activated and stimulated sensations inside the womb.

Alexander repeatedly tried to put his hands and his mouth directly onto the light-bulb and never cried on those occasions when I was unable to prevent him hitting the floor or banging his head. Dangers were rather limited, though, within the restricted space of my playroom. What was for me just the beginning of a terrifying suspicion, was soon confirmed by several desperate phone calls from his parents. As had apparently already happened before, Alexander one day simply put his face over the flame of a lighted gas-ring. Quite miraculously only his hair was burnt, as his mother, who was there next to him, intervened in time. Alexander did not show any fear and did not cry until he heard his mother's terrified screams.

A few days earlier, again while at home, Alexander had shown no reaction to the pain that a rather deep cut over his eyebrow requiring several stitches should have caused. As his mother told me, amongst desperate sobs, 'He's always been like this . . . whenever he cuts himself he is just amazed at the sight of blood . . . then later perhaps he cries . . . but just because he hears so much commotion all around him . . .' Though Alexander had already been neurologically tested in the past before coming to see me, and I was somehow almost sure of the non-organic origin of his symptoms, I suggested a second opinion to rule out any possibility of a syringomyelic type of dissociation of his thermal and pain sensations. (Thermal and painful sensations represent two vital survival mechanisms for the newborn and in general for man. This becomes most evident in those neurological conditions affecting them: mutilations and severe burns in people affected by syringomyelia are a sadly well-known fact: these patients, incapable of discriminating heat and pain, simply burn or mutilate themselves without being in the least aware of it.)

All the neurological examinations proved in fact to be negative, and Alexander's sensory pathways seemed to be quite intact. Only, somehow, quite amazingly, Alexander managed at times not to feel what he was actually quite capable of feeling and consequently in all innocence often managed to come very close to severe mutilation and death.

Other activities in the session also conveyed the same mixture of innocence coupled with extreme danger, as when Alexander would try to plunge his head under water after filling the sink, or even more worryingly, when he tried to hang himself while playing with the rather long cord of the curtain of my playroom. Alexander often held the cord while jumping from corner to corner of my room like Tarzan holding on to a liana. Sometimes though, he wound the cord around his neck and in the fraction of a second before I managed to intervene, Alexander simply smiled, as if the sensation of the cord around his neck had merely caused him a pleasant surprise. The possibility of strangulation seemed never to cross his mind.

When plunged in the 'inside', like a child with no brain, Alexander also quite often seemed to lose the capacity to understand the meaning of my very simple words, which he then treated as mere sounds more or less pleasant. Therefore quite frequently I found myself having to resort to very 'concrete' interpretations indeed, miming my impressions with simple gestures of my face and my hands.

Alexander, though, seemed unusually sensitive to any variation of the tone of my voice and my mood, and whenever he perceived even a slight alteration in my voice he looked at me immediately wide-eyed and uttered some of his very rare words, asking me, 'Still friends?'

At the end of each session I was never his 'friend', as I announced to him that he had to leave. As in the sessions above, he then quickly sat down in the yoga position and refused to leave.

One of Alexander's signs of progress in the analysis was in fact his increasing capacity to feel 'hurt', to experience painful sensations and react accordingly to them, as well as to become aware of heat and the potential dangers connected with it. Gravity too became less an alien concept for him and he became a bit more careful in his jumps.

Parallel to all this Alexander became slightly more 'symbolic' in his games. So far he had just played with some rather 'uterine' components of my room, such as the water or the cord, otherwise ignoring any toy. Now the first human figures began to emerge in his tentative games and these were engaged in in-and-out movements of plunging in and emerging from the water of the sink. Not that this could be considered a momentous step forwards, but at least, compared to the massive total projective identification dominating his mind just a few months before, one could begin to distinguish in it some kind of movement of to and fro, some 'in' and 'out', whereas before it had all been just aquatic and oceanic fusion.

As Alexander became more able to relinquish his past, his sessions gradually became more orderly and monotonously controlled following an obsesssive orchestration of them, with each second stressed almost like the monotonous ticking of a typewriter, one of the original 'loves' of his past. A long stretch of rather impenetrable obsessivity now probably lay ahead of us. But Alexander apparently had improved in the world outside, though he was still rather limited in his vocabulary and quite unimaginative in the range of his activities and games.

After three years of treatment, as so often is the case in the analysis of very young children, his parents expressed the wish to stop analysis, as, given his progress, they saw no point in continuing it.

From the little I have heard of him since then, Alexander has continued to make some progress in his life, though on the whole he seems to have remained a rather obsessive and backward child.

CASE NO. 5 – THOMAS (two years and three months old)

Thomas, a very attractive little boy, with bright red hair and big hazel eyes, started an analysis with me when he was two years and three months old. Thomas should have been an abortion. His mother, a young secretary, and his father, a trained nurse, a specialist in new trends in midwifery, had not planned or wanted his birth; Thomas was just the unwelcome result of what had started off as a casual and not even too passionate affair.

As Mrs M got the result of her pregnancy test, she tried at first to get rid of him with a not clearly described, but apparently rather crude 'do-it-yourself job', which Thomas survived. Then Mrs M, always assisted in all this by Mr M, made an appointment with the hospital: 'But it was already rather late . . . and nobody agreed to abort him any more . . . not that we didn't try to ourselves . . . I even started bleeding rather heavily at some point . . . but he must have been strongly attached to the womb as well as to his life . . . ' Apparently at the instigation of Mr M, Mrs M continued to try all sorts of horrific procedures to abort her child, including the insertion of needles and probes, abortifacient potions, and all kinds of possible foams. But again Thomas seemed to resist with incredible tenacity all these attempts.

Pregnancy, in spite of all the repeated attacks, continued well and the two parents now started living together. Mrs M, though, noticed that the child was now quite immobile inside her womb. 'To begin with I had felt some movement . . . but then nothing . . . I never felt those famous kicks . . . ' As the supposed date of the delivery approached, Thomas still continued not to move. 'Apparently he had retreated into a corner of the womb and stayed there completely immobile . . . I had the impression that he didn't want to come out at all . . . '

Time elapsed, and towards the end of the tenth month of pregnancy the gynaecologist decided to intervene and attempted to induce birth. Mrs M's womb, however, didn't respond. There were no signs of dilation nor of contractions. In the end, since a beginning of fetal distress was noted, the doctor decided to perform a Caesarean. 'But this was just typical of my family . . . none of us are capable of giving birth to our children . . . all my sisters and my aunts had to have a Caesarean too . . . ' In the end, Thomas was born and, as his mother said, 'He was easy and beautiful . . . he never cried . . . all the other children in the ward were brought to their mothers screaming with hunger . . . but never him . . . he sucked . . . he slept . . . and he ate . . . but never asked for anything . . . '

Once back home his mother continued breast-feeding him for the first two months and Thomas continued not to cry, but 'We were only too pleased about his silence . . . ' Then Thomas had to be weaned, as Mrs M resumed work, leaving Thomas in his father's care. (Mr M was still preparing for some exams and therefore was not working at the time.) Mr M often described how during the day Thomas would spend hours alone in his cot, mostly in silence, looking at something on the wall, or else asleep. Whenever he gave any sign of life though, 'I tried to put him back to sleep by every possible means . . . ' I was never told by what means, but from what I have been able to reconstruct through the transference, my strong suspicion was that masturbatory practices ranked rather high amongst his various means. Yet so far, in spite of his prevailing silence, Thomas had begun to make some sounds and seemed interested in the world surrounding him. Then, as Mr M said, 'Nothing more from the fourth month . . . ' All this though seemed to suit them only too well. 'Since he never cried, we never allowed him to express anything . . . we just gave him things . . . the moment he cried, we would give him a dummy . . . we called it his plug . . . ' All this rather horrific information was given to me bit by bit, over the years, and only after the treatment had started and was well under way. In the first interview both parents had tried to present an appearance of distress for the 'incomprehensible' catastrophe that had hit them.

To begin with they became particularly worried about Thomas's motor development, as by eight months he could not sit alone and by ten months he was unable to crawl. He was then seen by a neurologist, but nothing apparently wrong was found and all subsequent neurological check-ups – and Thomas had been seen by innumerable neurologists – always proved to be negative. When he was about eight months old Thomas was also examined by a psychologist, who diagnosed autism and suggested several books on the topic that his parents could read. Since then his parents had probably read nearly all the available books on the subject and by now will have certainly read many more.

When Thomas was first brought to see me and during all my subsequent contacts with his parents, I had the impression that their main, if not exclusive, concern was to exert all their 'diagnostic acumen' on him, trying to 'understand' in terms of psychopathology even the tiniest details of his mental functioning and constitutional make-up. Apart from seeing him as a 'case', they seemed not to care about him at all. When Thomas was one year old they tried by every possible means, and indeed succeeded, in having him officially recognized as handicapped, so as to obtain a subsidy from the state. Then they immediately parked him in a kindergarten and, to their surprise, Thomas seemed to improve a bit while there. Once back home, though, Thomas was left in a corner to play by himself. His parents never took him to the park, never visited other children with him, never read him a story, let alone played with him. His mother found him 'sticky' and thought that Thomas behaved a bit like an infant with her, 'But I understand him perfectly . . . there is no need for words between us . . . probably I should stimulate him to talk a bit more . . .'

When he was referred to me, as I said, at the age of two years and three months, Thomas was just beginning to walk, and though he had been diagnosed as autistic and mutacic, he was beginning to say a few words.

From the very first session, reported below, one could see quite clearly that Thomas could not be considered an autistic child. In this session Thomas responds quite clearly to my talking to him. In spite of all that has happened to him in his brief life, he seems to show an extraordinary tenacity in holding on to anything that could save him and help him to come alive.

Looking back at this session several years later, I am struck by how many elements of Thomas's history were present in it. Besides his tenacity, his resilience, and his basic good nature, his despair and hopelessness at being ignored and treated like dirt, all seem represented there. His main defences such as projecting himself totally inside his mother's body while losing his head, his intelligence, his perceptions, and his speech are also hinted at, while the newspaper reduced to 'pulp' resembles only too grimly an aborted mass.

I had seen Thomas just a few days before for a brief but intense consultation before deciding to start an analysis with him the following week. On that occasion Thomas had shown an almost passionate involvement with me and he had found it very difficult to part. Though no interpretative work had been done on that occasion by me, his analysis could almost be said to have already started then. Even on that occasion Thomas had shown a great tenacity in trying to make the best of the little that was offered him.

Thomas: first session – detailed report

Thomas arrives punctually, accompanied by his mother. When I open the door, he is standing next to her, with his back turned to the playroom. When I say hello to him, he gives me a very cross look. I say that he seems very angry with me because the other day I closed my door and didn't stay next to him as his mother is doing now. He glances at me, then points at the front door as if wanting to go, and while doing this he turns away from me more and more. I say that now he is the one who wants to go. He wants me to know what it feels like being left. He turns himself towards me and smiles. He leaves his mother and comes inside the playroom. His mother, ignoring my signals, says that she is coming too and brings her newspaper with her. She enters and sits on my chair, then starts reading.

Thomas goes to the small table and starts touching its holes, smiling at me. I say that he felt understood, so then it was no more like feeling forgotten and pushed down a hole. He nods and goes to the drawer. He gestures that he would like me to take out the crayons and pencils, and I give them to him. He smiles at me, goes back near his mother, pretends to be holding on to her coat, but then comes towards me smiling. I say that when he feels understood he doesn't need to stick to his mother or to me any more. He nods and smiles. Then he alternates between hanging on tightly to his mother's coat while putting some of his pencils in her lap with her accepting them passively without taking her eyes off her paper, and moving away from her and going and trying some of his crayons on his paper. While doing this he seems delighted and gives out little cries of joy. I say that he is showing me how he feels secure when he clings to someone, he is not afraid of falling down the hole, but then he can't try anything new, like for instance his colours. He smiles at me.

He takes one of the pages from his mother's newspaper (she doesn't react in the least) and wraps it all around his head. Then he indicates to his mother that he would like her to do the same. She follows, passively and absent-mindedly wrapping her head too. Both their heads are wrapped inside the same sheet now. I say that like this he still feels stuck to his mother, as when he was inside her tummy, but also I point out how, when he is sticking to her, he cannot see, or hear, or try anything new. Thomas glances at me. I say that he wants to make sure that if he comes out, I will look at him and pay attention to him. He wants to make sure that my head is not all wrapped up, as if inside a newspaper and closed to him.

He comes out and goes towards the light. He switches it on and off. Then he touches the buzzer slightly, switches the light off, goes over to his mother and curls up on her lap. He is now occupying all her stomach and she can't read her newspaper any more. He now turns his back to me. I say that he is going back inside now. He doesn't want to feel hurt any more by my switching the light on and off, by my opening and closing the door as I did the other day. But I also point out to him how he remains in the dark. He cannot move, or see the light as before. He leaves his mother's lap and goes and switches on the light again.

Then he touches the radiator. He goes to the sink and turns the tap on while smiling at me. I say that he felt understood. He could then come out without being all wrapped. Outside he can drink something new, milk, and still feel some warmth. I remind him of his turning on the tap and touching the radiator. He points at the glass and I give it to him. He drinks from it while smiling at me. Then he moves away from the sink slightly, and says clearly and distinctly 'Water', and he looks very proud. I say that if he feels nourished by me then he can also begin to talk.

He looks towards the door (we still have about ten minutes left). He touches the radiator, and says, 'It is too hot . . . ' He fills the sink with water, then goes and takes another page from his mother's newspaper and puts it inside the water. He looks at the disintegrating newspaper, looking very thoughtful. His mother now stands up and goes and waits for him in the waiting room, yawning, and looking very bored. Thomas apparently doesn't seem to realize that she has gone out, but I notice that his eyes more and more seem to lose focus. I say that at this moment he still feels inside and not born. In this way he doesn't feel that his mother or I go out. He doesn't feel thrown away in the hole. I make him feel too hot with excitement and then let him down. He raises his head and points at the bin while smiling at me. Then he takes the remains of his sheet and throws what's left of it inside the bin. I say that he really feels like rubbish when I say goodbye to him. He looks at the paper inside the bin and notices that it is all fragmented, as if reduced to pulp. He seems frightened. I say that now that he has to go he is afraid of falling to bits, like the paper did. I will just throw him away. He smiles at me and points first at the chair and then at the fragments of the newspaper. I say that I should hold him on my lap (the chair) and not throw him away now that it is time. He gives me his hand and we go back towards the waiting room. When I say goodbye to him, he stands there looking sadly at me.

The tone of this session, though, was certainly too luminous and light, as in fact it took me another five dark years before Thomas was able to regain sufficient trust in me and in life to be able to enjoy the colours of the world as well as to speak properly and behave like any other child. Utterances and cries of joy were not to be heard in his sessions for a very long time. First we were to deal for quite a long time with the 'pulp', with his fear of being mashed into a worthless mass and thrown away.

In the following months Thomas seemed to show how he felt 'in his bones' that he had been destined to be an abortion right from the start. Deep depression, if not downright hopeless despair, seemed to be his basic mood. Thomas would turn up for each session with his face covered with thick mucus and all sorts of almost putrid (often foul-smelling) secretions. Then he would spend the rest of his sessions curled up inside my bin, often mumbling 'my place', while crawling and curling inside it. He spent most of his sessions in almost complete immobility and silence inside the bin or any other narrow and uncomfortable hiding place, such as the space under my chair or my small table, where he would retreat in total immobility, curled up in the fetal position. The end of each session was almost invariably met with desperate, terrified screams as I tried to pull him out of his hiding place. Rather frequently, though, Thomas also mimed repeated aggressions with all sorts of potentially sharp objects, such as scissors and pencils which he often called 'needles' (one of his very few clear words), penetrating and stirring his secluded space. Such sharp persecutors seemed aimed at starting him from his hiding, bringing him to the open, and reducing him to a bloody pulp. Often, after mimicking one of these relentless attacks, Thomas would come out of his bin, with his face covered with thick yellowish mucus, and would then begin to scratch all the uncovered surface of his skin until it started bleeding. His parents in their constant search for subtle psycho-pathological explanations ascribed this habit to a psychosomatic rash. On the few occasions when Thomas would be out of his hide, he would spend the rest of the session dissolving a tissue of my Kleenex in the water of the sink which he had tinted with red, the only colour that Thomas seemed to recognize, if not like. Needless to say, the remains of the tissue looked as if it was drenched with blood.

My voice, mostly apparently ignored, was also equated at times with just another sharp intruder into his unprotected space or else for a long time seemed to be for him just too painful a reminder of a distant past which he could never bury inside his mind.

It took me several months before Thomas could be convinced that he was not going to be disintegrated and reduced to a kind of aborted mass if he dared move from his hiding place. During those long months I was often left holding on to those first impressions of mine as the only dim hope that he had not been damaged beyond repair and retreated chronically into an impenetrable, autistic hide-away.

Yet after a long gestation Thomas began to feel that his retreat at least was a safe space. The bin, so far his favourite place, with all its accompaniment of terror and persecution as well as the not so symbolic dread of really ending up in some kind of bin one day, was now replaced with more benign hiding places, such as my curtain or the blanket on my couch, which seemed to provide him with at least a warmth and a softness he had never experienced before. From a bad and persecuting womb he seemed to have moved into a more benign, safe, and good one.

Soon after, though, Thomas began to feel any breaks in his analysis acutely, often equating them with a violent birth. Towards the end of each session he would now look at his watch and then stand on the edge of the sill, as if on the verge of an abyss, looking pale and terrified. When his mother or his father then rang the bell, he began to scream and cry while scratching his face, and often they had to pull him out by force. Birth was often represented in his games as a kind of sudden earthquake shaking the baby out of the stillness of my lamp or of my bin. Once out, the baby was soon hurled against the wall. One day Thomas went as far as mimicking a kind of Caesarean delivery on my couch, with loud yells and screams, then suddenly the scissors intervened, the baby was taken out of his jumper and once more thrown away. As Thomas said, 'Nobody wants it any more . . .'

Yet Thomas, probably right from the very early stages of his life, had something very resilient in him and an almost incredible tenacity in holding on to hope for a new life. From the all-pervasive confusion of his early days, some tentative sanity began to emerge, and Thomas seemed to hold on to me and to my words with all the strength of someone holding on to a last, tenuous link with life.

Thomas's analysis was interrupted when he was seven years old and his parents decided to move to another town. By then, though, Thomas could be said to be like any other child. He was certainly very much liked by his teachers and very popular amongst other children at school. His school reports were quite satisfactory too.

Apparently his tenacity and his capacity to hold on to life and to make the best of whatever was available have continued to support him till now.

Contrary to my expectations, Mrs M has continued to keep in touch with me. She and Mr M have now split up. Thomas is living with her, and Mrs M has at long last decided to follow what I had suggested to her many times and is now in analysis herself. In the last note I received from her Mrs M told me that she and Thomas were doing well and that Thomas had helped her a great deal: 'Sometimes I think that he has been like a life-jacket saving me from drowning in my life . . .'

CASE NO. 6 – PETER (two years and eleven months old)

Peter, an attractive, almost miniature little boy, started an analysis with me just before turning three. His mother, a pleasant and pretty woman in her late thirties, was by then almost in despair. Peter, whose brightness and verbal capacity were far ahead of his young age, was constantly rowing with her and accused her all the time of being stupid and totally incapable of doing anything right. As she said, 'He never forgives me some original sin . . . he makes me feel a total failure as a mother . . . '

Peter's behaviour had apparently worsened recently, after he had been hospitalized briefly for a series of tests to determine the cause of his frequent headaches. Nothing physically wrong with him had been found, but the doctors had concluded that his symptoms were probably due to tension, as he seemed to be a bright little boy but very tense and unable to relax. By now Peter reproached his mother all the time, saying that it was 'all her fault', and his subtle argumentative capacity had almost convinced Mrs N that he might well have been right. The relationship with his father, a pleasant man in his early forties, seemed much easier and less charged with tension; as Peter's mother said, 'As a woman I am the one to be blamed . . . my husband, being a man, seems to be immune from all this . . . ' Peter's father, though certainly less involved and less hurt by such verbal fights, was clearly supportive of his wife.

Peter apparently had always been a rather difficult boy. His parents had been married for several years before deciding to have a child. Mr and Mrs N, both professionals, had kept postponing the decision to start a family as they were quite busy and quite happy with their lives. Peter's birth had therefore been planned mainly in consideration of Mrs N's age. Once pregnant, however, Mrs N had felt very happy about it: 'I was well established in my career and I knew that I could have easily taken even two years off before resuming work just part-time to fit in with the requirements of the child . . . '

Contrary to her original, carefully laid-out plans, Mrs N had to stop working right from the start, as her pregnancy was from the beginning a very troubled one. At first an ectopic pregnancy was feared, but this possibility was soon ruled out by a scan. Then, when Mrs N was three months pregnant, her gynaecologist told her that the child had probably died *in utero* as her womb had not only not increased in size, but if possible seemed even smaller than before. But on that same day Mrs N was examined with ultrasounds and the child could be seen: its clearly visible heart-beats confirmed that it was alive. Subsequently Mrs N was to undergo many, frequent scans, as her placenta was inserted low and *abruptio placentae* was therefore an almost constant risk with her. Mrs N also bled frequently and rather heavily almost all the time and was therefore bedridden, as she was told that she ran a great risk of losing her child. Apprehension therefore had been a constant throughout pregnancy. Amniocentesis, though, and the repeated scans had shown no apparent structural defect in the child. During each rather prolonged scan Peter was always seen to be completely immobile. Nor did Mrs N ever perceive any movements by him. 'He was totally immobile . . . yet, though I knew that this was not a good prognostic sign and that detachment of the placenta was a possibility . . . and quite a risky one for me too . . . I very much wanted to continue this pregnancy and to save my child's life . . . '

The doctors, worried by the child's immobility and also by Mrs N's rather frail aspect, had even suggested the possibility of termination. Then, when Mrs N was seven months pregnant, she was told that it was no longer necessary for her to be bedridden. 'On that day I decided to go out with my husband for a short walk . . . but as soon as we were out in the street the membranes ruptured and I rapidly lost all the amniotic fluid on the pavement . . . I was rushed into hospital . . . and Peter was born less than half an hour later . . . it was a really lightning birth . . . I had no labour pains . . . and I remember just pushing once . . . in a second he was catapulted out . . . '

Peter weighed slightly less than 2 kilograms and therefore was kept in an incubator for a while. Mrs N visited him as much as she could and in the end succeeded in obtaining permission to be in the nursery with him almost all the time. Peter, though, was gaining weight incredibly fast and, therefore, when he was fifteen days old was dismissed from hospital. Mrs N recollected how, as soon as they got home, 'He plunged into a deep sleep which lasted almost a whole day . . . it was impossible to wake him up . . . he seemed to want to forget all he had been through and put it all to the back of his mind . . . he seemed to want to forget about his past . . . ' As soon as he recovered from his deep sleep, Peter immediately clung to his mother's breast and apparently spent the next five months clinging to it tenaciously. 'He was clinging to it all the time . . . and while doing this he monitored me with his eyes . . . if I dared move my breast even an inch away, he yelled and screamed . . . it was a real tragedy each time . . . I must admit that I was quite exhausted at the time . . . and in a way I was hurt too, as I felt that he treated me just like a sort of milking cow . . . ' When five months old, Peter had to be weaned, as his mother's milk was by now quite insufficient for him. Peter apparently made some 'fuss' about his baby-food, but then soon got used to it, though he always ate very little and still did so when first brought to me.

When he came to see me Peter was still a tiny child. His minuteness contrasted even more sharply with his incredible verbal and intellectual precocity. Peter had started talking when he was nine months old and when one year old his vocabulary was as rich as that of a much older child. Apparently Peter also 'never slept from the start'. According to his mother, he was always 'on the alert', and even now continued waking at least four or five times per night. Each time he seemed to have woken in a fright and often his parents kept him in their bed during the night to soothe and comfort him. Peter found it extremely difficult to 'let go and fall asleep'. Apparently he had to go through countless rituals before being able to relax at night. This aspect greatly worried his mother, who said, 'He seems to want to check the world down to its tiniest details . . . '

Everything had to be done following a minutely pre-arranged order, and Peter went as far as refusing to wear any new shoes or clothes until they had been sufficiently tested and proved safe by him. As Mr N said, 'Novelties frighten him . . . if I insist and force him to wear something new . . . in the end he will . . . and once he has tried it, what was new becomes something mastered and therefore safe for him again . . . ' His control extended to practically all aspects of his orderly life, including demanding the constant attention of whoever happened to be taking care of him. Mrs N worried in particular about the constant efforts Peter had to make to keep everything under control. As she said, 'So much tension and effort . . . it's a real shame . . . I wish he could use his energies and intelligence in other ways . . . '

Though I was not aware of much of this at the time, as many details of his pre-natal and perinatal past were collected only later over several meetings with his parents, Peter's first session, reported in detail below, seems absolutely full of hints of the dreads and fears, as well as of the survival mechanisms, which may have been operative in his distant past. Particularly when looked at in retrospect, this session seems paved with vestiges which quite possibly belong to his pre-history.

Peter: first session – detailed report

Peter arrives punctually, accompanied by his father. When I open the door, he is in his father's arms and holding on tightly to his neck. He is screaming, and saying, 'I don't want to go . . . ' As I say hello to him, he says, urgently and without glancing at me, 'I have to do a wee . . . ' I show him the bathroom and he goes in there with his father. I hear him talking to his father and saying, 'This toilet is too small . . . but why? . . . ', and his voice sounds almost broken by sobs. His father replies, 'But why should it be bigger? . . . ' Peter says, 'I don't like it this small . . . easier to fall in it . . . apparently no blood around though . . . ' His voice sounds much more calm. His father says, 'But why should there be any blood? . . . ' Peter replies, 'You never know . . . ', and he comes out of the toilet. His father shows him his watch and explains to him that he will be back in fifty minutes. Then he tells him that today perhaps he will come back some ten minutes early and wait for him in the waiting room. Then he urges Peter to follow me.

Peter just gives me a quick glance, then looks as if he were frightened and holding his breath. He runs hurriedly into the playroom. He goes straight to his drawer and starts examining its contents, without ever glancing at me, and keeping his head fully bent and almost buried inside his drawer. I say that he seems to be really frightened of me, he keeps avoiding looking at my face, as if it could be frightening and full of blood. First he ran to the toilet and now he buries his head inside his drawer, so as not to see what I look like.

He replies, 'It is always better to play it safe . . .', then he looks at me, and asks, 'Do you have a child? . . .' I say that he felt safer after I spoke, but he is wondering whether I know how to look after a child. He says, 'When I am at home I go around with a parachute . . . so that if I fall, at least I fall on safe ground . . .' I say that he seems to be unsure whether he is on safe ground with me or whether I will just make him feel as small as a small child and then drop him, causing him to bleed. And I remind him of his fear of the small toilet.

He starts carefully examining all the contents of his drawer. I say that he wants to know every detail of my room, so as to make sure he is on safe ground. He looks around and starts making very clever deductions about me and my room. He says, 'This is a couch . . . not a bed . . . you have a sink . . . but no kitchen . . . the toilet could be all right . . . but on the whole I am sure that this is not your house . . . you must live somewhere else . . . now this drawer belongs to me . . . one . . . two . . . three . . . and two more drawers . . . you must be seeing six children in here . . .' I say that he seems to want to study my life and my room minutely, so as to be protected from any surprise.

His scanning becomes more frantic. His pencil-sharpener falls on the floor, under the small table and out of his sight. He seems terrified. I say that if something, like the pencil-sharpener, is out of sight and not under his control, he feels frightened, as he felt frightened by my 'new' face before. He looks at me and starts describing my face and my body in detail, 'Your face is rather thin . . . auburn hair . . . light brown eyes . . . you are not wearing any lipstick now . . . but you probably were before . . . pearl earrings . . . you are slim and rather tall . . . not enormous breasts . . . but nice legs . . .'

In the meantime he takes the fence and puts the figure of the mother inside. He looks at it and says, 'It's a prison . . .' He takes a small house and throws it away, looking frightened, and saying, 'It's an old house . . . I don't want to see it any more . . . it's frightening . . .' I say that he seems frightened now of being locked up with me in something old and frightening, something that he cannot control in every detail. He sits on the sofa, and says, 'It could be an earthquake . . . I'd better keep absolutely still . . . otherwise I may fall . . . fall out I mean . . . ' I say that he is afraid that something might happen all of a sudden and shake him out and make him fall. He adds, 'I may even die . . . like in an earthquake . . . ' Then he adds, 'I have many pillows under my bed . . . I fell out once during the night . . . and that was enough . . . falling once was enough, no more falling now . . . I have a safety net now . . . ' I say that he wants to make absolutely sure he will not experience anything terrible with me as he might have experienced in the past. He doesn't feel secure enough with me yet. He takes the cradle, and says, 'I don't sleep in a cradle . . . I sleep in a bed . . . '

I say that he seems terrified of feeling like a small baby again, he's trying, therefore, to grow fast and at the same time keeping an eye on and trying to keep under control every detail of the world around him. These both seem to be safety nets for him. He says, 'I am tired.' I say that it is such an effort, though, having to grow so fast and keep everything under control.

He curls up in the fetal position and points at the sofa, saying, 'It is full of monsters inside . . . ' I say that he is really frightened of something monstrous that may have happened in the old house, in his past, when perhaps he was still very small and still living inside. He says, 'The old house frightens me . . . ' He takes his pillow and holds it very tightly, as if hanging on to it. He is completely immobile. I say that he feels afraid of any tiny movement or of any distance from his pillow now, in case any movement or any distance might cause a deadly earthquake. He says, 'If the pillow comes off and slips out, I may die . . . I'd better hold on to it very tight . . . I may bleed to death otherwise.' I say that he seems to be talking about a distant past when he felt that any tiny movement might have caused his death. This past is sometimes still with him, particularly at night, or in any strange, unknown situation, as with me, and I remind him of his fear of falling down my toilet and of his falling during the night. He says, 'I have to go to my parents' bed at night . . . ' He remains immobile.

The door-bell rings. His father has arrived some ten minutes early. Peter reacts to the sudden sound of the door-bell with a start and then falls flat on the floor. He says, 'He's come too soon . . . I fell on the floor . . . ' I say that he is afraid that I will not hold him safely, but push him out too soon and too precipitously. He says, 'You are a woman . . . of course . . . and women are no good . . . you are just a useless and incompetent woman . . . it's better to go home now and sleep for at least a good solid twenty-four hours . . . ' I say that he wishes to sleep now and forget that he has been sent out so fast. Women are all incapable of keeping him in securely and holding him safely. If I were competent I would not let him fall out and would hold him tight. He adds, 'I hope no nightmares . . . ' I say that he cannot have a peaceful sleep while he has so many monsters and fears buried in the back of his mind. He jumps up suddenly, looking like a spring and starts running about singing and listing all the items of the room at the same time. I say that he seems determined not to feel pushed out now and left to fall on the floor. He says, 'Unless tops spin round, they fall . . . ' It is time to finish and he runs back to his father and almost jumps into his arms.

I will not make any attempt at commenting on the correctness or not of my interpretations, their timing, their phrasing, and so on. In this session I was just trying to follow what seemed like an eruption of volcanic and potentially explosive emotions. My focus here is just on trying to indicate how some of these emotions may have originated during Peter's pre-natal past or at least may be linked with it by an intangible thread.

Peter clearly seems to dread his past. He is terrified of being imprisoned again in an 'old house', as his 'old life' in the inside seems to have been charged with nightmares and monsters. Being small for him means that it is 'easier to fall', and death and blood. As Peter says, 'You never know . . . ', and something unexpected and potentially catastrophic like an 'earthquake' may happen to him at any time. His pillow may come off, leaving him bleeding to death. 'If the pillow comes off and slips out I may die . . . I'd better hold on to it very tight . . . I may bleed to death otherwise . . . ' It would be only too tempting to link his pillow with the precariously inserted placenta which caused his mother so much bleeding and anxiety during his pre-natal past. Women, as Peter says, are 'useless'. They all seem incapable of keeping him 'in' securely and holding him safely, as in the case of his old, shaky uterine 'house'. The delivery too seems to have been experienced by him as a too precipitous, premature fall, as Peter says, about his father's unexpected arrival: 'He's come too soon . . . I fell on the floor . . . '

Total immobility and carefully and constantly keeping a watchful eye on his surroundings seemed to be his only means of feeling some security in an otherwise uncontrollable and potentially lethal world. As Peter says, 'It is always better to play it safe . . . ' He is terrified when the pencil-sharpener disappears from the careful monitoring of his eyes. His primeval terrors, though, seem to have sharpened his senses and his mind.

230

Peter now seems incredibly bright in his observation and his deducing from details more general aspects of my life. Any other young child might well have taken months before formulating these deductions so clearly. This, as he says, makes him feel on 'safe ground . . .'. Yet Peter also seems determined not to experience such distant and nameless dreads any more, as he says, 'falling once was enough . . . no more falling now . . . I have a safety net now . . .'

It is in fact very difficult to remember that Peter is still very small, as he talks and reasons like a much older child. Peter, as he says, at home goes around wearing a parachute, so that 'At least if I fall, I fall on safe ground . . .'. Yet not all of Peter's defences can be considered as concrete as that. His same extreme verbal precocity and sophistication seem also a means of mastering and controlling his universe. Peter seems determined never to be caught off guard, and to this end always has to be at least one jump ahead, to prevent any cataclysmic surprise.

During the following months, Peter seemed really determined never to be 'caught off guard'. Yet in spite of all his cleverness and no matter how he managed to exert a careful and almost total control of all his time and space, at the end of each session he always managed somehow, to his and my great surprise, to find himself catapulted on to the floor. Other surprises too seemed to shake him and to leave him on the ground, bruised.

But other reminders of his past too found their way into the otherwise almost totally controlled space of his sessions. Peter often spent his time trying to glue his pillow to his overall, while saying, 'I don't know what happened . . . but it certainly was a mess . . . I have to glue myself to my pillow now . . . to stick to it . . .' or 'I will have to do some tricks . . . some magic . . . abracadabra . . . now I am well glued to it . . . and it doesn't slip out . . . [then looking rather frightened and tense] . . . but I mustn't move . . . otherwise the magic will not work . . . and I will die . . .' His otherwise rather manic-joking tone of voice always became deadly serious when saying all this. Yet in his games, as in an endless repetition of his past, Peter never managed to glue himself properly to his pillow, nor was the pillow ever 'firmly inserted' on the 'too mobile' surface of the sofa: just as in his nightmarish past each time it all threatened to end quickly in a bloody mess, as Peter said, 'I will be reduced to pulp . . .' Blind rage often accompanied such clumsy attempts at reaching a firm union with too mobile an object, and in those moments one had the impression of seeing once more the enraged infant catapulted too soon and too inexplicably into what may have already felt as a totally untrustworthy universe.

Peter would often also carefully seal the door of the playroom using his Sellotape, while uttering some chilling words such as 'No danger of falling out . . . and be washed away in a stream of blood . . . ' When saying all this his fears seemed real again.

Most of the time, though, Peter seemed intent on exerting all his possible control so as not to be caught unprepared and 'off guard'. As his father once said, 'novelties terrify him', and were felt by Peter as catastrophic and uncontrollable 'earthquakes'. Peter's extremely sharp senses carefully monitored any change in the micro-environment of his playroom. He noted immediately any change in my aspect, and reacted by carefully monitoring and describing such change down to its tiniest details, until the change seemed well under his control. He noticed differences in smells and was acutely aware of any almost inaudible distant sound. All these he called 'these bloody changes'. Peter particularly seemed to notice and be almost obsessed by any tiny change in the surface of the wall of my playroom as, as he said, 'Any crack might become an abyss, unless you monitor it . . . '.

Yet Peter also seemed determined to protect himself in many other rather effective ways. As already hinted at in the session above, Peter simply managed to throw his worries and fears 'behind' him, wearing a thick shield of mania, as he spun round as a 'top', talking and joking and moving non-stop. The persecuting 'old house' of his first session simply remained locked up inside his drawer, which he almost never used and only approached after long, sly detours just to take his pencils, his glue, or his Sellotape which he kept in one corner of it and which he could easily extract even while keeping his eyes tightly closed. Yet gradually some trust in me began to appear. So far I had been equated with yet another incompetent woman unable to hold him firmly. As he told me one day showing me a toy hen, 'This is a hen . . . my mother is a hen . . . and you are a hen too . . . hens are stupid . . . they only know how to push out eggs . . . eggs can break, though . . . their shell is very fragile . . . hens should keep their eggs inside . . . till the chick is born . . . ' His unnaturally premature birth when he was still too fragile, together with the insecurity and terror he may have quite probably experienced when still living inside, were, as I said, the 'original sin' which he never forgave any of the women he came into contact with. As he said to me, 'Your head is useless . . . you might as well cut it off . . . all I need from you is something else . . . a nice pillow . . . a tight hold . . . women should be like cows . . . no head . . . plenty of milk . . . and big placid tummies . . . cows know how to deliver and look after their young . . . '

Probably his mother's all-pervading anxiety during pregnancy may have also contributed to render his pre-natal past full of monstrous fears and endless tensions.

Yet after several months Peter began to give me the baby to hold. He then began to say, 'You keep it . . . after all women can be good at that . . . ', and parallel to this a new kind of softness began to appear occasionally during his sessions. As Peter said, 'I have a big tender heart . . . ', and the utter control that had characterized so many of his early sessions began to loosen slightly.

Unfortunately, though, Peter's parents soon decided to stop his treatment. Peter had been in analysis for two years and his parents found him greatly improved. Peter seemed much less tense and much more able to relax. His headaches were just a memory of the past. His mother in particular was very pleased about beginning of a new kind of relationship with him. As she said, 'It's like starting all over again with a new child . . . ' This was probably too optimistic, and I was worried about Peter's future reaction to yet another precipitate end, which for him certainly had 'come too soon', but I could also well understand his mother's wish to enjoy the privacy of a new start.

5

Concluding remarks

I should like now to sum up the findings of this exploratory research and speculate about its relevance for psychoanalytic formulations and further investigations.

Pre- and post-natal continuity

The main thread uniting all the material in this book, psychoanalytical and observational alike, is that there is a subtle link of behavioural and psychological continuity extending from fetus to infant and from infant to child. To summarize briefly the pre- and post-natal continuities of behaviour in the fetuses I observed and in the small children I treated were the following.

Giulia was one of the least active fetuses, her main activities being licking the placenta, sometimes pulling it gently towards her, and holding her hands between her legs; she was in an apparently peaceful state of at-oneness with the rhythm of her mother's breathing. Her mother said, 'She was too comfortable in there', and, indeed, her birth was slightly overdue and very traumatic for her mother, but Giulia looked very unperturbed by it in spite of all the commotion around her. Once out she at first licked rather than sucked the breast as she had licked the placenta. Later, with the assistance of her mother and grandmother, she acted as if her post-natal world was a womb in which all she had to do was eat and relish her food and other sources of sensual gratification. Her breakdown was precipitated by the birth of her brother, with its undeniable proof that someone else occupied her pre- and post-natal space, and much of her treatment with me was devoted to helping her to achieve a psychological birth and a somewhat less wholehearted devotion to sensuality as the only theme of her life.

While in the womb *Gianni* clung to the cord almost constantly, was rigidly immobile, and had to be delivered by Caesarean section, the obstetrician commenting on his 'tight immobility'. Gianni is still obsessively rigid and clings to routines and to people in much the same way as he clung to the cord. It is as if already in the womb he was holding himself together by what Bick described as a 'second skin formation' (Bick 1968), and he has continued to do so.

Pina was an adventurous, active fetus who became immobile after a detachment of the placenta nearly led to miscarriage. She has continued to be active and adventurous, though with considerable claustrophobic anxiety, near anorexia, and fear of being 'washed away'.

I have summarized the main findings about the four pairs of twins at the end of Chapter 3, but will briefly recapitulate them here. The most striking fact is that all DZ twins showed marked individual behavioural differences and characteristic patterns of relating to each other before birth, patterns which were continued after birth. Sharing the same womb did not seem to affect the basic temperament of each individual child very much, though after birth each child showed clear signs of being powerfully affected by sharing their space with another being.

As a fetus *Marco* was much less active and 'outgoing' than his twin sister *Delia*, and this difference continued in infancy and childhood in spite of the parents' preference for Marco. Marco was bigger than Delia and was born first, but after birth Delia forged ahead; Delia continued to be an alert and interested child, while of Marco, as his mother said, 'All he wants in life is sleep'. As small children they often collided when going through doorways and Delia, smaller and quicker, usually slipped through first.

Luca and *Alice* were temperamentally different before and after birth, though they were gentle and affectionate with each other in both periods. Luca was smaller, more active, and first to be born. They stroked each other gently *in utero*, just as they later stroked each other from either side of the curtain when they were a year old. At four years Luca was forging ahead of Alice in his schoolwork and social contacts. Their pre-natal past, however, is very much with them. Luca plays with cars and makes the little car win the race. Alice makes her teddy-bears hug and stroke each other as she and Luca did *in utero*.

The most striking pre- and post-natal continuity for *Marisa* and *Beatrice* was that they constantly hit each other when in the womb and have continued to do so throughout their infancy and early childhood, with the loving and often amused acceptance by their mother and grandmother of the naturalness of their jealousy and mutual dislike.

Giorgio and *Fabrizio* had a very unusual experience *in utero* because they shared not only the same genoma but also the same amniotic sac, so that they were intertwined and mixed up with each other throughout their uterine life. Fabrizio was usually the first to move, to be followed a moment or two later by Giorgio, a pattern that is still noticeable at four years of age. Giorgio and Fabrizio suffered a very strange and neglectful post-natal experience in which they were left alone in the dark for much of their waking life. After initial retardation of speech and other behaviour, they improved notably once they went to nursery-school, but each has a cruel expression and each experiences twinship as a monstrosity. They hate each other but cannot do without each other, still in a tangle.

In a sense my research findings about the continuity between pre- and post-natal life are obvious, but even today are not universally accepted, largely, perhaps, because of the lack of opportunity until very recently to observe the fetus. Most psychoanalysts and psychologists, while accepting the idea of temperamental inheritance, really seem to think of the infant's mental life as starting at birth. Many speak of 'psychological birth' as occurring sometime later when the infant shows rudimentary signs of differentiating self from object.

The 'impressive caesura of the act of birth'

Although birth brings with it an impressive environmental change as the infant is exposed for the first time to a radically different physical environemnt and to truly social and cultural interchanges, it did not seem, for the children I observed or treated, to represent in itself a complete mental or emotional change from the pre-natal state. One might perhaps think of it as a sort of crescendo, the climax of the pre-natal state, leading into the post-natal state, but not severing links with pre-natal patterns. The way each child reacted to birth seemed consistent with already well-shaped individual tendencies from their past. Despite the continuity of pre- and post-natal behaviour, however, birth was always an extremely important event, sometimes crucially so. Traces of it could be found in much post-natal behaviour, particularly in the case of children for whom it had been especially traumatic, perhaps especially Alexander (pages 210–17), Peter (pages 224–33), and Tina-Vera (pages 196–202).

On 'suffering from reminiscences' (Breuer and Freud 1893)

My findings both for the children I observed before and after birth and for those I treated psychoanalytically suggest that although it seems unlikely that children 'remember' their experiences within the womb and their birth, such experiences are constantly re-lived and re-worked as they grow and develop. This was especially clear in the twins; in their constant talk about overcrowding and lack of space, as in their preference for playing games connected with pairs and couples, they seem to be forever linked by the fact of having once been together as a pair inside too narrow a space.

In her claustrophobia and near anorexia *Pina* lived out her immobility and presumably acute tension and fear after the threatened miscarriage, and her relief at going outside her flat seemed to repeat her relief, described by the obstetrician who delivered her, at being out of the womb. *Gianni* views the world as a dangerous place like the womb, where he must always find something to hold on to.

But it is mainly with Giulia that one could attempt at establishing more meaningful links with a past which I knew about through her ultrasonographic scans. The intense gluttony characterizing the here-and-now of her transference relationship with me and her treatment of me as a kind of pleasurable placental background are strongly reminiscent of the real images belonging to her pre-natal days. Only now I have a way of observing not only her behaviour, but also of knowing something about the feelings associated with it. Though these are current feelings, they seem to convey something about her past.

In the case of the small children whom I treated psychoanalytically, I had of course no ultrasound scans to compare with their post-natal behaviour, but here too one can see links between the children's behaviour in the consulting room and their pre-natal behaviour as described by their parents. I think it unlikely that they could consciously or coherently recollect the events of their past, but they seemed at the very least unable to 'repress' or 'forget' some of the sensations belonging to such a past, and this fact seemed to have hampered their movement forwards towards life. Most of these children seemed in fact stuck in a weird re-edition of an incongruous past. The consequences of such clutching backwards were only too sadly evident in their often terrible condition. Isolation, concreteness, annihilation of the perceptual apparatus are some of the most important manifestations both in their everyday lives and in the consulting room.

In her frantic behaviour inside the consulting room *Tilda* seemed to indicate that she perceived my room as a kind of persecuting womb filled with too much animation and too varied stimuli. Only gradually did the womb acquire for her a more benign quality, and it took her exactly nine months before she was finally 'born'. *Tina-Vera*, with her constant wrappings with the curtain cord of my consulting room, showed many of the complex meanings that her pre-natal experience and birth, with the cord tightly wrapped around her neck, might have had for her. Unfortunately she and Tilda still seem very stuck in their past.

Thomas's resilience in the face of all the gruesomely perverse attacks he was subjected to both before and after birth seems clearly reflected in his capacity to make the most of the little that I and life can offer him now. But he cannot 'forget' all the needles and probes that repeatedly tried to abort him. *Peter* goes around wearing a 'parachute' in case he falls as he fell out of his mother's womb that was unable to contain him, and he now seems determined not to be caught off guard in his almost premonitory and constant control of his surroundings.

Both Peter and Thomas seemed to perceive the womb as a dangerous place totally unfit to provide any form of security or physical containment. It also took them months before working through some of their anxieties relating to their distant past. Though 'wombs' seems to be felt to be safer spaces, many of the emotions belonging apparently to their pre-natal life are now indissolubly linked with their current way of relating to life.

Unlike Peter and Thomas, *Alexander* seemed to perceive the womb as a kind of paradise lost where he could enjoy endless freedom from the too-varied stimuli of this world and freedom too from the laws of gravity, heat/cold, and pleasure/pain that govern life after birth. He wanted an unchanging life at home and in the consulting room as he had wanted repetitive, sonorous music when he was in the womb.

When does mental and emotional life start

As I have said, most psychoanalysts think of the infant's mental life as starting at birth or at some time after birth. In view of my findings that characteristic individual behaviours develop well before birth, can one assume that some rudimentary self-awareness is present before birth? If such experiences, including some kind of awareness of pleasure and pain, depend on a significant degree of brain function they cannot be present at any time during the entire first trimester – that is, thirteen weeks (Grobstein 1988) – the time when my first observations of Giulia began. This is a reminder that to speak of fetal life in general is a gross simplification, as the fetus cannot be considered a 'unicum' in its turbulent development and preparation for the conditions to be met in post-natal life. The fetus covers a period of enormous change by almost any criterion. Biologically speaking, even the embryonic period is now subdivided to include a pre-embryonic stage, and never again in post-natal life will so much happen in terms of growth and development as during the crucial nine months of pregnancy.

Is it possible that some rudimentary form of self–other differentiation starts in the womb? Obviously, observing fetuses with ultrasonographic scans can only tell us about how fetuses behave, not what they may or may not feel or think. This probably we shall never know. However, if one looks at behaviour as an expression or a forerunner of some kind of feeling and of thinking, one can also attempt to put forward certain speculations of a hypothetical nature.

Spontaneous movement seems difficult to understand without invoking some kind of source of inner activation. Ultrasonic imaging shows us the emergence of independent behaviour at as early as six or seven weeks. All this raises the question of independent volition and possible sentience, properties associated with psychic individuality and therefore with the beginnings of a possible me–not me differentiation. 'Me–not me' sensations may in fact reach the fetus each time it moves, through the proprioceptive feedback of its muscular apparatus. They can reach it from without through the varied sensory stimulations filtering through or deriving from the intra-uterine environment. They can reach it from within its own body through enteroceptive and kinaesthetic stimuli, and so on. From the moment the fetus begins to have sensory experiences (and these, as described in Chapter 1, have been seen to correspond in time with the beginnings of motricity), it seems to show highly individual preferences and reactions. Therefore it seems to be already acting on a pleasure–unpleasure basis at the least, and mere awareness of being, what has been called 'sentience', seems to be present, albeit perhaps in a minimal form. The fact that characteristic behaviour patterns are established so early and evolve developmentally but without losing their characteristic form suggests to me that they may well involve some very rudimentary form of 'me–not me' differentiation.

Can one establish psycholgical norms of fetal life?

Certainly, much further research will be needed before one can establish norms of fetal behaviour and development, not only for physical movement, but also of possible 'normal' psychological development during fetal life. So far only motor, sensory, and

239

behavioural milestones have been established for it. But it seems to me possible that certain pathological and defensive formations may start to develop in the womb. Sometimes these formations are clearly the result of spontaneous or induced uterine trauma, as in the case of Pina (near miscarriage), Tina-Vera (cord tightly around her neck twice), Peter (constantly threatened miscarriage), and Thomas (attempted abortion). On the other hand we cannot be sure of the factors involved in Giulia's pre-natal sensuality, Marco's search for an 'impossible inanimate peace', or Gianni's rigid holding himself together although Gianni's immobility may have been a response to uterine conditions created by his mother's anxiety. Much observation would need to be done to establish psychologial norms of fetal behaviour, but it seems to me possible that such behaviours as autistic closure, adhesiveness (Gianni), and feelings of fusion (Giulia) may not be normal conditions to be met in ordinary fetal life, but may represent, even at this very early stage of life, pathological defensive phenomena; perhaps, for example, Giulia in her fusional at-oneness with her intra-uterine environment may have already been resisting or blurring some kind of dim realization of 'me–not me' sensations. A complex pathology such as autism thus might already be deeply rooted in the child's pre-natal past. All views of autism as arising from post-natal and environmental factors alone may be too simplistic in ignoring all the complexities of pre-natal life.

Nature and nurture

In spite of paying lip-service to the interaction of inheritance and environment, most of us tend to view the individual as shaped primarily either by intrinsic forces and drives or by parental and, broadly speaking, environmental forces. All too often we tend to call 'genetic' all that is pre-natal, therefore not allowing for all the varied elements and stimuli belonging to the far-from-neutral intra-uterine environment.

Within the womb, however, the fetus is subject to almost constant and varied stimulation, and therefore nature and nurture in fact do mingle all the time from the start. The dichotomy between genetic versus environmental forces appears too artificial and simplistic if applied in an either/or way.

My observations have taught me to look at both observational and therapeutic situations with a much more open mind. Had I met a child like Giulia for a consultation and subsequent treatment without knowing about her pre-natal past, I would have probably wondered whether her constant search for sensuous pleasure and for food as testified by her obesity and by her whorish demeanour might have been, let us say, compensatory phenomena due to a lack of emotional bonding with her mother. Or I might have wondered whether her problems might have been due to envy or rivalry towards her mother, or to a generic lack of containment which she may have suffered during the early months of her post-natal life. The unusual opportunity to observe Giulia from her pre-natal days added an extra dimension and greater complexity to a tentative explanation of the phenomena observed in later life.

If I had met a child like Pina before having done this research, I think I would have underplayed the continuing effect of the uterine trauma. In view of the supportive attitude of her mother, I think I might well have attributed Pina's claustrophobia and anorexia to some sort of hereditary factor − and, indeed, if we are to regard her adventurousness as at least partly genetic, it may well have played a part in the uterine trauma.

Thus my observations have taught me to look at therapeutic situations in a much less simplistic light, realizing that behaviours that seem 'obviously' explicable in terms of present-day factors may have other and more complex roots.

Do the mother's emotions affect the fetus?

My observations were not designed to answer this question, but two sets of observations are relevant. In the case of Marco and Delia as described above, the mother had a temporary but near psychotic breakdown during her pregnancy, but no effect could be perceived on the behaviour of her twins.

In the case of Gianni it seems possible that the mother's anxiety − both her characterological anxiety and her acute anxiety about the position of the placenta − may have affected the uterine environment and therefore Gianni. Maternal anxiety as well as tocolytic drugs and other disturbances in the womb may have been a factor in Pina's sudden immobility after the threatened miscarriage. In the absence of ultrasonographic scans we of course do not know exactly what reactions Peter had when still in the womb.

Certainly, the effect of maternal emotions on the fetus merits further and more systematic study. My hypothesis is that some biochemical factor may be involved in the case of maternal emotions, and that it is likely to be only very strong and relatively long-lasting emotions that affect the fetus.

The post-natal environment and pre-natal patterns of behaviour

I made no attempts in my research to compare or assess the relative importance of the post-natal and pre-natal environments and experiences as my study was so preliminary. A simple behavioural description was all I was aiming to do, but I want here to make a brief summing-up of those aspects of post-natal experience that showed continuity or discontinuity with pre-natal experience.

Giulia's mother and grandmother very much reinforced and fostered her pre-natal tendencies towards sensuality and constant craving for an always available placental background. Both her mother and her grandmother, though well-meaning towards her, seemed to foster her tendencies by providing constant sources of sensuous enjoyment and continuous feeds. The sheltered atmosphere of their family world also seemed to reinforce Giulia's original tendencies of not wanting to 'come out' at birth.

The mothers of *Gianni* and the twins *Marco* and *Delia* provided support of a kind that allowed their children's tendencies to continue without either fostering them or counteracting them. Gianni's mother observed his rigidity, but did not think of it as something she particularly needed to try to help him with. She regarded it as his inborn nature and found it very confining; she was relieved to go back to her job, and Gianni improved somewhat when in the care of an au pair. Marco's parents observed Marco's withdrawing tendencies and Delia's outgoing qualities; they preferred Marco and somewhat disapproved of Delia, but seemed to make no sustained effort to alter the orientation of either child.

Pina was clearly helped by her understanding and very observant mother (and grandmother) to overcome many of the terrors belonging to her past. Contrary to her original plans, her mother waited well into spring before considering going back to work, and was always very attentive to soothe Pina and comfort her whenever her fears of falling or her claustrophobic anxieties seemed to overwhelm her.

The mother of *Luca* and *Alice* recognized the different characters of her twins and said explicitly (and showed in her behaviour) that both were lovable as they were. Similarly, the mother and grandmother of *Marisa* and *Beatrice* allowed each twin, and their older brother, to be as they were, with much toleration of the twins' mutual aggressiveness.

In contrast, *Giorgio's* and *Fabrizio's* post-natal environment seems to have introduced in their lives new forms of pathological experience. Not only did their parents not help them to establish more separate identities, but they also seem to have created additional pathological problems for them. When the twins in their feverish episode could not tell night from day, one was only too easily reminded of the earlier time when their room was in complete darkness at any hour of the day. When their mother comments on the fact that they hate each other now, yet cannot do without each other, one wonders how much of their mutual dependence may have been fostered by the fact that they were always alone in their room and therefore each could only resort to the other so that they had to depend on each other even to learn how to walk and talk.

Many of the parents of the young children I treated also seemed there to help. Though *Peter* might have been regarded as a 'normal' child by many standards, his sensitive mother was worried about the effects his contempt for her and women in general, as well as his constant effort at exerting some kind of control, might have on his future life. *Alexander's* mother, after noticing his frantic reactions while still in the womb to any discordant music, and perturbed later by his accident-proneness, brought him to treatment as soon as she could and was very supportive. Though their children rewarded them very little for it, both *Tina-Vera's* and *Tilda's* parents seemed ready to do anything to help them. Unfortunately, their children's condition seemed already from birth beyond any help that parents could give. Only *Thomas's* parents had provided traumatic experiences for him before and after his birth, but his mother's attitude towards him later improved markedly.

I consider the views put forward in this concluding section as tentative conclusions and working hypotheses for future work.

Postscript

By the time this book was finished all the research children were aged five to six years. Though for reasons of space I cannot report my detailed observations of these subsequent years, I have been greatly struck by one particular feature in the further development of all these children.

At some point between the ages of four and five a remarkable change took place in the research children's preoccupations with and possible memories of pre-natal life. The 'facts' of pre-natal life, which previously had seemed to dominate and pervade all their phantasies and games up to the age of four to five years, became intertwined and mixed with many additions and accretions belonging to later life. The composite picture one got at this later period, though still containing recognizable elements of their pre-natal past, seemed fundamentally different from their previous straightforward and almost all-pervading linear version of their past. Pre-natal life also seemed to lose its 'factual' realistic quality and became more and more coloured and changed by the phantasy affect attached to it. Therefore the 'womb' no longer resembled the womb either as I had observed it or as it had actually seemed to have been perceived by each child at the time of the earlier observations: in the case of some children it became idealized; in the case of others it became charged with persecution and claustrophobic anxieties. In both types of change the experience of the new 'womb' was quite remote from the original 'facts' as they were observed by me and recollected and worked through by these children even just a few months before these later observations.

Bibliography

Alberts, J.R. (1981) 'Ontogeny of olfaction: reciprocal roles of sensation and behaviour in the development of perception', in R.N. Aslin, J.R. Alberts, and M.R. Petersen (eds) *The Development of Perception: Psychobiological Perspectives*, New York: Academic Press.

Alberts, J.R. and Cramer, C.P. (1988) 'Ecology and experience. Sources of means and meaning of developmental change', in E.M. Blass (ed.) *Handbook of Behavioral Neurobiology*, Vol. 9: *Developmental Psychobiology and Behavioral Ecology*, New York: Plenum Press, pp. 1–35.

American Institute of Ultrasound in Medicine (AIUM) (1988) Bioeffects Committee, 'Bioeffects consideration for the safety of diagnostic ultrasound', *Journal of Ultrasound Medicine* 7 (suppl.): 53–6.

Anderson, C.M., Torres, F., and Faoro, A. (1985) 'The EEG of the early premature', *Electroencephalography and Clinical Neurophysiology* 60: 95–105.

Anzieu, D. (1985) *Le Moi-peau*, Paris: Dunod.

Armitage, S.E., Baldwin, B.A., and Vince, M.A. (1980) 'The fetal sound environment of sheep', *Science* 208: 1173–4.

Awoust, J. and Levi, S. (1984) 'New aspects of fetal dynamics with a special emphasis on eye movements', *Ultrasounds in Medicine and Biology* 10: 107–16.

Bench, R.J., Mittler, P.J., and Smith, C.N. (1967) 'Changes of heart rate in response to auditory stimulation in the human fetus', *Bulletin of the British Psychological Society* 20: 14.

Bick, E. (1964) 'Notes on Infant Observation in psycho-analytic training', *International Journal of Psycho-Analysis* 45: 558–66.

——(1968) 'The experience of the skin in early object relations', *International Journal of Psycho-Analysis* 49: 484–6.

Bion, W.R. (1959) 'Attacks on linking', *International Journal of Psycho-Analysis* 40: 308–15.

——(1967) 'Notes on memory and desire', *The Psychoanalytic Forum* 2: 272–3; and in E.Bott-Spillius (ed.) *Melanie Klein Today*, vol. 2, *Mainly Practice*, London: Routledge (1988): 17–21.

Birnholz, J.C. (1981) 'The development of fetal eye movement patterns', *Science* 213: 679–91.

——(1985) 'Ultrasonic fetal ophthalmology', *Early Human Development* 12: 199–209.

——(1989) 'Ultrasonic fetal neuro-ophthalmology', in A. Hill and J.J. Volpe (eds) *Fetal Neurology*, New York: Raven Press.

Birnholz, J.C. and Benacerraf, B.B. (1983) 'The development of the human fetal hearing', *Science* 222: 516–18.

Birnholz, J.C., Stephens, J.D., and Faria, M. (1978) 'Fetal movement patterns: a possible means of defining neurologic developmental milestones in utero', *American Journal of Roentgenology* 130: 537–40.

Boddy, K. and Dawes, G.S. (1975) 'Fetal breathing', *British Medical Bulletin* 31: 3–7.

Bots, R.S.G.M., Nijhuis, J.G., Martin, C., and Prechtl, H.F.R. (1981), 'Human fetal eye movements: detection in utero by ultrasonography', *Early Human Development* 5: 87–94.

Bowlby, J. (1957) 'An ethological approach to research in child development', *British Journal of Medical Psychology* 30: 230–40.

——(1960) 'Ethology and the development of object relations', *International Journal of Psycho-Analysis* 41: 313–17.

——(1969) *Attachment*, London: Hogarth Press.

——(1973) *Separation: Anxiety and Anger*, London: Hogarth Press.

——(1980) *Loss, Sadness and Depression*, London: Hogarth Press.

Bradley, R.M. (1972) 'Development of the taste bud and gustatory papillae in human fetuses', in J.F. Bosna (ed.) *Third Symposium on Oral Sensation and Perception: The Mouth of the Infant*, Springfield, Ill.: Thomas.

Bradley, R.M. and Mistretta, C.M. (1972) 'The morphological and functional development of fetal gustatory receptors', in N. Emmelin and Y. Zotterman (eds) *Oral Physiology*, Oxford: Pergamon Press.

Bradley, R.M. and Mistretta, C.M. (1973) 'Investigations of taste function and swallowing in fetal sheep', in J.F. Bosna (ed.) *Symposium on Oral Sensation and Development in the Fetus and the Infant*, Bethesda, MD: USHDEW.

Bradley, R.M. and Stern, I.B. (1967) 'The development of the human taste bud during the fetal period', *Journal of Anatomy* 101: 743–75.

Brazelton, T.B. (1962) 'Crying in infancy', *Pediatrics* 29: 579–88.

——(1974) 'The origins of reciprocity: the early mother–infant interaction', in M.Lewis and L.A. Rosenblum (eds) *The Effect of the Infant on Its Caregiver*, New York: Wiley.

Breuer, J. and Freud, S. (1893) *Studies on Hysteria*, Standard Edition of the Complete Psychological Works of Sigmund Freud (SE)2.

Bryan, E.M. (1983) *The Nature and Nurture of Twins*, London: Baillière Tindall.

Campbell, K. (1980) 'Ultradian rhythms in the human fetus during the last ten weeks of gestation: a review', *Seminars in Perinatology* 4: 301–9.

Campbell, S., Wladimiroff, J., and Dewhurst, C.J. (1973) 'The antenatal measurement of fetal urine production', *British Journal of Obstetrics and Gynaecology* 80: 680–6.

Carmichael, L. (1933) 'Origin and prenatal growth of behaviour', in C. Murchison (ed.) *A Handbook of Child Psychology*, 2nd edn, Worcester, MA: Clark University Press.

Chamberlain, D.B. (1983) *Consciousness at Birth: a Review of the Empirical Evidence*, San Diego, CA: Chamberlain Publications.

Coghill, G.E. (1929) *Anatomy and the Problem of Behaviour*, New York: Macmillan.

Colburn, D.W. and Pasquale, S.A. (1982) 'Monoamniotic twin pregnancy', *Journal of Reproductive Medicine* 27: 165–8.

Darwin, C. (1872) *The Expression of the Emotions in Man and Animals*, London: Murray.

——(1877) 'A biographical sketch of an infant', *Mind* 2: 285–94.

Dawes, G.S. (1968) *Fetal and Neonatal Physiology*, Chicago: Yearbook Medical Publishers.

DeCasper, A.J. and Fifer, W.P. (1980) 'Of human bonding: newborns prefer their mother's voice', *Science* 208: 1174–6.

DeCasper, A.J. and Sigafoos, A.D. (1983) 'The intra uterine heartbeat: a potent reinforcement for newborns', *Infant Behavioural Development* 6: 19–25.

de Grouchy, J. (1980) *Jumeaux, Mosaiques, Chimères et autres aléas de la fécondation humaine*, Paris: MEDSI.

Dehkharghan, F. (1984) 'Application of electroencephalographical and evoked potential studies in the neonatal period', in *Topics in Neonatal Neurology*, New York: Grune & Stratton.

De Snoo, K. (1937) 'Das trinkende Kind im Uterus', *Monatsschrift fuer Geburt und Gynaekologie* 105: 88.

de Vries, J.I.P., Visser, G.H.A. and Prechtl, H.F.R. (1982) 'The emergence of fetal behaviour. 1: Qualitative aspects', *Early Human Development* 7: 301–22.

——(1984) 'Fetal motility in the first half of pregnancy', in H.F.R.Prechtl (ed.) *Continuity of Neural Functions from Prenatal to Postnatal Life*, London: Spastics International Medical Publications.

——(1988) 'The emergence of fetal behaviour. 3. Individual differences and consistencies', *Early Human Development* 16: 85–103.

de Vries, J.I.P., Visser, G.H.A., Mulder, E.J.H., and Prechtl H.R. (1987) 'Diurnal and other variations in fetal movement and heart rate patterns at 20–22 weeks', *Early Human Development* 15: 333–48.

Dreyfus-Brisac, C. (1970) 'Ontogenesis of sleep in human prematures after

32 weeks of conceptional age', *Developmental Psychobiology* 3: 91–7.

——(1976) 'Ontogenèse du Sommeil', *Archives Françaises de Pédiatrie* 33: 637–46.

Dreyfus-Brisac, C. and Monod, N. (1970) 'Sleeping behaviour in abnormal newborn infants', *Neuropediatrie* 11: 101–29.

——(1974) 'The electroencephalogram of full-term newborn and premature infants', in A. Remond (ed.) *Handbook of Electroencephalograpy and Clinical Neurology-Physiology*, Amsterdam: Elsevier.

Edelman, G.M. (1987) *Neural Darwinism: the Theory of Neuronal Group Selection*, New York: Basic Books.

——(1988) *Topobiology: an Introduction to Molecular Embryology*, New York: Basic Books.

——(1989) *The Remembered Present: a Biological Theory of Consciousness*, New York: Basic Books.

Edwards, D.D. and Edwards, J.S. (1970) 'Fetal movement: development and time course', *Science* 169: 95–7.

Emde, R.N. (1980) 'Emotional availability: a reciprocal reward system for infants and parents with implications for prevention of psychosocial disorders', in P.M. Taylor (ed.) *Parent–Infant Relationships*, Orlando, FL: Grune & Stratton.

——(1989) 'Toward a psychoanalytic theory of affect: I. The organizational model and its propositions', in S.I. Greenspan and G. Pollock (eds) *The Course of Life*, vol. 1, *Infancy*, Madison, WI: International Universities Press.

Feijo, J. (1981) 'Le Fetus, Pierre et le Loup', in E. Herbinet and M.C. Busnel (eds) *Cahiers du Nouveau-Né* N.5: 192–209, Paris: Stock.

Freud, A. (1953) *Indications for Child Analysis*, London: Hogarth Press.

——(1965) *Normality and Pathology in Childhood*, London: Hogarth Press.

Freud, S. (1905) *Three Essays on Sexuality*, SE 7.

——(1912) *Recommendations to Physicians practising Psycho-Analysis*, SE 12.

Freud, W.E. (1975) 'Infant Observation: its relevance to psycho-analytic training', *The Psychoanalytic Study of the Child* 30: 75–94.

——(1989) 'Prenatal attachment and bonding', in S.I. Greenspan and G.H.Pollock (eds) *The Course of Life*, vol.1, *Infancy*, Madison, CT: International Universities Press, pp. 467–83.

Galton, F. (1876) 'The history of twins as a criterion of the relative powers of nature and nurture', *Journal of the Anthropological Institute of Great Britain and Ireland* 5: 391–406.

Gesell, A. (1945) *The Embryology of Behaviour: the Beginnings of the Human Mind*, 1988 edn, London: McKeith Press.

Gettinger, A., Roberts, A.B., and Campbell, S. (1978) 'Comparison between subjective and ultrasound assessments of fetal movement', *British Medical Journal* 11: 88–90.

Geubelle, F. (1984) 'Perception of environmental conditions by the fetus in utero', in P.O. Hubinot (ed.) *Progress in Reproductive Biology and Medicine*, Basel: S. Krager.

Gluckman, P.D., Gunn, T.R., and Johnston, B.M. (1983) 'The effect of cooling on breathing and shivering in unanaesthetised fetal lambs in utero', *Journal of Physiology* 343: 495–506.

Goodall, J. (1986) *The Chimpanzees of Gombe / Patterns of Behavior*, Cambridge, MA: Belknap.

——(1990) *Through a Window – Thirty Years with the Chimpanzees of Gombe*, London: Weidenfeld and Nicolson.

Goodlin, R.C. and Schmidt, W. (1972) 'Human fetal arousal levels as indicated by heart rate recordings', *American Journal of Obstetrics and Gynecology* 114: 613–21.

Granier-Deferre, C., Leanuet, J.P., Cohen, H., *et al.* (1985) 'Feasibility of prenatal hearing test', *Acta Oto-Laringologica* 41 (suppl.): 93–101.

Graziani, L., Katz, L., Cracco, R., Cracco, J., and Weitzman, E. (1974) 'The maturation and inter-relationship of EEG pattern and auditory evoked responses in premature infants', *Electroencephalography and Clinical Neurophysiology* 36: 367–75.

Grobstein, C. (1988) *Science and the Unborn*, New York: Basic Books.

Grotstein, J.S. (1981) *Splitting and Projective Identification*, New York: Aronson.

Harris, M. (1969) *On Understanding Infants*, London: Dickens Press.

——(1975) 'Some notes on maternal containment in "good-enough" mothering', *Journal of Child Psychotherapy* 4: 35–51.

——(1979) 'L'apport de l'observation de l'interaction mère–enfant à la formation du psychanalyste', *Nouvelle Revue de Psychanalyse* 19: 33–54.

——(1982) 'Growing points in psycho-analysis inspired by the work of Melanie Klein', *Journal of Child Psychotherapy* 8: 165–84.

Hertogs, K., Roberts, A.B., Cooper, D., *et al.* (1979) 'Maternal perception of fetal movement', *British Medical Journal* 93: 1183–5.

Hinde, R.A. (1982) *Ethology*, London: Fontana Press.

Hofer, M.A. (1981) *The Roots of Human Behaviour*, San Francisco: Freeman.

Hon, E.H. and Quilligan, E.J. (1968) 'Electronic evaluation of fetal heart rate', *Clinical Obstetrics and Gynecology* 11: 145–67.

Hooker, D. (1952) *The Prenatal Origin of Behavior*, Lawrence, KAN: University of Kansas Press.

Humphrey, T. (1964) 'Some correlations between the appearance of human fetal reflexes and the development of the nervous system', *Brain Research* 4: 93–135.

——(1978) 'Function of the nervous system during prenatal life', in U. Stave (ed.) *Perinatal Physiology*, New York: Plenum.

Ianniruberto, A. and Tajani, E. (1981) 'Ultrasonographic study of fetal movements', *Seminars in Perinatology* 5: 175–81.

——(1982) 'I movimenti fetali nelle gravidanze fisiologiche', in P. Zulli, A. Ianniruberto, and F.A. Catizone (eds) *Motricità e vita psichica del feto*, Roma: CIC.

Isaacs, S. (1933) *Social Development in Young Children*, London: Routledge and Kegan Paul.

Juppila, P. (1976) 'Fetal movements diagnosed by ultrasounds in early pregnancy', *Acta Obstetrica et Gynecologica Scandinavica* 55: 131–5.

Klein, M. (1926) 'The psychological principles of early analysis', *International Journal of Psycho-Analysis* 8: 25–37.

——(1929) 'Personification in the play of children', *International Journal of Psycho-Analysis* 10: 193–204.

——(1930) 'The importance of symbol-formation in the development of the ego', *International Journal of Psycho-Analysis* 11: 24–39.

——(1932) *Psychoanalysis of Children*, London: Hogarth Press.

——(1961) *Narrative of a Child Analysis: the Conduct of Psycho-analysis of Children as Seen in the Treatment of a Ten-Year-Old Boy*, London: Hogarth Press.

Kuo, Z.Y. (1932) 'Ontogeny of embryonic behaviour in Aves: the chronology and general nature of the behaviour of the chick embryo', *Journal of Experimental Zoology* 61: 395–430.

Landy, H.J., Keith, L., and Keith, D. (1982) 'The vanishing twin', *Acta Geneticae Medicae et Gemellologiae* 31: 179–84.

Lecanuet, J.P., Granier-Deferre, C., and Busnel, M. (1989) 'Sensorialité foetale. Ontogenèse des systèmes sensoriels, conséquences de leur fonctionnement foetal', in J.P. Relier, J. Laugier, and B. Louis-Salle (eds) *Médecine Périnatale*, Paris: Flammarion.

Lecanuet, J.P., Granier-Deferre, C., Cohen, H. *et al.* (1986) 'Fetal responses to acoustic stimulation depend on heart rate variability pattern, stimulus intensity and repetition', *Early Human Development* 13: 269–83.

Lev, R. and Orlic. D. (1972) 'Protein absorption by the intestine of the fetal rat in utero', *Science* 177: 522–4.

Liley, A.W. (1972a) 'The fetus as a personality', *Australia and New Zealand Journal of Psychiatry* 6: 99–105.

——(1972b) 'Disorders of the amniotic fluid', in N.S. Assali (ed.) *Pathophysiology of Gestation, Vol. 2: Feto-Placental Disorders*, New York: Academic Press, pp. 157–206.

Little, J. and Thompson, B. (1988) 'Descriptive epidemiology', in I. MacGillivray, D.M. Campbell, and B. Thompson (eds) *Twinning and Twins*, New York: Wiley & Sons.

Lombroso, C.T. (1978) 'Quantified electrographic scales on 10 preterm healthy newborns followed up to 40–43 weeks of conceptional age by serial poligraphic recording', *Electroencephalography and Clinical*

Neurophysiology 46: 460–74.

——(1985) 'Neonatal polygraphy in full-term and premature infants: a review of normal and abnormal findings', *Journal of Clinical Neurophysiology* 2: 105–55.

Lorenz, K. (1939) 'Vergleichende Verhaltensforschung', *Verein der Deutschen Zoologischen Gesellschaft Rostock Zoologischer Anzeiger* 12: 69–102.

——(1949) *Er redete mit dem Vieh, den Voegeln und den Fischen*, Vienna: Borota-Schoeler.

——(1978) *Vergleichende Verhaltensforschung: Grundlagen der Ethologie*, Vienna: Springer-Verlag.

MacGillivray, I., Campbell, D.M., and Thompson, B. (eds) (1988) *Twinning and Twins*, New York: Wiley & Sons.

Mahler, M.S., Pine, F., and Bergman, A. (1975) *The Psychological Birth of the Human Infant*, New York: Basic Books.

Mancia, M. (1980) *Neurofisiologia e vita mentale*, Bologna: Zanichelli.

——(1981) 'On the beginning of mental life in the foetus', *International Journal of Psychoanalysis* 62: 351–7.

Manning, F.A., Platt, L.D. and Sipos, L. (1979) 'Fetal movements in human pregnancies in the third trimester', *Obstetrics and Gynecology* 54: 699–702.

Marsal, K. and Genser, G. (1980) 'Fetal breathing examinations: research tool and/or clinical test?', in A. Kurjak (ed.) *Recent Advances in Ultrasound Diagnosis*, Amsterdam: Excerpta Medica.

Middlemore, M. (1941) *The Nursing Couple*, London: Cassell.

Milani-Comparetti, A. (1981) 'The neuro-physiologic and clinical implications of studies on fetal motor behaviour', *Seminars in Perinatology* 5: 183–9.

Miller, L., Rustin, M., and Shuttleworth, J. (eds) (1989) *Closely Observed Infants*, London: Duckworth.

Minkowski, M. (1928) 'Neurobiologische Studien am menschlichen Foetus', in *Handbuch der biologischen Arbeistmethoden* 5: 511–618.

Mistretta, C.M. and Bradley, R.M. (1986) 'Development of the sense of taste', in M.E. Blass (ed.) *Handbook of Behavioural Neurobiology*, vol.8, *Developmental Psychobiology and Developmental Neurobiology*, New York: Plenum Press.

Moessinger, A.C. (1983) 'Fetal akinesia deformation sequence: an animal model', *Pediatrics* 72: 857–63.

Moessinger, A.C., Bassi, G.A., Ballantyne, G., Collins, M.H., *et al.* (1983) 'Experimental production of pulmonary hypoplasia following amniocentesis and oligohydramnios', *Early Human Development* 8: 343–50.

Moessinger, A.C., Blanc, W.A., Marone, P.A., and Polsen, D.C. (1982) 'Umbilical cord length as an index of fetal activity: experimental study and clinical implications', *Pediatric Research* 16: 109–12.

Natale, R., Nasello-Paterson, C., and Turliuk, R. (1986) 'Fetal breathing and fetal body movements in the human fetus at 24 to 28 weeks gestation', *Proceedings of the 33rd Annual Meeting of the Society for Gynecological Investigations*, Toronto, Ont., Canada.

Nijhuis, J.G., Martin, C.H., and Prechtl, H.F.R. (1984) 'Behavioural states of the human fetus', in H.F.R. Prechtl (ed.) *Continuity of Neural Functions from Prenatal to Postnatal Life*, London: Spastics International Medical Publications.

Nijhuis, J.G., Prechtl, H.F.R., Martin, C.B., and Bots, R.S.G.M. (1982) 'Are there behavioural states in the human fetus?', *Early Human Development* 6: 177–95.

Panneton, R.K. and DeCasper, A.J. (1984) 'Newborns prefer intrauterine heartbeat sounds to male voices', paper presented at the International Conference on Infant Studies, New York, April.

Parmelee, A.H. (1975) 'Neurophysiological and behavioral organization of premature infants in the first month of life', *Biological Psychiatry* 10: 501–12.

Parmelee, A.H., Schulte, F.J., Akiama, Y., Wenner, W.H., and Stern, E. (1968) 'The maturation of EEG activity during sleep in premature infants', *Electroencephalography and Clinical Neurophysiology* 24: 319–29.

Parmelee, A.H. and Stern, E. (1972) 'Development of states in infants', in D. Clemente, D.P. Purpura, and F.E. Mayer (eds) *Sleep and the Maturing Nervous System*, New York: Academic Press.

Patrick, J., Campbell, K., Carmichael, L., Natale, R., and Richardson, B. (1982) 'Patterns of gross fetal body movements over 24-hour observation intervals during the last 10 weeks of pregnancy', *American Journal of Obstetrics and Gynecology* 142: 363-371.

Patrick, J., Campbell, K., Natale, R., and Richardson, B. (1980) 'Patterns of human fetal breathing during the last 10 weeks of pregnancy', *Obstetrics and Gynecology* 56: 24–30.

Pedersen, P.E., Steward, W.B., Greer, C.A., and Shepherd, G.M. (1983) 'Evidence for olfactory function in utero', *Science* 221: 478–80.

Peiper, A. (1925) 'Sinnesempfindungen des Kindes von seiner Geburt', *Kinderhuj* 29: 236.

Pèrez-Sànchez, M. (1990) *Baby Observation*, Perthshire: Clunie Press.

Piaget, J. (1936) *The Origins of Intelligence in Children*, 2nd edn, New York: International Universities Press, 1952.

Piontelli, A. (1986) *Backwards in Time: a Study in Infant Observation by the Method of Esther Bick*, Perthshire: Clunie Press.

——(1987) 'Infant Observation from before birth', *International Journal of Psycho-Analysis* 68: 453–63.

——(1988) 'Pre-natal life and birth as reflected in the analysis of a 2-year-old psychotic girl', *International Review of Psycho-Analysis* 15: 73–81.

——(1989) 'A study on twins before and after birth', *International Review of*

Psycho-Analysis 16: 413–26.

Polisuk, W.Z., Laufer, N., and Sadowsky, E. (1975) 'Fetal response to external light stimulus', *Harefuah* 109: 395.

Prechtl, H.F.R. (1984) 'Continuity and change in early neural development', in H.F.R. Prechtl (ed.) *Continuity of Neural Functions from Prenatal to Postnatal Life*, London: Spastics International Medical Publications.

——(1985) 'Ultrasound studies of human fetal behaviour', *Early Human Development* 12: 91–8.

——(1989) 'Fetal Behaviour', in A. Hill and J. Volpe (eds) *Fetal Neurology*, New York: Raven Press.

——(1885) *Spezielle Physiologie des Embryos*, Leipzig: Grieben.

Prechtl, H.F.R. and Nijhuis, J.G. (1983) 'Eye movements in the human fetus and newborn', *Brain Research* 10: 119–24.

Preyer, W. (1882) *Mental Development in the Child*, 2nd edn 1983, New York: Appleton.

Pritchard, J.A. (1965) 'Deglutition by normal and anacephalic fetuses', *Obstetrics and Gynecology* 25: 289.

Querleu, D., Renard, X., and Versyp, F. (1981) 'Les perceptions auditives du foetus humain', *Médicine Hygiénique* 39: 2101–10.

Rabinowitz, R., Persitz, E., and Sadowsky, E. (1983) 'The relation between fetal heart rate accelerations and fetal movements', *Obstetrics and Gynecology* 61: 16–18.

Rayburn, W.F. (1980) 'Clinical significance of maternal perceptible fetal motion', *American Journal of Obstetrics and Gynecology* 138: 210–12.

——(1982) 'Clinical applications of monitoring fetal activity', *American Journal of Obstetrics and Gynecology* 144: 967–80.

——(1989) 'Antepartum fetal monitoring: fetal movement', in A. Hill and J.J. Volpe (eds) *Fetal Neurology*, New York: Raven Press.

Rayburn, W.F., Rayburn, P.L., and Gabel, L.L. (1983) 'Excess fetal activity: another worrisome sign?', *Medical Journal* 76: 163.

Reinold, E. (1971) 'Beobachtung foetaler Aktivitaet in der ersten Haelfte der Graviditaet mit dem Ultraschall', *Paediatrie und Paedologie* 6: 274–9.

——(1976) *Ultrasonics in Early Pregnancy*, Basel: Karger.

Richardson, B., Campbell, K., Carmichael, L., and Patrick, J. (1981) 'Effects of external physical stimulation on fetuses near term', *American Journal of Obstetrics and Gynecology* 139: 344–52.

Roberts, A.B., Little, D., Cooper, D., and Campbell, S. (1979) 'Normal patterns of fetal activity in the third trimester of pregnancy', *British Journal of Obstetrics and Gynaecology* 86: 4–9.

Rosen, M.G. and Scibetta, J.J. (1969) 'The human fetal electro-encephalogram. An electrode for continuous recording during labour', *American Journal of Obstetrics and Gynecology* 104: 1057–60.

Rosen, M.G., Scibetta, J.J., and Hochberg, C.J. (1970) 'Human fetal electroencephalogram: pattern changes in presence of fetal heart rate alterations and after use of maternal medications', *Obstetrics and Gynecology* 36: 132–40.

Sadowsky, E., Laufer, N., and Allen, J.W. (1979) 'The incidence of different types of fetal movements during pregnancy', *British Journal of Obstetrics and Gynaecology* 86: 10–14.

Sadowsky, E. and Yaffe, H. (1973) 'Daily fetal movement recording and fetal prognosis', *Obstetrics and Gynecology* 41: 333–42.

Saint-Anne Dargassies, S. (1955) 'La maturation neurologique du prématuré', *Etudes Néonatales* 4: 71–116.

——(1966) 'Neurological maturation of the premature infant of 28 to 41 weeks gestational age', in F. Falkner (ed.) *Human Development*, Philadelphia: Saunders.

Salk, L. (1962) 'Mothers' heartbeat as an imprinting stimulus', *Transactions of the New York Academy of Sciences* 24: 753–63.

——(1973) 'The role of heartbeat in the relation between mother and infant', *Scientific American* 228: 24–9.

Segal, H. (1957) 'Notes on symbol formation', *International Journal of Psycho-Analysis* 38: 391–7.

——(1964) *Introduction to the Work of Melanie Klein*, London: Hogarth Press.

Smotherman, P.W. and Robinson, R.R. (1988) 'The uterus as environment, the ecology of fetal behaviour', in E.M. Blass (ed.) *Handbook of Behavioural Neurobiology*, vol.9, *Developmental Psychobiology and Behavioral Ecology*, New York: Plenum Press.

Smyth, C.N. (1965) 'Experimental methods for testing the integrity of the foetus and neonate', *Journal of Obstetrics and Gynaecology of the British Commonwealth* 7: 920.

Sorokin, Y., Dierker, L.J., Pillay, S.K., *et al.* (1982) 'The association between fetal heart rate patterns and fetal movements in pregnancies between 20 and 30 weeks of gestation', *American Journal of Obstetrics and Gynecology* 143: 243–9.

Sorokin, Y., Pillay, S., Dierker, L.J., Hertz, R.H., and Rosen, M.G. (1981) 'A comparison between maternal, tocodynamometric, and real-time ultrasonographic assessments of fetal movement', *American Journal of Obstetrics and Gynecology* 140: 456–60.

Spitz, R.A. (1955) 'A note on the Extrapolation of Ethological Findings', *International Journal of Psycho-Analysis* 36: 162–5.

——(1957) *No and Yes: on the Genesis of Human Communication*, New York: International Universities Press.

——(1965) *The First Year of Life: a Psychoanalytic Study of Normal and Deviant Object Relations*, New York: International Universities Press.

Stern, D.N. (1977) *The First Relationship: Mother and Infant*, Cambridge, MA: Harvard University Press.

——(1985) *The Interpersonal World of the Infant*, New York: Basic Books.

Timor-Tritsch, I.E., Dierker, L.J., Hertz, R.H., Deagan, C., and Rosen, M.G. (1978) 'Studies of antepartum behavioural states in the human fetus at term', *American Journal of Obstetrics and Gynecology* 132: 524–8.

Tinbergen, N. (1951) *The Study of Instinct*, 1969 edn, Oxford: Oxford University Press.

Torres, F. and Anderson, C. (1985) 'The normal EEG of the human newborn', *Journal of Clinical Neurophysiology* 2: 89–103.

Townsend, R.R. and Filly, R.A. (1988) 'Sonography of nonconjoined monoamniotic twin pregnancies', *Journal of Ultrasound Medicine* 7: 665–70.

Trudinger, B.J., Aust, F., and Knight, P.C. (1980) 'Fetal age and patterns of human fetal breathing movements', *American Journal of Obstetrics and Gynecology* 137: 724–8.

Vanderberghe, K. and de Wolf, F. (1980) 'Ultrasonic assessment of fetal stomach function: physiology and clinic', in A. Kurjack (ed.) *Recent Advances in Ultrasound Diagnosis No. 2*, Amsterdam: Excerpta Medica.

Van Dongen, L.G.R. and Goudie, E.G. (1980) 'Fetal movement patterns in the first trimester of pregnancy', *British Journal of Obstetrics and Gynaecology* 87: 191–3.

Visser, G.H.A., Goodman, J.D.S., Levine, D.H., and Daws, G.S. (1981) 'Micturition and the heart period cycle in the human fetus', *British Journal of Obstetrics and Gynaecology* 88: 803.

Visser, G.H.A., Goodman, J.D.S., Levine, D.H., *et al.* (1982) 'Diurnal and other cyclic variations in human fetal heart-rate near term', *American Journal of Obstetrics and Gynecology* 142: 535–44.

Vyas, H., Milner, A.D., and Hopkins, I.E. (1982) 'Amniocentesis and fetal lung development', *Archives of the Diseases of Children* 57: 617–18.

Walker, D.W., Grimwade, J.C., and Wood, C. (1971) 'Intrauterine noise: a component of fetal environment', *American Journal of Obstetrics and Gynecology* 109: 91–5.

Walters, C.E. (1964) 'Reliability and comparison of four types of fetal activity and of total activity', *Child Development* 35: 1249–56.

Warnock, M. (1984) *A Question of Life: the Warnock Report on Human Fertilisation and Embryology*, Oxford: Basil Blackwell.

Werner, S., Stockard, J.E., and Bickford, R.G. (1977) *Atlas of Neonatal Electroencephalography*, New York: Raven Press.

Windle, W.F. (1940) *Physiology of the Fetus: Origin and Extent of Function in Prenatal Life*, Philadelphia: Saunders.

Winnicott, D.W. (1958) *Collected Papers: Through Pediatrics to Psycho-Analysis*, London: Tavistock.

Name index

Subject index

abortion, attempted 218, 240; *see also* Thomas, Chapter 4 218–24
amniotic fluid 37
analysis *see* child analysis
anorexia 237, 241
anthropology 2, 8
anxiety, during pregnancy 88, 240, 241
autism 219, 240
awareness, pre-natal 18, 180, 238

behaviour: continuity of 23, 24, 234–6; fetal 1, 4, 7, 8, 11, 26–38, 239, 240; motor 26, 27–32; pre-verbal 3
behavioural: fragmentation *see* pathological formations; norms 239, 240; states 32–4
birth: psychological 234, 236; *see also* delivery
bonding, mother/child 241
breathing movements *see* movement

chemoreception, role in fetal development 36, 37
child analysis 1, 2, 7, 20, 21, 25, 181–233, 237; Alexander 210–17; Giulia 182–96; Peter 224–33; Thomas 218–24; Tilda 202–9; Tina-Vera 196–202
Child Psychotherapy Training 4
claustrophobia 237, 241, 242

communication, non-verbal 21
continuity, pre- and post-natal 23, 234–6
counter-transference 14, 186
cutaneous tactile stimulation 34

delivery: Delia and Marco 118–19; Gianni 79; Giulia 50–6; Pina 95–6
dizygotic twins *see* twins

electrocardiogram (ECG), fetal 33
electroencephalogram (EEG), fetal 33
embryonic phase 238
embryology 1
emotional life, emergence of 238
emotions, maternal 24: effects on fetus 180, 241; ethological research into 1, 2, 3, 4
environment, importance of pre- and post-natal 242
environmental forces, in shaping individual 240
extra-embryonic membranes 37

fetal: behaviour *see* behaviour; conditioning 35; distress 31; eye movements *see* movement; sensory functions 34; studies 3, 20
food, obsession with 187–8, 237
fraternal twins *see* twins
free-floating attention 14